MAYA
ROADS

MAYA

▲▲

ONE WOMAN'S JOURNEY AMONG
THE PEOPLE OF THE RAINFOREST

▲▲

ROADS

MARY JO McCONAHAY

CHICAGO
REVIEW
PRESS

Library of Congress Cataloging-in-Publication Data
McConahay, Mary Jo.
  Maya roads : one woman's journey among the people of the rainforest / Mary Jo
McConahay.
    p. cm.
  Includes index.
  ISBN 978-1-56976-548-7 (pbk.)
  1. Mayas—Guatemala—Petén (Dept.)—History. 2. Mayas—Guatemala—Petén
(Dept.)—Social conditions. 3. Mayas—Guatemala—Petén (Dept.)—Antiquities. 4.
Petén (Guatemala : Dept.)—Politics and government. 5. Petén (Guatemala : Dept.)—
Social life and customs. 6. Petén (Guatemala : Dept.)—Antiquties. I. Title.
  F1435.1.P47M44 2011
  972.81'2--dc22

                                        2011008043

Lines of the *Popol Vuh* are translated from the Maya K'iche by Dennis Tedlock in *Popol Vuh: The Definitive Edition of the Mayan Book of the Dawn of Life and the Glories of Gods and Kings*, Simon and Schuster, 1985

Cover design: Natalya Balnova
Cover photographs: Maya women cross a river on their way to a ceremony,
  photo by Nancy McGirr; Mayan ruins wall carvings, PHOTO #24
Interior design: Sarah Olson
Interior illustrations: Map and chapter illustrations by Rene Ozaeta;
  traditional Maya icons © iStockphoto.com/cloud3200

© 2011 by Mary Jo McConahay
All rights reserved
Published by Chicago Review Press, Incorporated
814 North Franklin Street
Chicago, Illinois 60610
ISBN 978-1-56976-548-7
Printed in the United States of America
5 4 3 2 1

*In memory of my parents, Dr. James Cornelius McConahay and
Dr. Mary Thérèse Rakowski McConahay, my guiding stars*

Contents

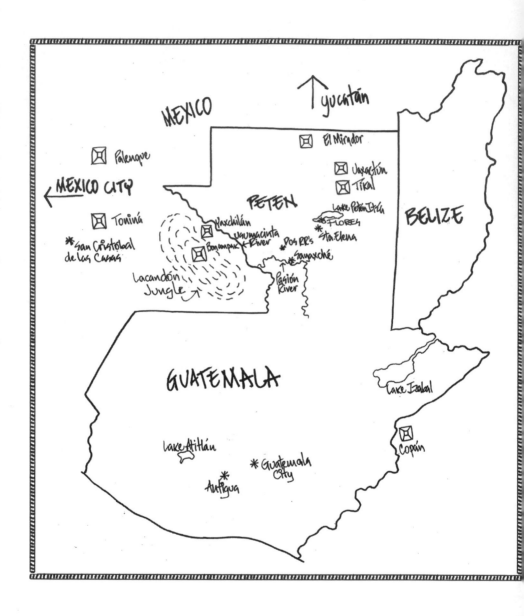

Maya Time and Place

TIME IS ACCELERATING, AS THE MAYA ERA IN WHICH WE LIVE, the fourth age of the world, rushes to meet its end on December 21, 2012, the Maya date 13.0.0.0.0. The Maya tropical forest has changed more since the 1970s, when I first knew it, than it had before then in the entire five hundred years since the European conquest. Maya believe time and place are inextricably linked. That any given moment contains all time, past and future, a sensation felt most clearly in hallowed places. In their civilization's jungle cradle, we can look backward and forward at once.

Mexico's southern state of Chiapas and Guatemala's northern state of Petén cradle the Maya tropical forest, one people on one land, separated only at the end of the nineteenth century when politicians marked a border through the rainforest. Even the relative newcomers homesteading Chiapas and Petén since the 1960s are much alike: peasant farmers with Maya blood, squeezed off their lands in other parts of Mexico and Guatemala, looking for a place to survive.

More than two thousand years ago, Maya Indians began creating settlements that became magnificent jungle cities like Palenque and Tikal, connected by networks of plaster roads on the forest floor. Their descendants in southern Mexico and Central America continue to speak related languages, sharing beliefs, calendar systems, and ways of life. Eventually I would see both halves of "Gran Petén," as the rainforest once was known. What hooked me to the place early, and for life, was a jungle corner on its Mexican side named for the small Maya group that called it home, the Lacandón.

The book's title, *Maya Roads*, refers not only to the author's paths but also to the *sacbe*, raised white clay jungle paths (*sac*, meaning "white," and *be*, or "way"), which ancient Maya traveled between points in their empires. For the Maya, great astronomers, the *sacbe* is also the white road in the sky, the Milky Way.

MAYA ROADS

Prologue

Into the Lacandón

AS A SMALL GIRL IN SOUTHERN CALIFORNIA, PLAYING PRINCESS in pink tulle, I never imagined someday my dream clothes would be loose khaki pants, my dream shoes canvas boots. But something happened when I hit my twenties.

Visiting Mexico City, on vacation with my sister, I saw an exhibit about the Lacandón Maya Indians in the National Museum of Anthropology. The year was 1973, but the native men still carried bows and arrows, their black hair long and wild. They wore tunics of white bark pounded so fine it looked like cloth. Women gathered their tresses at the nape of the neck, adorning them with the bright plumes of tropical birds. I lingered so long at the dioramas, I dreamt that night of white gowns among green trees, orange birds rising.

I had been studying Spanish in Cuernavaca, south of the capital, fleeing university life in California and a crumbled early marriage, living from odd writing jobs, like brochures and ads in English. My sister, just graduated from high school, came to visit. By her very presence she reminded me of home, the orange grove at the foot of sharp mountains, family. Perhaps I will return with her, I thought, surprise our parents, get back into step.

We went to the museum again the next day, she browsing room to room, I drawn once more to the figures of the Lacandón. How remote from civilization these forest people lived! How entwined with the nature around them. They honored ancient gods, drank sacred substances to achieve heightened states of mind. Fewer than four hundred survived in remote jungle. They were said to be the last of the Maya, whose ancestors had built the great Mesoamerican rainforest cities more than a thousand years ago. Nowhere could be farther from home, nowhere more distant from the predictable path of academia—and probably another marriage—awaiting me in the other direction. The rainforest beckoned.

"I must go there," I said to my sister, surprising myself. Once the words were out, however, it seemed the most natural idea in the world. My sister left for home.

Thus, like many of the best journeys, this one started alone, on impulse, chasing imagination. All the Maya roads I have traveled since, through history, revolution, and ineffable beauty, began in that first experience.

The road from Mexico City to San Cristóbal de las Casas, almost seven hundred miles to the south, took a day and a night on the bus. I arrived at a hotel at dawn, walking outside soon after to see the mountain town on foot. Thick fog chilled unexpectedly, lying heavy in hushed streets. In the distance, the outlines of three figures appeared, coming toward me. I stopped to make them out. Men? Women? Wearing what?

Whoever they were had seen me, too. They stepped from the high sidewalk into the cobblestone street, even though it ran muddy from overnight rain. Soon I saw that the figures were women with indigenous faces, not wearing the loose white Lacandón tunics I had seen in the museum but bright blouses and long, black wool skirts so feathery in texture they looked like fur. Even in the street, the women swerved as they passed, as if my body emanated an invisible resistance field, keeping them a precise distance away.

"*Buenos días,*" I said.

One replied with a rapid tightening of the mouth, which I took for a smile, although she did not look in my eyes. Several feet on, the three stepped up to the sidewalk once more. I experienced that disconcerting dance several times during the week I spent preparing for my jungle trip. Sometimes the dance was so subtle, Indians avoiding non-Indians, it seemed woven into the movement of the town as tightly as the woolen ponchos I saw on the streets.

San Cristóbal reflected its history as a Spanish colonial center for a region of subjugated Indians even five hundred years after the European conquest. White residents were called *coletos*, for the low-hanging ponytails (*colas*) favored by sixteenth-century Spanish aristocracy. Maya Indians, like the Chamula women who wore the dark, furry-looking skirts, came to town from their villages, sometimes hours away, to buy and sell. Or to experience one of their few contacts in a lifetime with the Mexican government, such as a court case or, rarely, to register a newborn.

Despite the fault line that ran beneath the community of *coletos* and indigenous, San Cristóbal claimed my senses. High atop hills east and west, simple white churches bracketed the town like sentinels, with staircases so steep they took the breath away.

Over the horns and human caterwauling of the marketplace, a grave cathedral loomed. Inside, Santo Domingo smelled of the incense that had smirched its gold-leafed walls for centuries. Outside, afternoon heat bounced off a sandstone-colored facade of scrolls, twisting ropes, scallop shells, Hapsburg eagles. I walked uneven cobblestone streets for the pleasure of it, past colonial-era buildings with elegant patio gardens seen through open, carved wood portals. At night, smells from street-corner braziers rose and mixed deliciously: green onions grilling, corn on the cob sprinkled with lemon juice, toasting over coals, tortillas slightly burnt, the kind that tastes best.

One day I entered a pharmacy seeking aspirin for a headache, probably from the altitude. As I browsed, an old native appeared at the open doorway, removed his straw hat, and waited for the pharmacist to acknowledge him. They did business six feet apart until the elder came inside, placed his coins on the counter, and grabbed a bottle of pills. Leaving, he bowed to the pharmacist and me, as if apologizing for entering our space, taking our time.

————

San Cristóbal might have held me, but in 1973 I did not have the experience to understand its air of danger and discomfort, the breach between Indians and *coletos*. Anyway, I had set my mind on the jungle. The more I thought of the coming journey, the more the city began to feel crowded. Celebrations, usually religious, seemed to erupt every other day, punctuated by fireworks, bringing back the headache once alleviated by the aspirin.

For the trip to come I bought a light string hammock and found a mosquito net for it in the market with sleeves at both ends that could be tied so tightly no bug could squeeze through. A package of dark green coils promised, when lit, to release insecticide against flying pests within a four-foot radius. I bought waterproof matches and a bus ticket to a cattle-trading town called Palenque, 125 miles northeast, outside the ancient Maya city of the same name. Palenque was near the Lacandón jungle on the map, the last place on my route that showed a bus station. As soon as I reached the town I walked to the ruins.

When the American adventurer John L. Stephens wrote of the ancient city in 1841, he said that if he and his artist companion, Frederick Catherwood, had not hired a guide, "we might have gone within a hundred feet of all the buildings without discovering one of them." For miles in every direction, giant trees grew in a forest impenetrable, "except by cutting a way with a machete." Trees had invaded massive structures, colonizing them, tearing stone facings from temples, twisting through portals in a way that made them seem living features of the old palaces.

The jungle still held the ruins of Palenque. From temple tops I could see the gray-green forest "in all directions" and imagined it in Stephens's time, stretching unbroken to the Gulf of Mexico, the Lacandón jungle, the river Usumacinta. Still virtually unreadable, the hieroglyphic carvings inside temples drew me like illuminated manuscripts in a strange language. In the mornings I explored the ruined buildings and in late afternoons walked in the surrounding rainforest on paths across brooks that once watered the old city. Some trails dead-ended in tree-covered mounds, structures still unexcavated.

Amid the broken temples, talking to other travelers, I heard the name Moises Morales, a local guide who studied the stars. He might know about the Lacandón Indians and how to reach them, Maya aficionados said. Workers told me where he lived, on the five-mile road between the ancient city and today's town, where the bus station is located. I found Morales sitting near his family home, under a *champa*, a roofed area with open walls. He was examining some sort of charts.

No sooner did I say hello—before introducing myself or saying why I had come—but Morales bid me enter and take a seat, the equivalent of inviting a total stranger into your living room. He was about thirty-five, dark-skinned, lean and fit looking, with quick brown eyes. His face already showed the grooves common to those who spend their lives in the sun.

When I laid out my plan, Morales said, "You remind me of myself when I was your age." He looked at me for a long time and shook his head. "It's too bad you are not a young man."

It was no time to take umbrage. Besides, after querying fellow travelers in San Cristóbal, I had met a British artist on holiday who agreed to come along on what he seemed to consider a fine lark. "Right," he had replied easily, when I proposed visiting the Lacandón in their rainforest, of which he had no knowledge. "You'll bring the maps."

Moises Morales asked me to return to his house that night to observe the stars through a telescope on his roof. I told him I would come back with a traveling companion who, he should be pleased to know, was "a young man."

———

Morales is an archaeoastronomer, a calling I did not know existed before that night, one who studies ancient beliefs about the sky. We looked through his telescope at the Milky Way, which Maya call the *sacbe*, the White Road. Constellations, planets, and stars, the travels of the sun and moon, each had meaning for the Maya, said Morales. Their astronomer-priests had observed the night sky for centuries, came to know its movements and recorded their details, even predicted future celestial events with remarkable accuracy.

"You must take fireworks," Morales said at evening's end. Apparently he had decided to help us with information. "That is one of two important things to remember."

The other: "Bring gifts."

"You light the fireworks at the edge of Lake Metzabok to let the Lacandón know you are present," he explained.

"Then they come and get us?" I asked.

"If they want to."

If they did come for us, presenting small gifts showed we honored them. Without the gifts, they would not respect us, which would be a difficult state of affairs in the middle of an unknown forest with no means of communication to the outside world. The map I had brought showed a blue drop where Lake Metzabok might be but no road anywhere close.

"How do we reach the lake edge?" I asked.

"That," said Morales, "you must figure out for yourself."

Morales was too busy to come, preparing for an unprecedented event in the history of Maya study that December, the First Palenque Roundtable. International scholars, enthusiasts, guides, and villagers had been invited to share insights on the art of the site. I had no idea at the time about Maya writing. Only years later would I realize the First Palenque Roundtable was a watershed in breaking the Maya code. Having worked separately for years, after eight days together participants established the entire dynastic line of Palenque, read from stones. It was Morales who suggested regents' names be rendered in Chol Maya, closest to the ancient rainforest language, not Spanish or English, the usual way, setting a precedent for readings of the glyphs. Deciphering the ancient writing had proceeded in fits and starts for decades, but after the Roundtable, it soared.

Of course I could have known none of this at the time. And even if I had, perhaps it would not have mattered, so single-minded was I about experiencing the Maya tropical forest.

The morning after we looked at the night sky with Morales, we headed for a point from which trucks supposedly drove south on a new road. My traveling companion strode a pace in front of me, carrying a trim shoulder bag. He had introduced himself by name when we met, but since then I had called him the Etcher, for his work. He had blond hair, was slight, shorter than I, with a confident British public school manner that said he had done all this before, even though he had not. For the first time since the dark café in San Cristóbal where we had made the agreement, I was looking at him as the man with whom I would share this trip—for safety and accompaniment, because that's just the way it seemed to me a woman traveled—accompanied.

"So what's that?" I asked, nodding at a large, square leather case I had just noticed, hanging from his other shoulder.

"My etchings," he said.

I almost tripped. "The naked . . . naked . . ."

"Nudes," he said. He had shown them in San Cristóbal, very lovely but wildly out of place in these parts, I felt.

"Why?" I said.

"In case we run out of money."

I suppose I should have been grateful for the gesture of consideration, but I could only think ruefully that I deserved this impractical fellow traveler on what was, after all, an impractical quest. The climate would quickly eat such unprotected paper. Our goal was a jungle whose inhabitants used money little and would be most unlikely to buy images of thin, undressed women. He brought them anyway.

An hour later the two of us, among other passengers, were struggling to keep our balance in the bed of a pickup. The truck flew along a dirt road so new it wasn't on the map, but already grievously pocked. We passed a few tiny settlements of newcomers cutting down jungle for land, but most of the time we ran between impenetrable-looking walls of trees.

"Fine!" the Etcher shouted over to me once, the picture of exuberance. He held the roll bar with two hands as the wind lifted his fine, longish hair. He didn't even bring a hat for the sun, I thought. Mad dogs and Englishmen.

"Yes, fine!" I shouted back.

The pickup's last stop was a house-front shop, with a few more houses behind and jungle beyond. Except for a young man carrying a burlap bag stitched closed, which might have carried canned goods from Palenque, we were the only two passengers left. One by one, we jumped down to the dirt.

At the shop, two shelves scalloped by termites held an assortment of whiskeys, imported rum, fancy cigarettes. The proprietor, a Spanish-speaking Tzeltal Maya Indian, said the fancy items were bought by hunters and, recently, by timber men and oil explorers who had begun to pass through. We were far from legal authority—and close enough to private airstrips, waterways, and the border—for the stock to be contraband. Cheap, too. We already had the fireworks Morales had advised, rockets bought before leaving Palenque. As gifts for the Lacandón, at the shop I picked up a shiny flat box of Benson & Hedges Lights and two of Sobranies, one containing smart black cigarettes with gold tips, the other soft pastels.

That evening we walked among the houses greeting residents, looking for food, but families told us they had none to spare. "With all the chickens running around, you would think someone could sell us an egg," said the Etcher.

I was on the verge of pulling out my salvation chocolate bar, to be eaten only in emergency, when a youth approached with eager eyes and an unsheathed machete. "Tell him to put that thing away," said my companion, who did not speak Spanish. Instead, I asked the youngster if his family might sell us a meal.

Shortly, we were eating beans, tortillas, and one fried egg each as the teenage boy gave instructions to his mother and sisters, reminding them to serve coffee afterward. The area had no resident priest or minister, he said, and the government teacher was away on his monthly eight-day rest, given to functionaries in remote posts. This news temporarily crushed my hopes of finding a worldly person who might advise on reaching the Lacandón Indians. Nevertheless, the youth said he would arrange for us to sleep overnight in the schoolhouse and pledged to find us a guide. I imagined returning in a few years to find the boy prosperous by local standards, running a growing town.

Without chairs, or hooks or poles to which we might fasten the hammocks, we slept on the schoolhouse's furniture, like picnic tables with benches attached to their sides. The large room indicated that all six

Ch...

Pickup By:
1/10/2024

.

.

.

.

.

grades probably were taught at once. Its concrete walls looked sturdy, and we could lock the door. As long as no snake or insect dropped from the thatch roof overhead—a possibility I did not mention—we were good for the night.

Just as I became comfortable, we heard a man's voice outside. "I come. I know the forest."

"*Quien?*" I asked. "Who is it?"

"My name is Emanuel. You want a guide." The Etcher looked alarmed, but I translated for him, slipped on boots to cross the dirt floor, and opened the door.

Emanuel was a fine-looking Tzeltal youth who spoke some Spanish, said he was soon to marry, and would be happy of any fee we might pay. He declined to sit and admitted under light questioning that no, he had never been to the villages of the Lacandón. At that, however, he rose to his full height and addressed my traveling companion. Apparently, Emanuel thought this was the person he must convince.

"I go far into the forest to collect wood," he said. "Sometimes I find the trails they use, when they come out to sell bows and arrows."

He was certain, Emanuel said, he could find Lake Metzabok. I asked the Etcher to shake hands with him as he left. I explained to my traveling companion that this man would be our guide and asked him please to blow out the candle on the floor before he went to sleep.

The schoolhouse was truly dark then, as only somewhere hours from electricity can be. In total absence of visual reference, the smallest rustle can sound loud. During the night I awoke, alert, several times, then talked myself back to sleep. When the morning light penetrated the room, I turned onto my stomach and slowly opened my eyes. The dirt floor was crawling with vile-looking black spiders.

"Tarantulas," I heard the Etcher say.

He sat wide awake, fully dressed, cross-legged on his tabletop, observing the floor. "Young. I'd say newborn. Quite interesting, actually. Those cilia will become the hairy look you see on full-grown adults."

I scrambled to put on my boots, which, fortunately, I had placed on the seat bench. Nevertheless I shook each first, lest something lurked inside.

"They're quite blind at the beginning, you know," he said. I did not know and was not sure he knew. I counted a dozen spiders crawling jerkily in various directions but not, as yet, climbing the table legs.

"Where is the mother?" I asked. I tucked the bottoms of my pants legs into my socks.

"Right," he said. "An interesting question."

———

I can't remember much of the trek on which Emanuel led us that morning, except that I felt weak. I brought up the rear, concerned mostly with keeping the men in sight. During the night I had begun to feel sick, even before I saw the spiders. Perhaps we should have skipped the local food when we arrived.

It did not take a mind at its sharpest, however, to see that the jungle we first walked through was serving as a wood outlet. Stumps abounded not only along the trail but as far as I could see into the forest. The biggest trees, which the Indian farmers could not fell with simple chainsaws and axes, sprouted short, ragged protrusions close to the ground, the remains of thick, low broken branches. Drag paths disturbed the forest floor. Settlers were mining the forest closest to the road for building material and cooking fuel.

In about an hour and a half of walking, evidence of woodcutting disappeared. The forest became thicker, the trail less obvious. We stopped for a rest. The Etcher photographed plants. I sat on a rock, hoping to calm a spinning head, wishing my stomach to stop rumbling. Silently, Emanuel walked a few paces in one direction, then another. His short, dark hair lay damp with perspiration. He looked at the ground, peered into the green.

"That way," he finally said, without explanation.

From that moment walking required more attention; not only did I feel sicker by the hour, but I had to keep from stumbling. Emanuel raised his machete often to slash through branches and vines. I switched the rockets from one hand to the other every few minutes. They were light, only sticks bearing a gray pouch shaped like a wasp's nest, carrying explosive powder. But they were awkward to carry, and I was becoming so tired I could hardly walk. Without warning, Emanuel stopped, lifting a finger into the air. I became instantly alert, straining to hear the footfalls of a bandit or the cracking branches of a passing jaguar, maybe a peccary.

"Smell," he said.

The Etcher turned in my direction and raised an eyebrow, as if to say, *Daft?*

"Smell," Emanuel repeated. "We are close."

Coming out of a thicket some twenty minutes later, I had to shade my eyes at the sight of Lake Metzabok, wide and sparkling. Undulating forest surrounded the water. Gray herons pranced close to shore.

As I gazed, eyes readjusting to the long view after hours in the dense, close-up forest, the Etcher took both rockets from my hand. "Shall we blow ourselves up?" he said.

"What?"

"Let's get on then. I don't fancy being alone here in the dark."

The Lacandón might decide not to allow us to visit their villages. Yet, I figured common humanity dictated they could not leave us defenseless for a night, even if they did send us packing in the morning.

"Very late. I cannot return today," said Emanuel. So he would stay with us, too, wherever it might be.

We planted the two sticks in the sandy beach, about six feet apart. The Etcher lit the first. I stepped away, covered my ears, and closed my eyes. Unbelievably, I heard both men yell, Spanish and English, "Run!" "*Corre!*"

The rocket had fallen onto the beach, ready to shoot, sideways. We scattered and covered our heads with our arms. Waited. Nothing. The fall, the damp shore, God's grace—something had made the pouch fizzle. Cautiously, we came out of our hiding places and circled the fallen rocket, as if it were a jumping viper that only appeared to be dead. We threw sand on its head.

The second rocket exploded high and well, a burst that cracked the sky, reverberating across treetops in every direction. Birds rose and flapped wildly. I felt embarrassed in front of nature for interrupting its tranquility.

As we watched, fog formed on the surface of the lake. The sky went pink. Slowly, out of the mist, a sleek, graying wood canoe emerged. It carried two long-haired figures in white, each rowing with a single oar.

Oh, they've sent the women, I thought, then berated myself for stupidity. At least I hadn't said it aloud.

From the museum display in Mexico City, I knew Lacandón Maya men wore their hair long, with loose, white tunics for dress. The closer the boat came, the more unmistakably male its pilots looked, with broad faces and frank eyes set wide. The younger appeared to be in his midtwenties, the other twice as old, but both powerful. Smoothly, they glided the canoe onto shore.

As the Lacandón men climbed out, I nearly smacked my forehead in dismay, thinking of the gift packs of boutique cigarettes I carried. Each Indian held a huge, hand-rolled cigar in his mouth.

"*Buenos días,*" I said. "Thank you for coming." They did not exactly look through me but didn't seem to hear me, either.

"We come from the road," said Emanuel, our guide.

The two Lacandón Maya and Emanuel, a Tzeltal Maya, conversed in a clear, musical Spanish, a second language for all three. Their native tongues were not mutually intelligible, but to my ear they clipped certain words in Spanish the same way and kept the same spoken pace, so their lingua franca seemed shared among them in a manner that mine was not. Emanuel was breaking the ice. In minutes, all of us were boarding the dugout canoe.

Crossing the waters of Lake Metzabok was like going through a tunnel in time and space. Nothing seemed familiar: not the oversized tropical foliage, not the massive, carved-out tree trunk in which we floated, not the shape of faces in the canoe—except the Etcher's, of course, but he sat behind me. I was entering a world mysterious, lonely, possibly dangerous, but seductive; I could feel it in my skin. I skimmed the water with my fingers, trying to touch the passage itself. Even at that moment, so many years ago, I sensed the tunnel was one-way, that having come through, I could never go back.

"*Cocodrilo,*" said the Lacandón facing me, a warning to keep hands inside the boat.

All the men were now smoking the absurd pastel cigarettes, gilt tips glinting in the fading sun. The two Lacandón smoked as they had smoked the cigars, no hands, the objects hanging from their mouths, pink, baby blue.

As we neared the opposite shore, I saw half a dozen women standing on the beach. Between them and our *cayuco*, a cormorant nose-dived into the water. It came up empty and soared away, as if the dive had been just for fun. When we banked and stepped onto land, the men dragged the bark to higher ground.

I stood alone before the women. They giggled and chattered in their *pura Maya* language. All the while they looked me over in a way I'd call rude were it not for the fact that it was I who had arrived on their doorstep uninvited and for no apparent reason beyond implacable whim. Like their men, the women wore loose, unembroidered white gowns, but multiple strings of red seeds graced their necks. Their hair did not hang loose and wild, like the men's. Instead, it was pulled back so their features—brows, noses, chins—looked chiseled and refined.

I stood my ground, about four feet away. I could not remember a thing from the museum exhibit about Lacandón Maya greeting customs.

"*Buenas tardes,*" I said. "*Mucho gusto.*"

No response. I wore a cap that covered my hair, no makeup, a Levi's shirt and jeans, boots. If they are new to me, I figured maybe I am new to them. Three of the women broke away from the others. One reached toward me, and I smiled, thinking she would touch my face. Instead, she gave a good hard squeeze first to my right breast, then the left. I felt my eyes go wide, the smile freeze in place. The other two who had stepped forward did the same as the first. As quickly as it started, the strange test—I think it was a test—was over. The women motioned I should fall into line, and they turned to walk.

Last in the queue, I looked ahead and saw an extraordinary picture that I have carried ever after: at the nape of the neck, where the hair was gathered, each woman wore a clutch of dead birds. Those birds just hung there from the knots where the long, black hair had been pulled together, lushly colored dead birds that must have been somehow magically preserved, whose wearing marked the women as natural members of the forest, yet its conquerors, too, a race of queens. Together we walked, they gracefully barefoot, I in my boots, toward their settlement named after the lake, Metzabok.

We came to a palm-covered *champa*, an open-air, thatch-roofed shelter where the women gestured that I should go inside. I watched them continue toward stick and thatch houses. Inside the shelter, as Emanuel helped the Etcher hang a hammock, the two Lacandón men who had rowed us across the lake sat on their heels, examining the black Sobranies, which seemed to please them.

In San Cristóbal, Indians would have bowed and expressed profuse gratitude at receiving any gift. Here, the Lacandón Maya uttered not a word of acknowledgment, let alone thanks. I had barely come into contact with the Lacandón, but it was already clear they were not the kind of subservient-acting Maya I had seen in the colonial city. I could not imagine them moving to the side on a path or a sidewalk to let me pass, as the Chamula women had done, stepping into the muddy street when I encountered them on my first morning in San Cristóbal. Having avoided outsiders since the conquest, the Lacandón were masters of the place they lived in, lords of the jungle.

Emanuel was tightening the ropes of a hammock. He glanced at the native men, who were on the other side of the *champa*, out of earshot. Emanuel said quietly, "They told me it was fortunate for us we did not arrive later. I have a feeling they would not have come."

A *susto*, a chill of fright, grabbed me at the idea of spending the night on that lonely shore. Yet I realized the Lacandón would have been right not to come, would simply have been acting in accord with their place in the forest order. Man the animal is not nocturnal, requiring daylight for best use of limited vision and poor olfactory capacity. We humans go inside at night or stay close to the fire.

I felt feverish by now, and must have looked bad, because one of the Lacandón men rose and showed me to a hammock already tied to poles. I crawled in gratefully, without removing my boots. That night I did not vomit but made several trips to the communal bathroom bushes. Diurnal animal or not, nausea and urgency trumped fear of the dark.

I passed the next twenty-four hours, my baptismal day in the tropical rainforest, softly rocking in and out of a dreaming state. No matter what I had expected, the deep jungle first entered me not through the eyes but the ears. The howler monkey's basso profundo. Chirps and bird calls, solo and in chorus.

I vaguely heard my traveling companion pay Emanuel from our shared expenses purse. Our guide came to me to say good-bye, but I could open my eyes only for a moment. He looked well rested, a giant Lacandón cigar hanging from his grinning mouth.

I felt my temperature running hot. I perspired, drank water, closed my eyes. The *slap-slap* sound of women making tortillas rose and fell, came and went. I heard someone trying to tune a radio until news spit forth, splintered by static, of a Caribbean hurricane, more Watergate. I awoke once in darkness to the reassuring sounds of others asleep, a hammock rope straining, breath caught in a throat, then gone regular again.

———

"You're well," the Etcher said to me next day as I rolled to the edge of the hammock and placed my feet on the ground. I did feel better, as if the previous thirty-six hours had passed in a single, long, miserable moment. Wobbly, somewhat hungry, I was ready nevertheless for whatever was at hand.

"One of the young bucks heads for Naha tomorrow, the place you wanted to see," he said.

"But we just got here," I said.

"You just got here. I have been in Metzabok two days. Fished, unsuccessfully. Drank with a bloke, couldn't keep up." His feelings were clear. "I say we go."

For someone who could not speak Spanish the week before and had probably expected an easier jaunt but could not get off the train now, this thin British artist showed fortitude, I thought. Looking down on the mass of fast-moving spiders in the schoolhouse, he had been surprisingly cool. Naha was the major Lacandón Maya village and home of the local honored chief, Chan K'in. If we stayed in Metzabok, who knew when we might find another guide to take us there? That afternoon, a couple of adolescent boys accompanied me for a last look at the lake.

"They have secret pictures over there," said one, pointing to low cliffs near the beach where the cigar-smoking men had picked us up.

"Who?" I asked.

"They, the old ones," he said.

"The ones who came before," said the other, as if this explained who the artists, or scribes, had been.

I walked steadily as the boys leaped over logs, tunics flying, long hair flopping onto their faces. Tying back the hair, I surmised, was a prerogative of women.

"They tell stories," said the first boy. "On the walls."

"Yes, stories," said the other. Both reveled in this special knowledge, something hidden from the outsider. I halted.

"OK, let's go see them," I said. I had watched even younger boys handily rowing *cayucos*.

It was as if I had popped the boys' balloons, had they ever seen balloons. They looked abashed, then nervous.

"Can't now," said the first.

"No boat," the other.

They walked by my side then, and I contemplated the cruelest question of all: had they ever seen those wondrous pictures? But it didn't seem right to deflate the boys' spirits further. Anyway, around the corner an apparition materialized that knocked the putative cave drawings out of mind.

More than a hundred flamingos waded in a shallow curve of the gray-blue lake. They fluttered, dipped beaks into the water, shook off drops, craned unbearably slender necks up to the sky. No longer a soft, insouciant hue, pink catching late light became a color as fierce and rich as any in the tropical forest. Sometimes a few birds flew in to swell the multitude. Or one flapped its wings and rose from the carpet, flying away carrying the gift of fiery pink to the darkening sky.

That night in the *champa*, I watched the older Lacandón man from the canoe illustrating something for the younger with a stick in the dirt. I approached and sat on my haunches, too. They looked startled.

"My name is Mary," I said.

The younger nodded, then stood and walked away. The elder did not introduce himself but did not walk away.

"What does Metzabok mean?" I asked. I had to ask a couple of times—I'm sure the accent on the word was awful—but finally he understood.

"Maker of Powder," he answered.

"Ah," I said, and we nodded somberly to each other, as if we were having a genuine conversation.

The lake and settlement, then, took their name from the Lacandón rain god, who creates black talc. Lesser gods dust it through the heavens with a macaw feather, making clouds dark.

"The cliffs, the caves across the lake," I said. "Do they hold pictures?"

The man regarded me as if he did not comprehend my words, although I believe he did. One future day, I would understand that queries, no matter how dignified their intentions, no matter how intense my quest to know, are not social intercourse. Information is precious, not easily shared. I already understood—and this wasn't hard—that women, at least outsider women, did not rate the same attention as men. I could communicate, in a certain way, with the women, but they did not speak Spanish, and I did not speak Lacandón Maya. And what did I provide of value, to make men or women want to talk to me at all?

I would not be seeing any ancient drawings to mark my memory of Lake Metzabok. Remembering its flamingos would have to be enough.

———

In the morning I awoke with the face of a handsome young Lacandón man bending over me. His long hair fell down to touch the hammock's edge. It brushed my shoulder.

"We are going," he said. "Now."

From the corner of my eye, I saw the Etcher tying the laces of his modish but thick-soled leather high tops. The Lacandón hovered another moment, then straightened and walked away. In a few minutes the three of us stood together on the edge of the village.

"Bor," the Lacandón said, pointing to his chest.

"Mary," I said, pointing to mine.

The Etcher said, "Bruce," and thumped his chest with an open hand.

Bor walked into the dark green forest. As soon as I crossed the threshold from village to jungle, following him, I realized why Bor wanted to begin so early, when it was barely light. The jungle floor, moist and soft as peat, was friendliest to bare feet like his in the first hours of the day. It had rained overnight. Gentle drops fell from leaves and branches.

In the forest, you see and hear in proportion to the silence you keep. I walked careful of treading hard. Electric-blue morpho butterflies rested peacefully until we were just upon them, then fluttered away unhurriedly. Birds foraging in the bush, brown and busy, flapped their wings but did not take to the air. Canopy birds sang and called out to one another. When the bright yellow-green of a toucan's beak caught my eye, I slowed down to point it out for the Etcher.

I walked between the two men, about ten feet from each. Sometimes Bor turned and peered at me with his Asian-looking eyes, as if to make sure I was there. I was, and I wasn't.

Taken by the forest, its dank but not unpleasant smells, the miasma of greens, I had become enchanted. Life took on its proper proportion, a feeling of being surrounded by living beings infinitely more numerous than one's own lumbering kind. For a moment, I sensed what it must be like to live at the bottom of the ocean. Vines ascending might be floating plants. Red and orange blooms looked like living coral. The curtains of trees and climbing lianas breathed the blue green of an enveloping sea.

We had walked for almost three hours when the trail met a stream. We hugged its left, using the flow as a guide. Bor called for a stop, descending from the trail to the running water. He took the hard half-shell of a gourd from his net bag, scooped, and drank. I hesitated, then descended, too, and filled my small canteen, which was almost empty. The water was the purest tasting I had ever tried. I wondered briefly if I were becoming so possessed by the place that my reason was addled. But I was thirsty. I refilled the canteen and drank it down once more. Then I refilled it again for the walk.

"*Mucho*," said Bor, watching. He rubbed his stomach and bent slightly, feigning pain.

Prologue

"Cramps," said the Etcher, looking down from the trail to the st
"He's saying you drink too much."

"Thanks, I got it," I said.

Yet I felt chastened. Keep your head, I told myself.

———

Despite double canopy protective shade, by noon it felt hot. Bor slowed down, for our sake, I think. The earth underfoot had turned hard, birds gone quiet. I wanted to rest, to eat the crackers I had brought, but didn't dare suggest it, so as not to appear weak. I was glad when Bor stopped, sprinkled stream water on a ball of corn dough he carried in a leaf, and ate from it with his fingers.

"Naha, close," he said, rinsing his hands in the stream.

The path turned difficult again, as it had done several times, with rises and slippery *bajas*, downhill slopes. Yet knowing the main village was in reach allowed the mind to relax, let down its guard. That is why I nearly trod on a snake, stopping just three feet away. A serpent so velvety, its diagonal design so mesmerizing, that I observed it a long time, it seemed, before becoming alarmed. The triangular head signaled danger, a viper that could jump.

Bor must have had eyes in the back of his head. He was there with his machete, bringing the flat of the blade down upon the snake's head, again and again, each blow marked by a whistle and thud. He whacked the rest of the body the same way. When he finished, the forest around us had gone silent. No segment of the battered serpent shuddered. He slid the blade under the flesh and flung it into the bush. I had not moved.

Bor fixed me with a steely look, his face sweaty, manner terse. "*Pica, muerte*," he said.

Bite, death.

———

We entered Naha in silence and said good-bye to Bor. A young Lacandón showed us to an empty, one-room structure. No sooner had we gone inside than rain began to fall, and the boy left quickly. In minutes, the rain increased to a torrent. The door did not close flush, and I could see that no one ventured out in the storm. We would be alone until the heavy rain stopped.

Inside, the simple room was buggy, so we hung our hammocks and crawled under their nets. For a little while, it would be light enough to read without the flashlight, whose batteries should be saved. There must be a way to rig a candle inside a mosquito net without risking fire, else how could Isak Dinesen or Gertrude Bell have borne their treks? I could not figure it out, however, and went to sleep with the dark, listening to the Etcher snooze. Once, deep in the night, awoken by fierce wind, I turned my flashlight onto the muslin net around me. Roach-like creatures and insects of all sizes covered its outside surface. Wherever I shone the beam, the circle of light crawled with movement. I prayed to the knots at either end of the net, meant to keep bugs from coming inside. Hold tight.

By dawn, the vermin had retreated to their holes or wherever they spend daylight hours. The rain had stopped. I checked the net—clear—and the floor, also clear, slipped on my boots, and walked outside.

Under the morning sun, mud and forest litter stood drying around the houses of Naha, about half a dozen that I could see. White walls with palm roofs, spirals of medium-gray smoke, the color that cooking fires make. Plants near doorways, some in cans. The jungle on all sides, hills in the near distance.

I needed to pay respects to the community elders. There was Chan K'in, of course, and another named Mateo, whom I found sitting alone outside his house. Mateo's face was twisted and scarred, as if by fire. With the skin pulled and stretched, his eyes seemed enormous. I wanted to look away, out of repulsion, or superstition, because whatever had happened to him might happen to anyone. Or I felt embarrassed that my own face was whole and smooth. Mateo spoke so kindly, however, his looks quickly became secondary to his manner. He swept a hand around the entire enclave before I left him, in a way I took to be a gesture of welcome.

Chan K'in, the Little Sun, sat on a planed log outside his house, whittling smooth a three-foot branch. The house behind him looked no finer than others, despite the elder's station as village chief. No windows cut in its wood plank walls, the roof thatched palm. The old man looked small, fit, with no gray in his thick, black hair, although I understood he was in his eighties. Children ran and played around him, but Chan K'in seemed unfazed. A toddler, wearing only a string of red beads around her neck, leaned on the chief's arm and closely watched him work. Chan K'in did not send her away or say, "Be careful of the knife." He indicated to me, with an almost imperceptible lift of the chin, another log where I should sit.

"Thank you for allowing us to sleep here," I said.

He understood. Many of the men used Spanish when they left the rainforest to sell their prized bows and arrows at the ruins of Palenque or in San Cristóbal, although it was hard to think of Chan K'in hawking wares.

"I wanted to know where the Lacandón people live," I said.

"Naha," he replied.

Only recently—well after the turn of the twentieth century—have Lacandón clustered in villages. As a child, Chan K'in likely belonged to the last Lacandón generation that had maintained a clandestine existence in the rainforest, extended families possessing little, moving when the need arose, refusing to be ruled by outsiders. Somewhere nearby, somewhere I was unlikely to see, the men would still have their secret God House, where they commune with supernatural figures from the beginnings of Maya civilization, three thousand years ago. In the God House they drink the sacred *balché* liquor, leading to dreams where they live for a while, returning to consciousness with greater understanding of the world. The Catholic Church never conquered the Lacandón.

"We want to stay a few days," I said. The Etcher had appeared from his morning stroll, and I asked him to take out our traveling purse.

"We want to compensate the village for any trouble," I said to Chan K'in.

The old man called out, and the boy who had showed us our lodging place the day before came running. They spoke in their own tongue, until the boy addressed the Etcher in Spanish. He was a bright-looking youngster, ten or eleven, and he took the Etcher aside to do business.

I watched Chan K'in whittle. Eventually he said, "There are boats."

"Boats," I said.

"Boats."

He looked up from the knife and saw me expectant. He lifted his chin to the east, where I could see only forest and hills.

"Boats," I said, on the verge of driving myself crazy.

"Boats. At the lake."

A lake lay near Naha on the map. Chan K'in was suggesting we see the lake, using a boat. Except for his three wives, all named Koh, who earnestly tried to teach me to make tortillas, this was the most direction, or attention, any adult gave us at Naha.

———

The bright-looking boy and his friends took us along when they fished, and instructed us how to row the *cayuco*. Some mornings we brought soap to the shore and bathed. One morning I saw two men return from the forest with a *tepesquintle*, a forty-pound, supposedly tasty nocturnal rodent, hanging by its feet from a pole they carried between them. Another day, they brought in a dark-haired jabali, like a sleek-faced pig, two sets of tusk-like teeth protruding up and around the snout. We were served only beans and tortillas with hot peppers, however, and occasionally fish or an egg, cooked by Nuk of the Twisted Jaw, a pleasant unmarried woman in her thirties with an unfortunate birth defect.

As long as the Lacandón had their forest, they would not starve, although I saw no evidence of abundance beyond battery radios. There were few manufactured goods, no commercial toys for the children, no school for that matter. I couldn't connect anything in Metzabok or Naha with the beauteous cities of their forefathers, like Palenque. Among the Lacandón I met, I had a hard time seeing a reflection of the great, diversified Classic Maya societies that included accomplished artists and scribes, architects and astronomers. Lacandón existed from, and within, one of the most complicated, even dangerous environments on earth, which meant they had to be highly intelligent, with sharply honed senses. Yet without speaking their language, or living with them a very long time, I had no way of knowing what they might carry inside themselves of those who came before.

One night after dinner, the bright-eyed boy looked over my shoulder as I studied a book about Maya sites, including vases and paintings. "Go ahead, sit down," I said. He took a stool alongside me at the table just cleared by Nuk of the Twisted Jaw.

"Your grandfathers, many generations back, sculpted these stones, or painted the walls," I told him, pointing to pages.

The night before, the boy had shown me pictures he had drawn of jaguars. He told me he had never seen a bicycle, but he drew airplanes well—he had seen them. He entered my illustrated book with abandon, reading the pictures with his hands. It takes a practiced eye to look at certain examples of Maya art and know where one figure ends and another begins. But the boy quickly traced the form of a wildly plumed bird, a seated man, a kneeling man, a turtle, and corn silk tassels, where I had seen only whorls and lines. He told me the Lacandón sometimes walked to the site of Yaxchilan to pray, but I couldn't imagine the boy could tease out elements and visages in the book—which came from all over the Maya world—from familiarity with a single site on an oxbow in the Usumacinta River, where there were no painted walls or urns, anyway.

Or could he? Or maybe the images were familiar from stories heard? Perhaps recognition ran in the blood. The traveler ends with more questions than answers.

Some call the Lacandón of Naha the Last Lords of Palenque, descendants of Maya who lived in the ancient city until at least the ninth century. Others say the Lacandón are a mix, descendants of those escaping the Spanish who intermarried with jungle residents and created an entirely new jungle population, now only five hundred years old. Whatever their provable lineage, Lacandón clearly carry knowledge, perhaps secrets, of Maya from the past.

———

Chan K'in's youngest wife was younger than I, a teenager who stared at me endlessly, even adoringly, as if I were a siren. (Her infant regarded me more like the Creature from the Black Lagoon, howling whenever I moved quickly.) I liked to frequent the kitchen of Chan K'in's wives.

You could say we conversed, although we had no common language. I watched them prepare food in a dark and smoky cooking shed.

"Where are your children?" I knew they were asking.

"I have none," I mimed.

They reacted with disbelief, alarm, laughter, talk in their own language.

"How many children?" the oldest asked, trying anew.

"None. I am not married."

More of the same.

"Husband?" They were asking about the Etcher.

"No, he is a friend," I said. Of this, they seemed to understand only "no."

This set off such a display of dismay, wonder, humor, and more conversation that the women seemed to forget I was there. The rich smell of beans cut with episote leaves rose from a pot. When one of the wives turned to stir it, I marveled again at the shining dead birds in her hair.

These incidents of communication produced little to no hard information, yet they took a long time. Sometimes I could hardly breathe with that acrid smoke in the shed, although it didn't seem to bother the women. I fought the asthmatic's urge for fresh air because I wanted to stay inside, for the pleasure of their company.

One night when I needed to urinate, I steeled myself to go out into the dark. I shook my boots and put them on; lifted the muslin mosquito net, disturbing a thousand crawling bugs; stepped outside and closed the door quickly behind me. Halfway down the path to the communal latrine, in a stand of trees some hundred feet off, I looked up and saw a single moving light, too small to be a torch, too large for a firefly. I stopped. It disappeared. As I took another step, the point radiated and faded again. An immeasurable moment later the glow intensified only inches from my face, illuminating the wild black hair and lined skin of the eldest Koh, smoking a thick cigar as she walked. The old woman raised a hand in sleepy greeting as she passed, and continued on the path.

The days passed quickly; the Etcher and I spent less than a week in Naha. Had I known what would become of the thick Lacandón rainforest over the next thirty years, I would have stayed longer, looked harder.

As it was, one night Chan K'in came to the door to say he would take us out of the jungle. I had been asking around for a guide, but those most likely to take the task had not returned from Palenque, where they were selling arrows. We would leave, said the chief, at dawn.

The trek took a direction different from the way we had come, through forest just as varied, however, just as hypnotic to me. Chan K'in walked quickly, large bare feet gripping the path with toes wide, sometimes using a walking stick, yet hardly breaking pace when climbing or descending. The bright-eyed boy came, too, holding the chief's stave when he didn't want it. As I once pressed favorite leaves and flowers in a book, I tried to impress images in my mind, wanting never to forget: a *matapalo* with multiple, woody arms magnificently strangling a less fortunate tree; a cloud of tiny orchids, blue as the sky, suspended above my head in a tree; the old man and the young boy, tunics rippling, dark hair flowing, one with the jungle passing.

In a couple of hours, the rainforest turned ragged, with stumps and even a discarded toothbrush trailside, a sign we were nearing the road. I felt as if I were waking from a dream faster than I wanted. We came over a steep hill and saw a dirt road below. Chan K'in stopped and said good-bye. He assured us that any truck would take us on.

Chan K'in and the boy crouched, observing the Etcher and me descend without a path, slipping on loose rocks, leaning backward to keep from falling. When I gained my balance at the bottom, I looked up to wave, but the two figures in white were already cresting the hill, backs to the road. I watched them disappear.

"I'll be back!" I called out.

1

Looking for Itzam K'awil

Wouldn't we be afraid to go inside there into a lordly house?
Wouldn't we be just wide-eyed? Take pity on us! Wouldn't we look
like mere dancers to them?
Don't be afraid. Don't be ashamed. Just dance this way . . .
— *Popol Vuh, the sacred Maya book*

IN THE YEARS AFTER LEAVING THE LACANDÓN RAINFOREST,
my life moved fast. I became a journalist, reporting on newly oil-rich
Middle East countries in the 1970s. I was a war correspondent in Central
America in the 1980s, covering Nicaragua, El Salvador, and Guatemala.
By the 1990s, Central American rebels and governments were moving
toward peace agreements. I had seen enough of death.

I found myself thinking more often of that filtered green jungle light
that had once enraptured me. I wanted to return to the rainforest, to the
seductive maze of trees and mystery, as many times as I could, as long as
my legs and unpredictable asthmatic lungs would carry me.

It had been almost twenty years since my first experience of the Maya rainforest. No longer was I a young girl traveling on a whim. I would not return immediately to the Lacandón villages, Metzabok and Naha, if I ever returned to them at all. I feared disappointment, that they could never match my memory of them. And why should they? Their forests had sparked my desire to breathe jungle air and my curiosity about one of the world's great civilizations, to know more about what the Maya Indians had once been. More than that a person should not ask of two jungle hamlets in a lifetime.

In the years since I had left Mexico, its magic never left me. I read every book I could find on the Maya, listened to any story that took place in the jungle cradle of their ancient culture. I came to know epigraphers—scholars and aficionados bent on unraveling Maya hiero-glyphs. I became friends with environmentalists who were creating rainforest reserves to stop timber barons and cattlemen from cutting it down. I hovered around archaeologists who used Antigua, the Guate-malan colonial town where I lived, as a relaxing base when they came in from the field.

One day in 1993, I took coffee and the newspaper out to my Antigua garden, in view of a blue volcano. I read that a renowned archaeologist, Arthur Demarest, was excavating a site called Dos Pilas in the Petén, Guatemala's northern jungle province. He would be attempting noth-ing less, said the account, than to solve a central puzzle of archaeology, the Great Collapse: how the Maya civilization reached a spectacular peak between AD 200 and 900—city-states rich with fine architecture, astronomers, mathematicians, the first written language in the Ameri-cas—and by AD 1000 had simply disappeared.

I hurried to search out a number for Demarest and left a message. That night when the phone rang, I woke in an instant, a journalist by habit. Midnight. What could be happening that might be making news?

"Returning the call," Demarest said, with a Louisiana drawl.

"Do you know what time it is?"

"It's not late, is it?" said the innocent voice. "I don't sleep, myself."

The next morning, I walked across town to Demarest's rented house near the market. A maid answered the door. She led me through an interior stone patio open to the sky, freshly washed, singing with parakeets. Sheltered on worktables in a protected corridor, red-brown ceramics sat whole or laid out carefully in pieces.

I entered the kitchen to the smell of chicory. "It's strong," Demarest said, pouring coffee from a blue enamel pot.

He wore a long, dark, belted lounging robe. His eyes looked heavy, as if he had been having sex and had not yet quite snapped out of it. Later, I would realize this was just the way Arthur Demarest looked: heavy-lidded brown eyes, sometimes far away, thick curly hair always slightly mussed.

"Have a seat," he said, motioning to a massive wooden table in the middle of the room. I had the feeling other team members lived in the house, because condiments sat on the table the way they do when residents eat at different times. He turned off the heat under an iron pot on the stove.

Demarest said he had already been on the phone for two hours, engaged in "archaeological politics." He exhaled impressively to show that his role as expedition leader weighed heavy. Such a "host of characters," he said, such rivalries, agendas, and sponsors to juggle on an expansive project like Dos Pilas.

He pushed a box of cereal on the counter out of his sight and heaped hot red vegetable stew from the pot into a bowl. He sat across from me and laced the stew with two kinds of piquant chili sauce. I raised my eyebrows, stunned at the firepower.

"I'm from a Cajun family," he offered. "My father always says we eat real food for breakfast, not animal fodder."

Demarest had read my reporting from Nicaragua and El Salvador. As a young archaeologist, he excavated at a Salvadoran site called Santa Leticia, founded around 500 BC, the ceremonial home of distinctive, ten-ton potbellied figures crafted by a culture that would become the Maya. When an El Salvadoran death squad, the White Hand, killed two of his laborers, he said, Demarest closed down the project. I had the feeling he was not afraid for himself but for his workers. Over his kitchen table in Antigua that morning, we discussed Central American wars, which I knew well, war in general, Maya war.

I longed to accompany an actual dig in the region of classic Maya civilization, especially like the one at Dos Pilas. It was a throwback to expeditionary archaeology, with dozens of specialists, hundreds of mounds. Demarest managed cavers, glyph readers, "a great fauna person," soil experts, bone specialists. His own particular quest was for the second regent of the Dos Pilas dynasty, who might be named Itzam K'awil.

The rules of Maya warfare appeared to have changed under the king Demarest sought, spreading what had been a limited activity among elites until it included civilians and attacks against population centers. When kings began aiming to kill on the spot, when war became a constant, the civilization spiraled toward destruction. Thus the regent was key to Demarest's theory of the Great Collapse, that increasing war led to the fall of the city-states, the disappearance of the classical Maya world. Arthur Demarest was about to excavate the pyramid where he hoped to find Itzam K'awil.

I knew Demarest could tell I was taken by the same questions that motivated his search. *Why do people go to war? How and why do they limit wars once they start?*

"You can sleep in the nurse's cabin," he finally said. "Just a bunk, no frills. Bring a candle if you want light."

The next week I boarded a vintage Cessna with Demarest and half a dozen team members. We flew out of the sprawl of Guatemala City over jagged brown mountains. Turbulence shook the aircraft, quieting talk. In less than an hour peaks and clouds fell behind, and below us spread the wavy jungle cover of the northern third of the country, twenty-three thousand square miles called Petén.

To the east lay the Lacandón rainforest of the Mexican state of Chiapas, ecologically a single vast swath with the Petén rainforest, although one part was in Mexico, the other in Guatemala. In fact, the Maya tropical forest stretched from southern Mexico across northern Guatemala to western Belize, the largest contiguous rainforest north of the Amazon. Once, the land lay at the bottom of the sea. It rose to the surface just three million years ago, recently in geological time, joining North and South America.

The new land drew animals and plants unique to the north to mix with those unique to the south. The forest became one of the most diverse regions on earth, comprising only 0.5 percent of its surface, supporting 7 percent of its species. Some plants and animals of Gran Petén, as the connected jungle of Mexico, Guatemala, and Belize is called, are found nowhere else.

When we sighted Guatemala's Pasión River, the pilot descended slowly until a clearing appeared. We landed on a dirt runway with hardly a bump. When the door opened, it let in air so heavy and humid my lungs soon felt ready to pop. It took a few moments to capture a steady rhythm of breathing. By the time I stepped down from the ladder, the others had already claimed their backpacks. Even the ground felt hot through my boots.

Soon seven of us—a South Texas speleologist (like a spelunker, but less casual), four archaeologists, the camp doctor, and I, interested observer—stood in the bed of a fast-moving, jumping Toyota pickup. We held onto its flanks, the back of the cab, the roll bar overhead. On both sides of the jungle road, trees grew thick and dark green, their highest branches meeting overhead, cooling the temperature twenty degrees. Talk was impossible.

Dr. Arthur Demarest, wearing a brimmed jungle hat with a leather band, looked in command. Not too tall, with a knife at his waist in a weathered scabbard, he fit the adventure-movie image of an explorer: intense, imperfectly handsome, deep brown eyes. As the truck lurched, his knees bent and unbent for balance like a fencer's.

We hit soft mud and fishtailed. Nearly everyone cried out at once. But we didn't flip, and those who had cried out laughed in embarrassment and relief. Demarest caught my eye and winked, as if to say, "This is part of the fun."

I thought back to the last instructions he had given me in Antigua, 150 miles away. I should call him Arthur, he said. Other orders were brief:

Don't get lost.

Don't get fatally bitten or stung.

Don't get in the way.

We bailed out at the edge of a wide, grassy square fringed with high, eroding structures. One building rose in the pyramidal shape of a sacred temple. I was breathing hard, arm muscles wrenched from hanging on in the truck, but feeling excited finally to be among the ruins. The plaza was littered with stone tablets called stelae, each one taller than a man, fallen or tilting at crazy angles, engraved with strange symbols, some with human figures costumed in feathers and animal masks. Graven stucco stairways cast sharp, stepped shadows in the late afternoon sun. In the northern sky a storm loomed, throwing intense purple-gray light on giant ceiba trees. A death mask wrought in stone lay fallen among brown leaves.

A bright yellow saucer spun through the air. A youth with a Mohawk haircut dove and caught it just as the disc veered toward a thirteen-hundred-year-old engraved monument. Demarest shouted.

"I told you guys not to fool around out here when lightning's coming!"

The young men guffawed, bowing in obeisance to the sky.

"My Alaskan volunteer," Demarest said drily. "And my fauna person."

We took a path to the archaeologists' camp, a ten-minute walk. Twelve cabins on stilts took up three sides of a commons; on the fourth side stood a long, screened-in laboratory for examining finds from the excavations, the only building with a generator for electricity.

Thirty-two square miles of ancient civilization spread nearby. But the well-funded Demarest was said to have the only camp in the jungle with genuine showers, and I had never felt so hot and sticky, my lips tasting of salt. I asked for directions.

What a delight it was to stroll through dense foliage and come upon two rows of shower stalls, completely roofless, nothing between bather and sky but branches of cedar trees, high above. Making sure I was on the women's side, I stripped. Heat wasn't the problem, I realized, it was clothes. Standing naked, I unpinned my hair and spread my arms, flapping them like a cormorant.

Inside the shower, a twist of the tap pulled stored rainwater through a pipe, spraying from an overhead spigot. Above I saw yellow-billed toucans, flying in pairs, while water ran like a tonic over my body.

"I'll be fumbling around my tomb the next few days," Demarest told me later, in a tone meant to sound casual.

"Can I go?" I asked.

By 8:00 A.M. the next morning, I stood atop the pyramid in the plaza. Alongside, a nervous-looking Demarest had sweat through his safari shirt. He bit at his full, dark mustache. His Guatemalan codirector, an elegant Sorbonne-trained archaeologist named Juan Antonio Valdés, pulled at the wilting indigo kerchief around his neck.

A week before, the men had sunk a shaft from the top deep into the temple's heart. Now Demarest, Valdés, and their local sidekick, Rat Man, stared down into its blackness. Rat Man looked the most relaxed. Demarest claimed Rat Man's bones folded in like a rodent's, so he was capable of slithering through narrow channels. But it was not Rat Man's turn yet; he would stay on top, in the open. Cicadas screamed in the heat. Demarest and Valdés climbed into the shaft.

I followed with some trepidation. There was no ladder. We felt for irregularly placed beams with our feet, grasping at others with our hands. The deeper we went, the darker it became, as if we were entering the underworld. Thirty feet down, we reached bottom, a damp, confined space. The floor felt soft. The air smelled dank but not oppressive. I could breathe.

Valdés shouted up the shaft to Rat Man. "Lower the generator!"

We watched the orange metal machine swing its way down, alternately blocking and revealing light from the top, a shifting eclipse. Valdés caught the thing by its rope, placed it gently at his feet, and bent to rev it up. Gradually, weak light emerged from a single bulb hanging waist-high on the wall.

By crouching, it was possible to gaze directly into the tomb through two fist-sized holes near the floor. It looked gloomy inside but did not smell musty, as I had expected.

Demarest stretched a shaving mirror through one of the holes into the crypt, as far as his arm could reach. I peered through the other hole. A rat shied from the mirror's glint, kicking up dust. Another cut to a corner, disappearing into a rocky wall. If anything else was in there, it was hidden by dirt. Six feet up in the crypt loomed a huge capstone, sealing it from above.

"I want to shrink up and crawl through," Demarest murmured, taking his arm from the hole. "But all I can see is this big rock on top that's going to fall and kill me."

Two tunnels into the tomb had already collapsed. Workmen had reinforced another slender cavity with cedar planks a foot at a time. Metal rebar, transported with us on the Cessna, would give it more strength. This is where a royal burial might be expected—the very center of the base of the pyramid. Within days, Demarest figured, he would enter.

We came out of our stooped positions, stood, and stretched our legs. Valdés, who is also an architect, reached behind me and picked at a shoulder-high substance that flaked under his finger. The temples at Dos Pilas had been built in a hurry, mostly with rubble, and finished with fine facades, so this was not the sturdiest pyramid in the jungle. As warfare spread under Itzam K'awil, the theory went, people fled their homes and invaded the sacred spaces around the temples, which were being deserted by their elite inhabitants. Commoners tore the exterior face stones from structures like this one to erect defensive walls around the temple complex, trembling behind them in fear of the enemy.

Innumerable tons of loose fill—no facade to fight the elements and no matrix—hung over our heads, all around us. Demarest knelt to squint into the tomb again.

"We can put in beams—maybe rebar—to take pressure off that vault stone," he said.

"How much does it weigh?" I asked.

"Enough to ruin your day," he said.

"Let's hope the grave robbers haven't gotten here first," Valdés said.

Even in the odd yellow light from the generator lamp it was easy to see Dr. Arthur Demarest, asker of great questions, blanch.

"Surely not this deep," he said.

But Valdés was not so sure, and he seemed to enjoy twisting a small, psychological knife.

"Good-bye, Indiana Jones," he said.

"Hello, Geraldo Rivera," said Demarest.

Both were anxious to enter the tomb. They debated the use of long drills, and wooden feet on the rebar to protect whatever might be lying on the floor of the crypt. They considered additional tunnels coming in from other directions. They longed aloud for a mining engineer with nineteenth-century skills to figure out how to widen the peepholes into a crawlspace, without power tools and without sparking a cave-in, and then shore the tomb walls to hold the giant overhead slab in place.

The rainy season, which makes digging impossible for six months, approached. News that the archaeologists had found *something* was already spreading through villages. Slash-and-burn settlers were destroying the rainforest around Dos Pilas in a tightening circle. And the temple stood in the middle of one of the last zones where the war still sputtered: an *enfrentamiento,* or confrontation between squads of army and guerrillas, even an accidental meeting, could occur at any time. Even if no one were hurt, an *enfrentamiento* would spook local workmen and cost the expedition days of work.

They would start the next day, the men decided, chipping an entrance into the tomb big enough for Rat Man, whose real name is Raul Aldana, then the archaeologists to crawl through. In several days, they would begin to excavate inside the tomb.

"With luck, he's in there," said Demarest, speaking of Itzam K'awil. Then he went somber, eyeing the huge capstone.

"What a nightmare," he said. "To lose a life for no king and a couple of rats . . ."

One morning after most of the scientists had gone out to the field, I found Demarest sitting alone in the mess hall.

"So hey, good, you found it," he said.

"Arthur, I've been here a week," I said. "This is where I eat."

"Oh," he said. "Want some coffee? My personal stash."

He poured from the blue enamel pot. Demarest was certain he was allergic to eggs, he said, although he had never been tested. For that reason, only a plate of toast sat before him. "That's the way they'll kill me," he said.

"Who?"

"Any one of them. My graduate students. Or for sure the settlement people. Slip the powdered version into my gumbo. Force me to eat quiche."

The "settlement people," archaeologists who determined where, how many, and how ordinary people lived at Dos Pilas, needed to map large numbers of house mounds to determine important demographic patterns. They had to cover a huge expanse of territory, so they were refusing to take time out to help dig individual burials, which can take several days each. The situation was "throwing my osteology people into trauma." They still needed large samples of bones from individual burials to know what diseases people died from and the quality of their everyday nutrition.

"And snake guards. 'Wear your snake guards,' I tell everyone. I bought snake guards for each and every person. Do you think anyone wears their snake guards?" He looked down at my jeans. "Where are your snake guards?"

With the end of the season approaching, Demarest was starting to act like a warlord maddened by the pressures of his expanding kingdom. He had taken on the character of a certain successor of Itzam K'awil, a regent known so far only as Ruler 4, who once scurried for months around his overextended, disintegrating kingdom, trying to keep it together. When he came home, his own people chopped off his head.

"Cookies," he said.

"Pardon?"

"They could do it with cookies with a lot of eggs in the batter."

"Arthur?"

A National Geographic TV crew walked in, carrying a gleaming machete. They had been working in Dos Pilas for a couple of days and now wanted to shoot Demarest slashing his way through the rainforest.

"The most dangerous animal in the jungle is an archaeologist with a machete," Demarest said. "It's not what we do well."

He would clear a swath through the forest with his bare hands instead.

"Just remember not to use terms like 'Classic' or 'Pre-Classic' on camera," the producer reminded him.

When the crew left the room, Demarest buried his head in his hands. He looked through his fingers.

"I just want to do archaeology," he said.

That night I drank coffee with scientists surrounding Héctor Escobedo, a Guatemalan with thick dark hair and a gentle manner, who excavated at another corner of Dos Pilas from Demarest. Escobedo was happily recounting his day at a structure called P-5-3.

"I was poking around. I was almost sure it was a burial. Suddenly I saw the top of a vase. 'God!' I prayed. 'Let it be a polychrome!'"

We carried our cups to the lab.

The vase was eight inches tall and four and a half inches across, unbroken, with a band of red-orange glyphs. Escobedo handled it gingerly, like a baby that needed to be bathed. Inside were remnants of a substance, probably cocoa, part of the sacred food and drink meant to accompany the deceased on the journey to the afterlife. Not only did he discover the vessel intact and in situ, but Escobedo, trained as an epigrapher, also recognized a formulaic sentence painted upon it, dedicating the pot and its contents to a patron's soul.

"This vessel might read, 'This is the vase of so-and-so,' identifying the name of the person buried in the mound," he said. "It will take some time to clean it, and study to read it. But it carries a *name*."

Escobedo had the wavy hair and tall stature of a ladino, a non-Indian Guatemalan, but also the almond eyes and wide, sensuous lips found on the jaguar-mask figures of southern Mexico. Like almost all Guatemalans, Escobedo probably carried the blood of both Indian and non-Indian in his veins. He worried, he said, that some of his countrymen—especially indigenous Maya—felt this work of digging up ancestors' graves was profanation.

"We're doing it for scientific knowledge," he said. "It would be profaning burials if we just took things out to sell on the market, without respect." He gestured at the bones and shards around us in the lab.

"As a Guatemalan I may treat all this with even more respect than someone from the outside, because this is part of my own culture, my own past." As a kid, he said, he made plaster pyramids in the courtyard of his parents' house in the capital.

In the morning I walked to the site known as Hector's Burial. The trail led from the plaza where Demarest was busy digging for Itzam K'awil into the jungle in the direction of the Bat River Cave. Along the way I saw scattered tablets and carved stones, unmarked by signs, some half-hidden, entwined by roots. These were the excess furniture of the

empire, too unimportant now—apparently not associated with structures or graves—to warrant examination. The very ordinariness of their
presence created a feeling that the entire Maya rainforest, the miles that
could be reached on trails and the countless inaccessible miles, must
be rich with memory, peppered with information. It was the kind of
landscape described by nineteenth-century explorers, who tried to hack
their way through jungle-covered mounds only to discover they were
hacking away at temples. Or, for want of a dry place, slept on rock slabs
carved—the morning revealed—with priceless hieroglyphs.

Héctor Escobedo knelt in a pit, removing soil from a skeleton with a
toothbrush and a dentist's scaling tool, oblivious to tiny, stingless sweat
bees buzzing around his face. He showed me where I could spread my
plastic poncho on the ground above the pit and watch. Kekchi Maya
Indian men worked near me, and, a few feet away, another team excavated a similar-looking pit dug into a house mound.

The person whose remains were appearing in the dirt where Escobedo worked had been buried in the house where he or she lived, a
commoner's version of a royal burial inside a pyramid. Escobedo noted
the compass position of the cranium—116 degrees east. Both regal and
commoner tended to bury their dead with the head toward sunrise. He
stretched a tape measure along a femur and checked the color of the
surrounding soil against a Munsell chart, like a book of sample paint
squares in a hardware store. The dirt matched square 10YR34: Dark
Yellowish Brown.

Watching such plodding routine chips away at romantic notions of
the job. I could see that each small piece of the picture of Dos Pilas society at the time of the Great Collapse would be a product of hundreds of
hours of work, beginning by systematically spooning up dirt in a jungle
corner like this one. Escobedo seemed a counterweight to Demarest's
archaeologist as boyish swashbuckler.

"Half of my work is paperwork," Escobedo said.

But he had transcendent moments. Using a tiny paintbrush, Escobedo uncovered a tooth in the dirt and picked it up. Was it incised?

A bone expert called over from a nearby pit. "Naw," he said. "It's
probably just broken."

Escobedo persisted, brushing more dusty granules from the tooth as I watched him work. Triumphantly, reaching up, he placed it in my hand.

"I told you so," he said.

A perfectly circular depression showed on the face of the enamel where a piece of jade once shone whenever its owner flashed a smile. What tool or procedure could make a perfect cutout in a tooth twelve hundred years ago, a task that today would require a skilled dentist and a diamond drill? Later examination of muscle attachments in the skull, and other points on bone, would tell whether the smile had been a man's or a woman's.

In another hour, a human skeleton lay clear. Bits of obsidian, a single jade bead, and pottery shards had been churned around it in utter disorder, broken and shifted from their original positions by the movement of dirt and roots over time. Escobedo plotted and drew them before digging to layers below.

The rhythm of the work was as steady as a metronome. Whenever dirt filled a bucket, a workman lifted it from the pit to a companion, who emptied the contents and sifted through them once more, in case some bone fragment or ceramic shard had been missed. Soil samples went into white cloth bags, tied and numbered in order. The harmless bees buzzed.

At a certain moment, the atmosphere became electric. About three feet from the pit, a low, steady rustling drew all eyes. From dead leaves, a serpent emerged, triangular head, unmistakably a fer-de-lance. The words of Bor, my Lacandón guide of twenty years before, hurtled into my mind: *Pica, muerto.* The snake slithered rapidly across two feet of open ground, disappearing under a flat rock. Everyone seemed baked in place, exactly where he had stood or knelt moments before, like figures caught by lava at Pompeii.

Slowly, purposefully, Escobedo began again to dust dirt from bones.

"Leave it," he said, without looking up. "He likes to be cool. He'll sleep."

I imagined that he was right but also that he did not want to expose the open grave to the scramble of an attack. But nerves were already frayed. No one spoke. A workman nearly spilled the contents of a white cloth bag. Another repeatedly stopped combing dirt for artifacts to look around. Most of the laborers were Kekchi Maya who had come to the Petén rainforest in this generation or the last, squeezed out from the highlands, looking for land to farm. The jungle was almost as foreign to them as it was to me.

"There are tiger here," one said, using the local word for jaguar.

At least one worker would have to stay on guard against tomb robbers at day's end, alongside the bones. Only the evening before, shots had rung out in the direction of the Cave of Blood. It was probably just poachers, chasing the tasty *tepesquintle*. But the workmen, like all peasants in a war zone, feared being caught in crossfire or mistaken by either side for the enemy, so the sound of any shots was alarming. And now there was the snake under the rock.

Escobedo finally ordered the fer-de-lance killed. With a long pole, a young worker lifted the flat stone, looking nervous because vipers can jump. This one, however, lay still and beautiful. The triangle of a head whispered poison, but the snake's dark gray and gold skin seemed to call out for a caress, it looked so sumptuous. With the barest movement, it stirred. A second worker raised his machete into the air and brought the flat of it down fast and hard on the velvety head. He was careful not to sever it, because Maya believe the serpent's head separated cleanly from the body will turn, jaws open, and come after you. They scooped the limp, mottled body, head intact, into one of the white cloth bags.

Demarest appeared, trailed by the television documentary crew. They were friendly, professional; they noted Demarest "sweats in irregular patterns" and asked him not to dirty his matching khaki shirt and pants. The chief archaeologist went down on one knee anyway, to get a better view of the skeleton. It lay in a relaxed, peaceful-looking position, on its left side, legs bent in fetal position, two vessels at its head and one at its feet, a vase, a bowl, and a plate.

"Incredible," Demarest said.

Héctor Escobedo beamed. Clearly, Indiana Jones would have liked nothing more than to jump into the pit and go to work.

"It's fascinating science, but it doesn't scream death," said the television producer. Demarest and the documentary crew moved on.

At that moment, unbeknownst to anyone at Dos Pilas, a message was on its way from Guatemala City informing Héctor Escobedo that his young daughter had died from a heart condition with which she was born. He would leave camp the next day. To keep his balance in the pickup, he would hold onto the back of the cab with both hands, helpless against the tears on his face.

On the night he had unearthed the burial, however, the usually shy Escobedo was riding high on the excitement of his finds. He wanted to show off the snake, too. As the other scientists came in from the field, they pulled folding chairs into a circle near Demarest's cabin. Escobedo shook out the white cloth bag. The fer-de-lance lay in the grass. All were remarking on its color and size when it jumped. The circle broke, chairs fell. The serpent had only been stunned. Someone—I couldn't see who in the rush and the dark—grabbed a machete and killed the snake all over again, cutting it to pieces as once the Lacandón had done.

Demarest, sitting on his cabin steps, hardly seemed to notice.

"Hector's Burial—that's the kind of stuff that makes the project," he said. "Not the tombs of kings."

On a bright day when the sun had dried much of the mud from an early rain, we took the pickup out of Dos Pilas to the port of Sayaxche on the River Pasión, an hour and a half ride. Demarest made a head count (eleven) of the scientists and workmen who had come to spend two days at another site called Aguateca. From the beach he picked out the three strongest-looking canoes, with outboard motors, and contracted their skippers.

We took a clear tributary of the Pasión, without white water. The jungle came so close it left only a strip of beach along the river, used by turtles as a launching pad. At the sound of the motor, they poked wrinkled necks from their shells and began a wobbly run, propelling themselves into the drink in a low, flailing arc. Near shore, green-brown crocodiles kept a sun-drugged watch, baking on half-submerged rocks.

That night Demarest displayed a tranquil, expansive side I had not seen in Antigua or Dos Pilas. Maybe because he was far from the headquarters camp, which seemed bustling compared to Aguateca, where fewer scientists lived in even simpler conditions. Or maybe it was the magical, calming effect of the river at night, which argued for flowing thoughts. Quite probably it was also the golden Glenlivet he lifted from a rucksack after dinner and placed on a rough table overlooking the shore.

"I am not a Mayanist," Arthur Demarest said formally as he poured. "Remember I am not interested in dead kings. Kings were rich; kings had nice pots. We know that. And I am not really interested in the history of the Maya. I want to know about beginnings and ends, and why complex societies formed, and why they fall apart."

Suddenly, he wanted to take it back—literally. He asked me to tear out the page where I wrote in my notebook, because there were colleagues who would not understand, he said.

This struck me funny. Was Arthur Demarest embarrassed at being seen as one who asks the big questions instead of a more narrowly defined but respectable "Mayanist" in the limited world of scientific archaeology?

"You're laughing because my career is over," he said.

He lowered his face in mock dismay. Clearly, Demarest wanted to exhibit the boy in the man, enjoyed being taken for a maverick. The deeper the night became, however, the more he talked only of the Great Collapse, as if obsessed with the event.

"If they had kept to their limited rules of engagement, the Maya could have had their kind of warfare forever: it was an ongoing activity that defined who their elite were, a means of resolving dynastic succession and maintaining access to the trade routes," he said.

I thought he made early Maya war sound like a duel among gentlemen, without consequences for the society they stood upon. Wasn't it economic, too? What wars were not?

"Oh, economic in a sense, because the elite got their quetzal feathers and jade and they won dynastic disputes that gave them access to tribute labor, but all those were things to reinforce their status. That's not the same as war over agricultural land or irrigated or raised field systems. For most of their history, people were not drafted, and rules of engagement were limited, although royal captives did die in brutal ways—did I tell you about the king they rolled up and kicked around for the sacred ball game?"

Kings played the role of preachers in the theatrical settings of the great plazas. They pierced their tongues and genitals, surely painful even with the help of hallucinogenic enemas. That way they regularly sealed with dripping blood the necessary pacts between the humans of their kingdom and their gods. The horrible death of a king at the hands of another ruler must have been traumatic in the extreme for his subjects, even if they were not physically harmed themselves.

Nevertheless, Demarest was saying that, over a period of two thousand years before the Great Collapse, the Maya in their fragile, interdependent, rainforest environment had figured out a way to have "war" without shooting themselves in the foot, without destroying the planet they knew. They did not ruin the enemy's fields, or take a chance on harming its population, because this brought a Maya chief no prestige, so long as war remained about status and charisma.

As we spoke, the scientists and workmen slept in the distance, curled into hammocks that looked like low-swinging oropendola nests. The sleeping area stood out of earshot, which was good, because Demarest suddenly raised his voice.

"The ones who destroyed all this! They were silly self-aggrandizing chiefs, imposing themselves on everyone around them, like chiefs everywhere." He hit the tabletop with a fist. "And they destroyed the ecology around them with their wars!"

Sitting among the dark trees, under the rippling reflection of a full moon on the flowing river, I felt how perfectly balanced the Maya world must once have been. Resounding bellows from the howler monkeys turned to mere crooning by the time they reached our ears; the aroma of night-blooming jasmine wafted up from the bank. I was beginning to understand better, even sympathize with, Demarest's urge to see what he might find in Itzam K'awil's tomb. I guessed he was angry at the old skeleton, in some unscientific way, for presiding over the change in the ethic of warfare, change that doomed the Maya's delicate balance with their world.

That imbalance was probably inevitable, Demarest said, once war had become a way of life. The megarich demanded "more stuff," even from far away. They wanted the phosphorescent, jewel-like gleam of the feathers of the quetzal, a bird that lives only in highland cloud forests. Profoundly green jade, the color of life after rain. Black obsidian from distant volcanoes. Not only did the elite expect such luxuries, they were lazy and overly fastidious, with retainers to carry them in wicker settees so their feet didn't touch the ground. They developed an entire service economy to cater to them, dumb jobs that removed people from productive work.

It had become very late. The moon shone so brightly that the passing river and gently moving branches of the trees looked like a film shot in day for night, rich in detail, metallic in color. The first bottle on the table had emptied itself; another appeared from the backpack. Only the finest Scotch, in the middle of nowhere.

Eventually, Arthur Demarest gave up on drawing the big picture; instead, he gazed in the direction of the darkened ruins of Aguateca, then toward the river, as if it were easier on the eyes. He rolled out curt, verbal captions for sketches he must have been seeing in his mind: "Warfare affects ecology and brings about the collapse of society. . . . Warfare became endemic. . . . Warfare became uglier. . . . It was not a change of technology, but of the ethic of warfare . . ."

I drew myself up to contribute. "What about our own time, when we demand more oil, more minerals, more precious wood every day? Are we like Maya princes squeezing too much out of our world?"

Demarest glanced up at me from his glass, then away, as if he couldn't be bothered with the obvious. Even though dawn was not far off, I think he resented the fact his audience had dwindled from several, who had sat around the table in the early evening, to one, me. Why wasn't everyone as interested in all this as he was? I could hardly keep my eyes open; I declined another drink and announced I would head to my hammock. He forbade me by launching into soliloquy. Curiously, it was an optimistic speech.

"Think about the unconscious limited-good model that once reigned among Maya kingdoms, which forbade them to intensify warfare beyond a certain point because it would destroy the environment," he said.

"Then consider that there is today an emerging limited-good ethic that is coming down from ecology. It hasn't been sold to the world's leaders yet, but it is being sold. Yes! The notion that this is a universe of limited resources is going to have an effect on warfare. That's the path to peace. Not the ethical argument, which is tied up with religions, and not the political arguments—we'll never get agreement on those."

I struggled through a haze of fatigue and single malt. Demarest was saying that the need to keep a balance in nature must finally curb man's propensity to go to war. I thought of Kuwait's burning oil fields after the first Gulf War, filling the sky with black smoke. I thought of El Salvador, plagued by violence, forests gone, land eroded. "Where is 90 percent of Salvadoran territory?" goes the grim riddle. "In the sea."

The howlers ceased, the moon had gone, and the water rolled by in silence. At this darkest hour of night the Maya might have been speaking from their graves: *Watch out. Power is ephemeral. Survival depends more than you think not on who beats whom but on how much you all abuse the earth.*

Demarest raised an eyebrow like a question mark and lifted the bottle. For the Maya, fermented drink was a sacred substance, a potion that helped the mind's eye see. I pushed my glass toward him with a single finger.

———

Few places make you so aware of the quality of muted sound as a jungle trail after rain. Leaves do not crunch underfoot. Small animals moving are felt rather than heard. Rain collected in the canopy seems to fall from the trees, not the sky, gently and quietly in the dark green curtain. The clatter of spider monkeys overhead becomes only rustle; they eat fruit and throw down big, hard seeds. However, the seeds land with only faint report on damp ground, like cherry pits.

When we returned from Aguateca, the commons at the Dos Pilas base camp had gone swampy from rains. Archaeologists still paused there, however, coming in from the field in the late afternoon, clothes stained with variegated colors of mud and full-body sweat. They flopped onto chairs or into hammocks, trading stories from the day. One day at dusk, a workman set the head of a fresh-killed *tepesquintle*, a large rodent, on a fence post. Ants swarmed over it for ten minutes, leaving behind a new face of hairless, skinless, grinning bone.

"Found some wonderful fauna—could be Pleistocene—big, too," said an unshaven man. Muck dappled his shirt and pants. He introduced himself as Jim Brady and said his job was caves.

"Stop by the lab," he said. "Found something else today, too."

After dining in the mess on macaroni and cheese, washing it down with Tang, I took out my flashlight in the moonless night and walked toward the screen-wrapped building. It glowed in the blackness like a flying saucer. Inside, artists sketched, the Alaskan volunteer sorted shards, and the speleologist who had come on the plane with us sat at a Toshiba 1600, mapping the cave where he and Brady had made the day's find. On a long, wide shelf rested a dozen human skulls, in the order Brady and the speleologist had found them in a dry chamber, the eye sockets of one staring into the back of the head of the next, and so on down the line.

"Obviously some ceremonial site, way down there," Brady said. "What we're trying to do is locate important finds and features below ground, so later we can locate surface features directly above them."

Brady invited me to come the next day and see the wide-mouthed Cueva de Rio Murcielago, Bat River Cave. "Aw hell," said the cave scientist dismissively, without taking his eyes from the computer screen. "That's hands-in-your-pocket walking, that one."

That night in my bunk I opened my notebook to a page where I had pasted part of the obituary of a Maya archaeologist who had loved caves. One day in 1978, Dennis Puleston climbed the Temple of Kukulcan at Chichen Itzá with his two small children to show them an incoming storm. At the top, lightning struck Puleston dead on the spot. The children were not harmed. The part of the obituary I had saved was from Puleston's journal.

I tied my pack to the inner tube. . . . Moving out of the (underground) tributary channel into the main river, I made up my mind to go . . . without a light at all. . . . I blew out the lamp and was soon paddling my way upstream into thick darkness. Blacker and blacker it became. My only fear was running into a fer de lance. . . . I imagined the effect of darkness on Maya initiates; how would they react? Probably with some fear, although I did not myself feel particularly terrified now. I was simply experiencing the inky blackness, the feel of the water and the feeling of the tunnel as a passage through the earth. A wind now stirred. . . . Gradually it got lighter.

It was at this point that I began to toy with the idea that Xibalba (the lowest level of the underworld) as described in the *Popol Vuh*, the Maya Bible, was a land reached via such underground rivers as these.

The trail I took to the Bat River Cave wound through deep rainforest uninhabited since the Great Collapse. Immense *matapalo* trees wrapped themselves around other trees, slowly sucking away their lives. Palms with skinny trunks and leaves as sharp as obsidian looked disgustingly tumorous, laden with bulbous insect hives. I heard no human sounds, but sound was everywhere. The ground on this trail was dry, so lizards, harmless mudsnakes, and other small creatures too quick to identify skiffled through fallen leaves. Hidden birds, presumably resplendent, sang high in the canopy. Cicadas alarmed the air in waves, slow breakers of sound that rose until they vibrated like a scream, then receded, as if going out to sea again.

Sometimes the trail surprised. In a spot where bright sunlight broke through the greenery, a family of spider monkeys dipped and leapt among high branches. Nearby, white stones lay in the shape of a grave, marked with a cross of bleached mule bones. A year before, an intrepid Dutch traveler had dropped dead on the trail, and workmen who came upon him buried him on the spot. ("Next are the lords named Wing and Packstrap," says the *Popol Vuh*. "This is their domain: that people should die in the road, just 'sudden death,' as it is called.") Three days later, the workers dug him up and packed him in ice at the boat landing, transferring him to the top of a bus where he rode to the airport and home. But the workmen, who are Maya, keep the place where he fell looking neat, as if something important happened there.

The trail stopped at a cliff draped with ferns and hanging oropendola nests. I descended a rope ladder, holding hard to its sides, not trusting the fraying hemp rungs. I was sweating by the time I reached the bottom, twenty-five feet down. The mouth of the Bat River Cave yawned nearby. Clouds of black and yellow butterflies veered and tacked through the air, counterpart of the bats that would sweep from the cave at dusk.

Brady, tall and thin, still unshaven, wearing a red hard hat, fretted over a small orange generator. The spark plugs seemed fouled by bad gas; the problem was serious, considering the number of discoveries one makes in a cave is related to the light one carries inside. Fortunately, Brady said, today he would be working in the twilight zone, the crepuscular blue that extends only a couple of hundred yards in from the entrance.

The gaping mouth of the cave, forty-five feet across, looked magnetic and repulsive at once, inviting the hesitant into its shadows. Yet it marked a kind of border with the security of the ordinary world.

"Once you break that plane with the earth you're in the underworld and in the realm of the gods," Brady said.

Twenty years of exploring the dark had led Brady to a conclusion that differs from traditional thinking about Maya caves. Far from being unimportant side pockets of Maya life, or trash pits, as many assumed, Brady believed caves were so important in the cosmology and subconscious of the Maya that their positions determined the placement of the great ceremonial sites above ground. The Dos Pilas expedition studied surface layout and architecture as if they were extensions of the dark, mysterious cells underground.

"We're not just talking caves; we're talking spiritual geography here," he said.

Bits of pottery lay scattered over the ground. Brady made a surface survey, mapping the bigger artifacts. An unbroken dish. A broken *metate*, the flat, three-legged stone used by Maya women to grind corn even today. Some modern Maya make ceremonial bread for their rituals—they were probably making it here, too, a thousand years ago.

"Women are not supposed to go inside, of course," Brady said, grinning, knowing that was exactly why I had walked the long trail and climbed down that rotten ladder.

Just inside the cave, stalactites hung from the roof like limestone icicles. Watery mineral drops fell as they had fallen in the same places for eons, adding to calcium mounds rising from the floor like a garden of phalluses. Some of the growths had embraced pieces of ceramics over the centuries, joined now as one substance in hard stone. Most, however, rose pure, white, smooth to the touch.

Brady rejects the "caver" label.

"I love what the caves tell me, but a natural caver I am not. The proof is I get too claustrophobic."

The cave mouth is a place where you have to speak the truth.

"I feel my stomach knot up during the nasty little crawl to get at some bones," he said. "Yet I get pulled in almost against my will. Pulled by the thought of the thrill of coming upon a place and knowing no one else has been there for twelve hundred years. It's just exactly the way it was left, its altars and chambers."

We say rain comes from the sky, but for the Maya it comes from caves, the birthplace of water. Most of Mesoamerica traces its ancestry to caves, and most of the *Popol Vuh* takes place underground. In Maya mythology the road to Xibalba, the region of awe, the underworld, goes through a cave. At the cave mouth, Brady was not the crisp, no-nonsense scientific type I had taken him to be.

"Sometimes I feel things shouldn't be disturbed," he said. "Often we burn incense and light a candle before we go in. Sometimes workers absolutely won't go inside and won't tell you why, so you don't insist they enter. This is one of the real deep mysteries. Very difficult to get at."

We were already walking slowly toward the dark interior, Brady in the lead. He turned and warned me with a look from under the hard hat.

"These are very powerful places where some people are extremely uncomfortable."

He was right to smell ambivalence. The string of chambers, past the mouth and its tubular maw, was strong as a magnet. Who knew how far back it went? It felt like I could stand too close and it could suck me in with its deep breath. I did feel afraid. I feared being helpless in the wet underground, prey to an unexplored subterranean river that could rise unexpectedly, fill a chamber in a few seconds, afraid of holding my breath, feeling in panic at the slimy walls for an exit, sucking at the last air with my mouth against the ceiling of the cave. I have always been afraid of the water. Odd for a sailor's daughter. I blame it on the asthma, the experience of gasping for breath.

Brady was heading into the cavern's dark entrails, farther than I had expected to go. I willed my lungs to hurry, to adjust to the clammy air.

I followed him as closely as possible, or rather I watched the glow from his flashlight. Our boots made a squishing sound. A wet, mineral smell blew lightly but did not sting. We ducked to pass under a low ceiling; just keeping up with him was a job. I moved forward even when unsure of the floor, not to lose him. Hands-in-your-pocket walking, my eye. The beam of my torch shone too narrow and dim, confusing rather than helpful. Then I saw no light ahead at all.

I took a single step one way, then another. In every direction, only darkness. Disorientation happened quickly; I didn't know any more which way took me forward, which back. There might be side tunnels, I thought. I could get lost. I should stand still. I should call out to him, and I will if this goes on too long. But I did not want to hear my plaintive voice echoing in the cavern.

Brady's light reappeared, comforting as a lifeline. He must have stepped behind a limestone growth for a moment, or around a corner and back, blocking the glow.

"Stay right where you are," I called.

I caught up at a point where a shallow underground river surfaced. It trickled in one place, in another flowed with the velocity of a stream. Where the water pooled, Brady was picking out achromatic life with his flashlight. To compose myself, I made an effort to observe more sharply what I could barely see, as if I would have to tell someone later what it all looked like.

Life underground pallid, miniature. Catfish the size of little finger, whiskers floating like filament. Wan fungus on wall. Blind blanched crabs the size of shirt buttons. Brady collects translucent female shrimp, full of eggs, on hunch it might turn out to be a new species. Pops her squiggling into vial of acetone. Dies instantly. Floats in beam of flashlight.

Time passed, but I could not tell how much. Perhaps total silence throws off the sense of time. But the silence of the cave is an illusion. In time the ears sharpen to the gray spitting sound of rock walls perspiring into rivulets, the in-and-out hush of the cavern breathing from deep in its unseen lungs.

As Brady had warned, I did feel we had crossed a line between worlds. Outside, the jungle changes daily, even hourly: trees fall, animals move, vines flower and wither, sometimes in the same day. Cicadas march in line up a woody trunk and then suddenly exit their shells and scurry away in response to a signal only they can hear, leaving carapaces behind in static formation, like the remains of an armored caravan struck by a neutron bomb. Inside the cave, time might be measured by a stalagmite's growth over a century. But not by the disintegration and change we are used to in the world of light. Skulls do not deteriorate in a cave. They are not a measure of time.

I was glad not to be alone, although another person would not be much help if the river rose suddenly. In certain seasons, after strong rain, it has risen and flowed out the cave mouth in a torrent so loud it is heard outside Ruler 2's pyramid, almost half a mile away. I wanted to turn back but did not suggest it. I felt like a child whose curiosity had led her too far, who didn't mind being a little scared but who now decided she was unprepared to find whatever it was that had titillated her, who just wanted to go home.

I heard a rushing sound. "Water?" I whispered.

"No," Brady said. "Bats."

Thousands of them, disturbed by our coming.

"It's time we leave, anyway," he said.

In the *Popol Vuh*, the Lords of Darkness test the hero twins with snatch-bats, monstrous beasts with snouts like knives, instruments of death. One plucked Hunapu's head right off his body as the youth looked out the muzzle of his blowgun, trying to see how long it was until dawn. I aimed my flashlight overhead.

In the circle of light, the ceiling looked plastered with hills of shining black coral. Staring, I saw the mounds were not solid but writhing. Suddenly they broke apart, becoming bats descending and flying past us toward the late afternoon light outside, at first just a few but then black clouds of them, screeching at high pitch, making me feel I was stumbling through a nightmare. I wore a wide-brimmed hat, but in the dark it was still upsetting when occasionally, its sonar gone awry, one of the bats slammed into my head.

"You OK?" called Brady. "This is the part some people might not like."

When we reached the main camp, we heard that while we had been inside the cave, Demarest's team attended a ceremony with candles and incense at the base of the pyramid in the plaza. Then they entered the tomb.

"When you don't know, you're afraid," Rat Man told me later that night, about his first moments in the crypt. He had been helping archaeologists for a decade, but he was Maya, too, and full of respect for the ancestors. Within minutes, he said, it was clear the tomb held a burial undisturbed.

A dozen archaeologists and workmen waited for news atop the pyramid, a graduate student told us. They "froze" when the sky darkened quickly.

"Everybody realized it at the same time—we were standing at the highest point around," he said. They scrambled down the lumpy temple face, reaching camp as the rain began.

———

The night before I was scheduled to leave Dos Pilas, Demarest felt moved to go down to the crypt where he had been working, despite another storm. Of all times, this was the moment he decided I might come too. In raging rain. He guided us out of the camp with a lantern, past the fallen graven stones commemorating old victories. I climbed after him up the wet and sloppy pyramid wall.

On top, Rat Man had built a palm roof to protect the shaft opening from rain. As quickly as we could, Demarest and I ducked underneath and began the descent, lantern light jumping on the walls around us. My muddy, slipping boots made climbing down less sure-footed than ever. I didn't feel afraid, just unsteady. It seemed to take a long time to reach the bottom where I felt secure again, if you didn't count the hundreds of tons of rubble above our heads.

Demarest crawled into the tomb. I followed. He gestured to a place I could sit on the floor without endangering priceless artifacts. He pulled a portable stereo out of a knapsack and popped in a Doors tape. As I watched the archaeologist set to work with a small brush and trowel, time lost its ordinary measure once more, and Jim Morrison drowned out the thunder.

> You know the day destroys the night,
> Night divides the day.
> Try to run, try to hide.

Demarest uncovered Itzam K'awil's skeleton, and it looked virtually intact.

"You can't find a better one in a cemetery," he exulted, brushing dust from the perfect femurs.

Razor-sharp obsidian shards laced Demarest's hands with tiny cuts. Loose stones had crushed the skeleton's skull, but its attendant jade earplugs looked fine. A stingray spine lay nearby, a symbol of the genital piercing the king had performed in life. Demarest dug around the remains of a collar that had covered the monarch's chest, made of heavy jade beads. At the bones of the feet sat a pot from another Maya site, called Ik, a piece of "political information," he said, confirming tribute from a conquered kingdom, shoring up his theory that the skeleton ruled during a period of extended warfare.

Whether the excavation would prove that Itzam K'awil changed the long-standing rules of Maya warfare, spreading it, and thus tipped the first domino that caused the Great Collapse was not yet clear. But that was not what mattered in the heart of a rainforest pyramid. Arthur Demarest looked the calmest I would ever see him, a methodical archaeologist, working in dirt.

There was something culminating for me about the moment, gazing at the emerging bones, the modest treasures, the man working silently, the dust. This is where the Maya had got to after two thousand years of building civilization and mastering life in the rainforest. To a point where goods and prestige had become more important than peace, or life itself. Surely in years to come someone would warn, "But it wasn't that simple." They would say the weather changed or a celestial sign sent Maya packing or overpopulation exhausted the soil. Or all of these together caused the Great Collapse.

That is why I am glad I was able to spend time in the tomb, where factors and truths felt stripped to their simplest elements. My generation grew up afraid of annihilation by nuclear accidents or atom bombs, as if the products of technology had minds of their own. In the tomb, it felt clear that if we are to be done in, at some deep level it is acquisitiveness that will do it, unchained, human greed that clouds our reason, leads to war, devours the Earth as if it were one more object of consumption, making bloodless, glaucous lumps of our hearts.

Demarest turned to clip tiny roots around the remains of the large headdress. Its once-iridescent quetzal feathers and wooden frame were gone to dust, but pink-red spondylus shells and two-inch wide ovals of mother of pearl shone as if they had been buried yesterday. It was all too wonderful, too solemn to take in at once. He wanted to savor the moment. He reached into his pack and uncorked a bottle of Chilean red. We sipped from small beakers. He went back to work as music floated around the cool, damp crypt.

> *When you're strange,*
> *No one remembers your name.*
> *Faces come out of the rain . . .*

Weeks later, news of the tomb would hit the press in the United States, and charter planes ferry in photographers, embassy officials, and the more hardy sponsors, and Arthur Demarest would be swept up in the furious present. Over the five years of the project, ending in 1994, Dos Pilas would provide details of Late Classic Maya life deeper and wider than any other site. Brady would explore twenty-two caves and, together with Demarest, prove that important buildings indeed followed the sacred landscape of the underground rivers and caves. For the moment, however, Arthur Demarest looked content to sit in the dirt and slowly brush away the ages from the exquisite platters and bowls appearing under his fingers.

The tomb felt muggy, and I wondered if Demarest was going to work all night. I realized I didn't really care. There was a feeling in the tomb that echoed the moment the travelers dared to enter the palace of the underworld lords in the old Maya book, dancing right in, as if the adventure were just beginning.

2

Usumacinta, River of Dreams;
or, The Man They Killed

We had to force our way through branches of trees projecting out of the water, and often we had to use our machetes to remove the obstacles impeding our way. In spite of all our exertions we were frequently whirled round by the force of the current and carried downstream.

—Teobert Maler, exploring the central Usumacinta, 1903

THE SECOND-CLASS BUS–THE ONLY ONE THAT MADE THE RUN–came to its final stop at the Pasión River. Passengers stepped off and waited for a ferry to cross over to the town of Sayaxache. Long boats with curved prows and canvas roofs rode up and down before us. Except for outboards on their sterns, they looked like paint-chipped Egyptian barges, laden with maize instead of wheat, cobs poking out of burlap sacks stacked in mounds.

Months after leaving Dos Pilas, I returned to the scruffy river port I had passed through with Arthur Demarest and members of his team. This time I came alone, on a journey much less well planned.

From the ferry, I stepped onto the beach at Sayaxche with one man's name in my pocket, Donaldo Martinez, a government agriculture agent. A friend had promised that Martinez, who traveled the region, was sure to know how to find a boat from the Pasión down the great Usumacinta, the grandfather of Central American rivers. I had always wanted to know the river, the central highway of ancient Maya kingdoms.

Teobert Maler, an Austrian soldier who left the service when Mexicans executed his Hapsburg emperor in Queretero, reached Sayaxche in 1895. He called it a miserable collection of "a dozen cabins inhabited by Negroes who have straggled hither" from British Honduras, where former slaves remained subject to discrimination. A century later Sayaxche was a town of four thousand, with few blacks I could see, its population mostly ladinos—non-Indians—or Indians dressed as ladinos, and disproportionately male.

Part of the name of the town, Sayaxche, comes from the old Maya word for *ceiba*, the tree that grows at the center of the world. Walking its streets, however, I could make no connection to idyll or myth. Passersby did not return greetings as they do elsewhere in Guatemala, making me think more of Sayaxche's reputation as the end of the line, beyond the law, where village assassins and others on the lam can find jobs running contraband in and out of Mexico, no questions asked.

I checked into the only hotel with locks on the doors. I borrowed the phone at the desk, found Martinez's office number, and after several dropped calls made an appointment with him for later in the afternoon. I settled into a rocker on the hotel porch, which was raised on pilings for a view of the river. Time moved slowly, bright sun in white sky.

I was nearly dozing off when a cook in an apron came from the kitchen, carrying a live turtle in her arms. She placed the animal on a table covered with plastic and began to butcher it. She grinned at me occasionally over her knife, salt-and-pepper hair and yellowed teeth, proud of the work.

She lifted the breastplate and severed the membrane attached to the intestines so they spilled over her hand. She wielded the knife like a professional performer, avoiding the flailing legs, keeping hands out of reach of the turtle's jaws. The animal snapped in self-defense even as she dismembered it. When the cook flipped it over, the turtle blinked and turned a conical head on its long neck, a miniature dinosaur helpless on its back. She tipped the struggling remains so the creature's blood emptied into a gourd, for soup.

A boy brought a vat of boiling water, placing it at the foot of the table. The cook shoved in everything but the shell.

"The meat is still alive," she announced gleefully, forearms shiny with slime. I stood, stepped over to the vat, and looked. The white flesh still palpitated.

"For the best taste," she said, because the people of Sayaxche liked their turtle meat fresh killed.

The cook and the boy carried the vat to the stove. I went back to the rocker. The woman returned to scrub the plastic tablecloth with a brush and rag.

"I was eleven when I cut up my first," she said to me, drying a hand on her apron to brush hair from her eyes. "I'm thirty-nine now. Imagine all the experience."

Two burly men in cowboy boots came onto the porch. Shoulder holsters peeked from under their vests. They took chairs at the table where the turtle had just been slaughtered. The big guys didn't seem to notice, or didn't mind, the bits of gray-white flesh hanging from the corners of the plastic cloth or the shiny pool of viscous liquid on the floor at their feet. In a few minutes, they lifted their beers toward me in invitation. I declined and turned to look out again over the shoddy beach.

When I went to Donaldo Martinez's office, at first he seemed suspicious of me. I had no ulterior motive, I told him, only wanted to find someone to take me down the river for a few days. I think trust bloomed when I promised to send him certain books impossible to obtain in Petén.

"I have been a reader of books for four years now," he said.

Martinez, who looked about forty, told me he had first heard of Petén as a child in the 1960s, in his home village on the Pacific plain. Neighbors gathered in front of his parents' house after work, he said, and one of them with a year or two of schooling read the newspaper to the others. Everyone wanted to hear the stories datelined Flores, Petén's capital. They were not real news articles but government promotional dispatches, propaganda designed to lure population to the vast north.

El Petén is one-third of Guatemala's national territory, some twenty-three thousand square miles, but in the 1960s, only twenty-five thousand people lived there. Mexico wanted to build a dam on the Usumacinta, and Guatemala needed a populated littoral to reinforce an argument against it. Such a manipulative reason for inviting settlers did not matter to landless peasants.

"Petén was another world, the stories said, where there were snakes with wings, and tigers, and hundred-pound frogs, and where the earth was white," Martinez said. "People marveled at those ideas and thought Petén must be very mysterious, even wonderful."

———————

In his eloquent historical account of the continent, *The Open Veins of Latin America*, the Uruguayan writer Eduardo Galeano said, "Arbenz's fall started a conflagration in Guatemala which has never been extinguished." *Veins* appeared in 1971. Galeano might have written the same line today.

In 1954, a CIA-sponsored military coup ended Guatemala's "Ten Years of Spring," a decade of reforms that had abolished debt bondage, established social security, and introduced the idea of health care and schooling for the general population. The coup also ended the leftist government's attempt at land reform, which the democratically elected president Jacobo Arbenz hoped would develop agricultural production, bringing the nation "out of feudalism and into a modern, productive capitalist system," as he put it. At the time, 2 percent of the population owned 70 percent of the land, keeping millions of acres unused. The Guatemalan congress under Arbenz compensated owners of the idle tracts at the tax values they had declared, distributing it to landless farmers.

When the Boston-based United Fruit Company, the biggest owner of idle land in the country, was affected, Washington—long suspicious of Arbenz's independent, leftist attitudes—unleashed the coup. Land reform was reversed. For Donaldo Martinez, Petén was a better choice than remaining landless on the coast.

"Had my parents stayed in the village, they would have been exposed to total servitude, passing that on to their children and their grandchildren, servitude like many are in now, subject to what landowners and plantation owners decide," he said.

Martinez's father and six other men from the community journeyed to Petén to determine whether the newspaper stories were true. On their first nights, they heard the deep call of the *zaraguate*, the howler monkey, so they took turns staying awake, thinking it was a jaguar's roar. They didn't know how to hunt jungle animals for food. They were unaccustomed to the extremes of heat and rain and the visitations of insects.

One of the men died, conditions were so difficult. The others returned home with scales of the hugest fish anyone had seen. They carried back moon-white stones from the Petén's karstic limestone crust.

"People said, 'This is really another land. We should take the chance,'" said Martinez.

He still had the peasant's quiet voice and habit of looking down or to the side when he talked, too polite to meet another's eyes. His hair thinning, pudgy rather than stocky, Martinez infused sentences with long words that might have come from his readings. Documents and files stood around the office in leak-streaked cardboard boxes; clerks jumped in surprise when the telephone rang, because it was usually out of order. The central government in Guatemala City may have been on Mars for all the attention and funds it sent to provincial offices. Farmers awaiting clerks stood because there weren't enough chairs.

But Martinez said he loved his job, informing faraway villages about deliveries of organic fertilizer, holding meetings on how to feed healthy children from household gardens. Behind his desk hung a table of distances by water from Sayaxche to various settlements, and a handwritten evocation: TO PRODUCE IT IS NECESSARY TO LEAVE THE OFFICE FOR THE FIELD, GET HANDS DIRTY AND SWEAT.

I sent out for soft drinks all around. Spirits lifted as palpably as if someone had ordered champagne. Martinez said he would arrange a trip downriver with a restaurant owner and his elderly father, who had business to do in their old cooperative. I could pay for the gas, and we would do Martinez the favor of handing out flyers about an upcoming meeting to the agricultural cooperative settlements. I could sleep in *chozas*, the farmers' palm huts, along the way. The trip should take less than a week. We sipped our sodas wordlessly, like old friends.

"So, why did you leave your cooperative on the river?" I asked.

Martinez took a chart from a bottom desk drawer and placed it before me. All the Usumacinta co-ops—about a dozen—had shrunk in population from hundreds of residents each in the 1970s to just a few. Some were no longer there.

"What happened?"

Suddenly everyone in the office—clerks, farmers, the storekeeper who delivered the sodas—was speaking at once. "Talk to the man they killed," someone said, although in the bustle I couldn't see who said it.

"*Señores, por favor,*" Martinez said, quieting the room without moving from his chair. The men returned to their business in twos and threes, while the chief cleared his desk of papers. He folded his hands on its surface but did not raise his eyes.

"Maybe you do not know," he said. "Violence was not absent from Petén during the worst time, as those in the rest of the country believe."

"Is there something I should know about these places on the river?" I asked. "Who is the man they killed?"

"Some want to talk, others do not," he said, giving the impression he belonged to the latter. "Maybe it interests you, the first big fiesta on the river? I was only about seven or eight." He spoke for another hour, recollections infused with the affectionate glow often surrounding antebellum memories, wherever they may be.

———

We pushed off at dawn in the soft, new light, old Serafino Reina and I sharing the center plank seat, his son Jaime, about forty, behind us in the stern. Jaime, as hefty as his father was thin, manned a twenty-five-horsepower outboard engine that easily propelled the fiberglass boat, just fourteen feet long. Packets of food sat protected in the bow. Rice, beans, and scrambled eggs, said Serafino, wrapped by his wife in large, shiny green leaves.

Out of Sayaxche, the Pasión River flowed downstream in indolent curves. I liked Serafino right away. Sometimes I called him *Don* Serafino, using the honorific.

"There wasn't a hut or a clearing on these banks the first time I came down," he said, raising his voice over the sound of the motor. Unrolling before us like a ribbon, the river seemed to jog his mind. "There we were sitting in the boat that first time, the men from our village, looking only straight ahead," he said.

When Don Serafino smiled, decades dropped from his wrinkled face. "We were hiding our fear from each other, hour after hour, because we were each so startled at how endless the river was."

We fell into a comfortable, side-by-side silence, pointing out the occasional snowy egret to each other. On this stretch in the 1890s, Teobert Maler had to force his canoe's way through masses of mahogany logs waiting to be floated to the Usumacinta then downriver another four hundred miles to the Gulf of Mexico. No mahogany was in sight now, but thick stands of mangroves filled the river's swampy side pockets. Their thin, arched roots grew above ground, reaching out like spiders' legs trying the water.

I wore a wide-brimmed khaki hat tied under my chin, and Jaime a baseball hat that miraculously never blew off, but his father traveled bareheaded, squinting as the light grew brighter. Serafino's thin gray hair lifted in the wind. We ran for miles alongside verdant blocks of jungle, living walls of slim bay trees with powder-green leaves and tall gray-barked *sapodilla* trees, the kind that produce chicle for chewing gum. Palms grew everywhere, spreading wide fans close to the ground or slim, sensuously waving fans high in the canopy. Crowns of pink boulders rose above the water's surface; green lizards lay upon some of them, motionless in the sun.

Serafino pointed to a wooden sign on shore that said MANOS UNIDAS, Joined Hands. So this was it, I thought, a spot that played a small part in my own country's history.

In 1961, the US Central Intelligence Agency maintained a jungle prison here for recalcitrant Cubans de-selected from the Bay of Pigs invasion force. The hapless would-be invaders didn't like Fidel Castro but didn't want to take orders from officers of the former dictator,

Fulgencio Batista, either, and rebelled against racial discrimination from US troops. From the CIA training camp hundreds of miles away, in Guatemala's southeast, the mutineers were flown to the jungle. They slept in tin huts, but not behind fences. The loneliness of the place, its distance from civilization, the crocodiles and thick jungle, all were as good as prison walls.

I first heard about the Cubans from the founder of the Manos Unidas cooperative, the former Maryknoll missionary, Thomas Melville, a black or golden legend in Guatemala, depending on your perspective. On a visit to California in 1992 I had interviewed Melville, who told me he went to Central America in 1958 as an idealistic young missionary. Eventually, however, he and two other Maryknoll priests became known as the rover boys, not only for piloting planes and riding motorbikes. They cooked up projects to improve the lives of their peasant congregations, outside the reach of stuffy superiors.

"Simply saying Mass and burying children" who died from poor food and no vaccinations was "not enough," said Melville. (Another rover boy, Minnesotan Bill Woods, accompanied peasants settling the Ixcan lowlands, southeast of Petén, on land coveted by ranchers and military officers after American companies discovered oil nearby; in 1965, Woods died in a still-mysterious crash, in fine weather, ferrying supplies.)

Thomas Melville told me that one particular Sunday stuck in his mind, a turning point in understanding his highland parishioners' point of view, before Petén. Truckers with connections to local authorities had been attacking the farmers' nascent independent business, even running their hard-won communal truck off the road. Peasants pressed the padre: what moral rights of resistance did they have? There was no recourse in the legal system, moribund then as today.

Melville had just preached on the Good Samaritan when a farmer approached. Courteously removing his hat, the man asked, "What would the Samaritan's obligation have been if he had come around the bend an hour earlier and found those guys beating up on the man on the road to Jericho? Should he just stand there?"

"Well, what do you think he should do?" Melville said.

"With respect, Padre, I got the impression that if the Samaritan came in the middle of things, he should rub his hands and say, 'Don't hurt him too badly so I can pour oil on his wounds later and take him to the dispensary.'"

"I didn't say that," Melville retorted.

"Don't you think it's one man's obligation to try and save the other one's life?" the farmer asked.

"Well, how would you do that? These guys are attacking and may kill him."

"I think you should wade in and try to stop them. Your intention is not to kill the robbers but save the man."

"Yeah, I could agree with that," Melville said.

"So why don't you preach the right to self-defense?"

As a Catholic priest, Melville was committed to nonviolence. He said he saw the cooperative movement and Petén as real hopes. He went scouting for land on the Pasión late in 1961 when he saw the recently abandoned CIA camp, huts with cement floors, a water tower nearby, and a pump down in the lagoon.

"That would be nice to start out with," he said.

The straightforward colonel in charge of Petén colonization said, "It's yours."

In the 1960s other Roman Catholic priests, too, helped congregants establish co-ops. Fidel Castro's revolution had triumphed in Cuba, and a scramble had begun in Washington to keep other hemispheric dominoes from falling. President John F. Kennedy's Alliance for Progress dates from this time, an avalanche of aid and attention poured on poor Latin countries, aimed at heading off popular revolution. In that atmosphere, priests had a green light to help organize cooperatives: the ultra-conservative Guatemalan Catholic church had been an ally in the 1954 coup, a recognized bulwark against communism.

Thomas Melville's hair was gray when I interviewed him, but when he spoke of Petén, he described a young man's dream. "Ya know, it was almost Shangri-La when we first went there," he said.

As we passed Manos Unidas in the boat, I imagined Melville young and vigorous, scrambling up the shore, fired with the joy of leading dozens of dirt farmers to the promise of their own land. The jungle then was "absolute," he said. Settlers went hunting *jabali* with a .22—hard to bring down a wild boar with a .22, but they did it. They could get lost for two days, only an hour's walk from their houses. In the first year, some swelled so severely in reaction to insect bites they looked disfigured, until their bodies adjusted to lowland venoms.

By the mid-1960s, big landowners were coming into Petén, Melville said, many with tracts granted by friends in the region's military administration. During long evening conversations, the ranchers spoke freely because they were Catholic and he was a priest. "They planned to use arriving peasants as an underpaid work force," Melville said, looking indignant three decades later.

Without the technical assistance and infrastructure farmers had at Manos Unidos, however, the new cooperatives were doomed to at least partial failure. Members would have to work on the big new private Petén ranches to make ends meet. The labor system of the highlands and south coast—just what peasants were fleeing—would be replicated in their promised land.

Melville's frustration burst out at the Maryknoll house on a visit to Guatemala City, when Sister Marion Peter of the elite Monte Maria girls' school asked for help operating a radio. She needed to communicate, she said, with students away on a literacy project in the highlands. Melville said he scoffed, calling such efforts "band-aids when the problem was cancer." Off the cuff, he suggested the emerging bunch of Guatemalan "revolutionaries" held the answer. The nun replied that if he felt that way, she would introduce him. The guerrillas knew of his work in Petén, she said, and wanted to meet him.

"Whoa," Melville recalled saying. Despite his unorthodox vision of what a missionary's life should be, he did not jump at meeting guerrillas.

"I argued with Marjorie [Sister Marion Peter's original name, which she reclaimed when she left the Maryknoll order]. To say the revolutionaries had the answer was one thing, and getting mixed up with them was another. I told her we were naive, and neophytes in this kind of stuff, and how did we know they wouldn't use us?"

Nevertheless, Melville met with guerrilla commander Cesar Montes after hours in a Guatemala City high school. The *comandante* said if the guerrillas won, the priest's work would be important and respected in the new order. Montes made no plea for collaboration, Melville said, which the *comandante* later confirmed to me. Yet the priest invited students sympathetic to the guerrillas' cause to the cooperative to give sessions on literacy and political rights. Eventually, when the same youths became more clearly part of the rebel organization, they proposed returning to Manos Unidas to explore a passage between Petén and Ixcan, the contiguous lowland jungle where guerrillas were active.

"I said, 'Yeah, all right,'" Melville recalled.

"How could you have endangered the dream of the settlers of Manos Unidas like that?" I asked him.

"It never crossed my mind," he said.

Had he lost faith in the cooperative system?

He had lost faith in the idea that Petén was going to be the answer to land problems for people in the highlands, he said.

Before I left Melville's house that night in California, he gave a version of a meeting famous in Guatemala history, when foreign priests and nuns supposedly made a pact with the Marxist guerrillas. Melville insists it was this meeting, around Thanksgiving 1967, at which his brother Art, also a Catholic priest, and Sister Marion Peter were present, that caused their expulsions from the country, and not his work in Petén. It was a "philosophical" gathering of missionaries, he said, not political. Nevertheless, a mid-level guerrilla cadre attended. A Spanish priest ("I consider him an agent provocateur") declared, "We'll all be in the mountains by Christmas," a way of saying the missionaries would be joining the rebellion.

"We discussed the role of someone, at that time, who was supposed to be a teacher," Melville said.

About 85 percent of Catholic clergy in the country were foreigners, the population almost all Catholic. Priests and nuns faced the kind of questions the farmer had asked Melville after his Good Samaritan sermon, about the right to self-defense. The religious workers saw their parishioners poorer by the day, subject to state violence. What should they teach if they believed the revolutionaries were closer to answers than the government? What should their relationship be with the guerrillas?

"We felt we could be some kind of moral influence on the revolution-ary movement, and that would be our role," Melville said. "We were not sure we would be accepted, not because we were priests and sisters, but because we were foreigners. We would never carry arms. And we weren't sure we trusted the guerrillas entirely."

After they were expelled from Guatemala, Sister Marion Peter and Thomas Melville left their religious orders and married in the United States. They spoke out in interviews and a book on land and violence in Guatemala. But interest was on Vietnam, where Americans were dying. As two of the Catonsville Nine, Catholic peace activists who went to prison for pouring napalm on Selective Service records in 1968, the Mel-villes tried to draw attention to Guatemala but failed.

In Guatemala, meanwhile, some called Melville "the guerrilla priest," adding to the assumption, or propaganda, that activist Catholics and rebels were formally aligned. Dozens of priests and catechists died at army hands.

Serafino asked me if I wanted to stop at Manos Unidas. No, I said, not knowing his feelings about Melville.

"Too bad," he said. "That's the biggest co-op on the river. A very rich and beautiful place. They had a good start. A priest who worked hard. An American, like you. But he's gone now."

Soon we came to the confluence of the Pasión with the Salinas River, and the Lacantun, which drained the Lacandón jungle in Mexico. Each of the three streams seemed to possess its own temperature, its own density. They melded around the boat. I pulled the map from my back pocket. For the first time, it read *Usumacinta*.

This was the heart of the ancient kingdoms' commercial network, linking some of its finest royal centers: Altar de Sacrificios, Yaxchilan, Piedras Negras. I thought of the great river, more than six hundred miles long, as a road like the Maya causeways hidden now under jungle growth. Like the celestial *sacbe*, the white way, the Milky Way flowing across the night sky. Old Serafino grabbed his side of the craft. I felt Jaime straining to maintain control in the current, growing stronger.

Teobert Maler reached this point in 1895, pushing up the Lacantun to discover a carved limestone foreshore, revealed only in the dry season.

Copies of drawings he made, in books covered with red leather, rested in an Antigua library: nobles with feather headdresses, fabulous snakes, small animals unidentifiable or since disappeared, a series of concentric circles. Maler figured the illustrated limestone table was sacred, where Maya sacrificed to propitiate the water gods. He called it *El Sacrificio*.

"Can we pull in here?" I asked Serafino.

"No," Jaime said.

I longed to roam around, even to camp, to feel this part of the river at night. Serafino said nothing, deferring to his son. I turned to face Jaime.

"Why not?"

"We don't know people here, on the other side," he said.

"Just for a few minutes."

"No," he said. "*Dificil*."

In Guatemala, "difficult" means impossible. No way, forget it, not in this lifetime.

"*Drogas*," he said.

Drug runners landed planes on secret airstrips in the vicinity. They stored marijuana and cocaine on the Mexican banks. Without knowing exactly where the stashes were, we could meet trouble.

I would have to imagine what El Sacrificio felt like at night. In my mind I could see moonlight bouncing off the river, reflecting on the line of trees along shore. Maler had camped at a maize depot, where canoes arrived from the *monterías*, lumber camps deep in the forest, to buy corn. Before oarsmen loaded the cobs, they stripped the leaves to save weight, throwing the husks onto great piles on the rocks. At night they set the heaps afire. The landscape, wrote Maler, "appeared as if illuminated by a magic light."

Jaime slowed the boat as we rounded a bend. A bluff, cleared of jungle, loomed on the Guatemalan side. Flags waved over wooden sheds. Palisades of hewn trunks climbed a steep hill.

"We have to put in here—it's the law," Jaime said.

We debarked and climbed, threading a way among log fortifications with peepholes and gunsights, like those in restorations of forts in the American West. But these stood ready for use. Halfway up the hill, under a thatch roof, an official in charge of monitoring river traffic lazed in a rope hammock. For a while, he gazed at the woven fronds above our heads through half-closed eyes, rearranging his testicles, slurring orders to subordinates. Then he received the bad news, that one of the travelers carried a U.S. passport. He sent a runner to the top of the hill.

The commanding officer appeared, uniformed, startlingly tall and blond among dark-complected troops. Under his arm, he carried a biography of Genghis Khan.

"What do you do?" he asked me.

"Writer," I said.

"What do you write about, ancient times or modern times?"

"Modern times, sir."

"Well, there is nothing to write about here in modern times. Nothing has happened here in modern times. If you tell me you are writing about the Maya, about the ruins, that's one thing. But modern times? Do you work for Amnesty International?"

"No."

"You are entering a conflict zone," he said. "Americans give us trouble. You can be killed, and everyone will blame the army."

I decided not to blink first. Until it came to me that this man possessed the authority to turn us all back to Sayaxche. I blinked many times.

"Look," I said pleasantly, pointing out the author's name on the cover of the officer's book. "That's an American, you know."

"Yes, I know." He had read another by the same writer, he said, a biography of Cicero.

Instead of Cicero easing the situation, the lieutenant and I fell into parrying absurdly over the relative merits of members of the First Triumvirate: Julius Caesar, Pompey, and who? Yes! Crassus. I disliked the officer not because he was an ignorant boor but because, worse, he seemed intelligent, calculating, and intimidating, throwing his weight around on the edge of the universe. Serafino and Jaime looked as if they wished they had stayed home.

All green eyes, the lieutenant returned my passport.

"They had to kill him, you know," he said.

"Who?" I asked.

"Cicero."

"Why? Because he had a gift for saying things?"

"Because he could move the masses."

––––––––

The first cooperative we came to was named Los Laureles, for the tree of aromatic leaves. Donaldo Martinez had grown up in this village, where his warm fiesta memories returned as I walked dirt paths among small stick and adobe houses. The cooperative's anniversary party had been announced two months ahead, he said. People arrived by canoe, Mexican families from the opposite shore, but mostly they came from settlements like Los Laureles, on the Guatemala side.

"Those farthest downriver, near the white water, started at dawn, rowing against the stream," he had said. "At five o'clock in the afternoon, people were ready to dance."

They celebrated, "children too," with a battery-operated record player, until five in the morning. Martinez's dreamy look in his Sayaxche office when he described Los Laureles had said the place was once lovely beyond words. To me it looked like a dump.

After twenty-five years, the settlement still had no lights, drinking water, or road out, but, according to a woman selling soda from her window, it did have dengue—breakbone fever—and *camayote* flies that lay larvae inside wounds. I bought a bottle of warm Fanta Grape. The woman said a neighbor had died from cholera the week before.

"We put her in the cooperative's boat, but the engine failed," she said, leaning elbows on the sill. Men rowed the patient upstream to a hospital on the Mexican side, too late.

I gave her one of the flyers from Martinez, about an upcoming meeting on natural fertilizers. She regarded it carefully, top to bottom, smoothing its folds on the window ledge.

"I can't find anyone to sign this," Jaime said, his loud voice startling me from behind. "None of the men can read."

He waved a document with an official seal attesting that we had delivered flyers to residents of Los Laureles. He would have to return the form to the agricultural extension office, so Martinez could account to his supervisor for the paper used to make the flyer. Sometimes Guatemala's bureaucracy felt as thick as its jungle. Jaime ordered a Fanta Orange. "Can you sign this?" he asked the woman.

"*No leo*," she said. I closed my eyes. All that time studiously examining the flyer, and she can't read.

Jaime reached toward the ledge. The woman extended her hand, palm up, as if submitting to familiar ritual. Wordlessly, Jaime inked her thumb with a ballpoint pen, pressing it onto a line where a signature should have been.

Beyond Los Laureles, the river began to take on the color of the smoke in the air. Farmers burned to clear land for planting before the rainy season. The blazes created warm winds, which blew up waves where you least expected them. Under a matte sky, the water lost its sparkle. Sometimes it seemed we glided in a stream of tarnished silver, or lead.

Don Serafino appeared to tire, so Jaime and I delivered the flyers at more cooperatives. They seemed alike except for lyrical names, given by peasant farmers once elated at a second chance: Bonanza; Ixmucane, the Maya goddess of corn; Bella (Beautiful) Guatemala; Flor de Esperanza, Flower of Hope, after the line from a country tune, "I have a little plot of land filled with weeds and trouble, where there grows a flower of hope." I began to think "the man they killed" was not a real person at all but a symbol for something that had died on the river.

Serafino's eyes flickered with fresh life when we pulled into El Arbolito, his former home. He clambered out of the boat even before Jaime did, fastened the rope to a young tree, and disappeared up the bank. Up top, I saw him in a knot of old-timers sitting under a *chicozapote* tree.

I set off to walk alone, to hear nothing but bird songs, to feel the cooling late afternoon air coming in off the river. This was not jungle, born and living wild, but land once tamed, going feral again. Burning red hyacinths jumped from old garden beds and raged across paths like flames through brush. Morning glory vines wound purple-bloomed trailers around scorched trunks, through blackberry bushes, up and around any plant of height, a miasma of morning glory vines, the living warp of a mad weaver. Orange trees grew flush with shiny leaves, but their branches held undersized green balls. I peeled one; it was almost all skin. I wondered what race of plants the familiar trees, untended, might become if the land reverted to rainforest.

Taking another route back, I noticed what first seemed like volcanic rocks. But there was no volcano. The stumps stood at points of quadrangles. I had seen this before, in El Salvadoran towns burned to the ground by the military. Charred houseposts. There were dozens of them.

That night when I asked Serafino about the time he first came to Petén, in 1969, he replied with details that sounded as if they came from the nineteenth century, not the twentieth. "We packed flour sacks with seed and the few pots we had, and the children carried the chickens in their arms," he said. "The women wrapped extra clothes around the corn-grinding stones to cushion them for the trip, as if they were made of gold."

They brought enough corn and beans to survive on at first, he said, and seed to plant for themselves and the families to follow. They even brought chairs and tables if they had them, dismantled, right into the cabin of the military transports that flew them to the airstrip at Sayaxche, the adults white-knuckled, the kids crazy with happiness at the adventure. Launches took the pioneers downriver, dropped them on the beach without cutting the motors, and left.

The farmer families looked around at virgin jungle, no roofs for shelter, no roads out, and no boats, no lifelines to the outside world. "We founded our cooperative on the Day of the Tree, so we named it *El Arbolito*, the sapling," Serafino said.

"Then, on June 17, 1981, it all came apart."

This is the story of what happened the day everything changed for El Arbolito. I put it together from conversations over a few days with families at their houses and around the fire at night in the *choza* where I slept. I took the feeling from most that they sympathized with the rebels' stated goals at the time, ending military dictatorship, land reform to assure peasant farmers land ownership. They said they did not belong to guerrilla organizations, but I had no way to confirm this. Certainly these farmers were politically aware, believing the status quo must change and that they might change their own lives working together cooperatively. As Catholics in that time and place, they would have been exposed to liberation theology, in which the faithful examine their own lives in light of gospels that demand dignity for even the poorest on earth.

Also, local residents may have been among those countrywide who once, or many times, fed or guided guerrillas out of solidarity with them, without joining more overtly. One thing I know from my own ears is that peasants along the river did not use the rhetoric of the guerrilla groups and seemed truly unfamiliar with concepts such as communism, socialism, capitalism. Those I spoke with said they never carried arms against the government. "I support the authorities, right?" one farmer said at El Arbolito. "If one commits an error, he must pay for it. But that's not what happened here. Why did we, the just, pay for the sinners?"

Most of the other cooperatives I saw were attacked in the days after El Arbolito. Not too subtly, Serafino and Jaime Reina made sure I would hear the story by telling family and acquaintances I was *de confianza*, one who might be trusted. I sensed father and son, although they seemed so different, one kind, one gruff, shared a belief that the prospect of a written account gave their suffering and dead a kind of honor, or at least a record.

At 8:30 A.M. on June 17, 1981, three columns of soldiers disguised in tattered civilian clothes entered El Arbolito in pincer formation from its jungle side. They carried army-issue Israeli Galil rifles. They had walked in from a temporary camp at a village called Vista Hermosa, Beautiful View, three hours inland, one of the last places trucks might arrive by road.

The river was not a battlefront, said the farmers. There had been no skirmishes between the army and guerrillas, no sounds of even distant battle.

The troops brought two young men with them, Erasmo Aguilar, eighteen, and Rene Mejia, nineteen. The youths had lived in El Arbolito until, several months earlier, they said, they were heading for

Guatemala City to look for cash-paying work. Now Aguilar and Mejia were returning with hoods, *capuchas*, over their heads.

Soldiers ordered the population onto the soccer field, where they were "spread all over the grass like clothes drying," as one man said. They brought women from a line at the mill, still holding their plastic dishes of corn, teachers and students from school, where they had been practicing a Father's Day skit. At first, some parents hid well among the trees, but when they saw their children under the guns, they walked into the open and joined them.

Soldiers dragged Reginaldo Aguilar, Erasmo's father, out of the cooperative store, away from its real showcases of farm implements and one or two outboard motors—no longer had settlers been making the expensive, arduous trip to Sayaxche, or paying the exorbitant prices of the trade boats, to buy goods. Troops looted the store, pulling new shirts and pants over their clothes, donning the stock of bright tennis shoes, leaving their own behind in a mocking heap. The raid on this store stayed in people's minds—everyone I talked to mentioned it with regret, as if a family business had been destroyed.

On the grassy field, the *encapuchados*, Mejia and Aguilar, walked slowly, accompanied by soldiers. Facing each man, one by one, the hooded ones either shook their heads no or gave the fatal nod.

Over the years, I have interviewed dozens who witnessed *encapuchados* betray others. Survivors said they recognized the men (always men) despite the hoods. Listening to residents at El Arbolito, for the first time it occurred to me to question, why then the disguise? Who in Arbolito, with fewer than one hundred families, would not recognize the body shapes, the walks, of two boys who had grown up among them? Perhaps the black hoods with their ragged eyeholes were a perverse detail intended to intimidate, to rob the condemned of even the dignity of facing the accuser.

Another possibility. The hood may be ordered to ensure the *encapuchado* performs without breaking down emotionally, becoming incapable of performing the final betrayal. In the end, the dark cloth *capucha* may not be for the victim at all, but for the traitor. A mask on the face to keep the knees from buckling. To soak up tears.

Fourteen men received the nod that day at El Arbolito. Each was grabbed by the hair, thrown on the ground, handcuffed, hauled to his feet again, and herded to the Catholic chapel on a hill.

A few soldiers stayed behind with the neighbors on the grass. The armed men identified themselves as guerrillas and then pointed their rifles at the men and women, calling *them* guerrillas, demanding the whereabouts of arms and ammunition. Those I spoke to brought up the same curious detail: no one, man or woman, escaped the feeling of being punished that day, as if for something he or she had done.

Troops in the chapel trussed the captive men together, marching them out and toward their inland camp. Days later, six of the prisoners straggled back to the river, with burn marks around their necks where a noose had been tightened and released repeatedly, so they would fall in and out of consciousness. Maybe they were spared because they confirmed what the army wanted to hear about the others.

Were Erasmo Aguilar and Rene Mejia guerrillas? Their names divulged under torture by some other rebel or found on a list of would-be recruits in a raided safe house in the capital? There is no way, for me at least, to know for certain. What might have induced them to point out the others can only be imagined. The boys disappeared with the rest of the captives, whose bodies have never been found.

Which side were the cooperatives on? It may be more important to ask which side the military presumed they were on. Before the attack, guerrillas had turned up on the river, buying from co-op stores. When farmers saw them crossing the Usumacinta into Mexico, they were unlikely to report it to authorities. Some almost surely acted in sympathy by keeping information to themselves; others may have seen silence as a way to stay uninvolved.

Jaime said that before the army hit the river towns, sign-up lists appeared in the hands of *enganchadores* (literally those who hook or rope in) who claimed to be recruiting agents for the rebels. Young men especially were encouraged to register for tasks or training to be specified later, he said; if they were reluctant, the *enganchador* might act threatening or claim everyone else in the neighborhood had signed on.

"Recruitment lists" may have been an army ploy to determine who would side with the rebels given a chance. They had used the trick elsewhere. If the lists were genuine, however, the army would have regarded them as incipient rebel organization of the cooperatives. Or perhaps Jaime was lying. Whatever the details, the war had come to the river inescapably with the mere presence of the rebels.

Cooperatives are by nature reformist, not revolutionary, organizations, with a capitalist view. They exist so members can make a profit as individuals and as a group, to buy seed in bulk at a discount, for instance, or expand crops. El Arbolito was not a miserable, hopeless place. Any child could attend school up to sixth grade, above the average level in Guatemala even today. Both cooperative and individuals owned boats and motors, and many owned cattle—Don Serafino had 120 head. There also was a sense the place was becoming important beyond itself: a soils-testing laboratory served the entire littoral; volunteer labor had built a twenty-bed hospital with funds from a Belgian religious organization; a class of paramedics had just graduated, and classes for paramedics and midwives from up and down the river were in session when the soldiers came.

The army looked at the big new clinic and accused the villagers of training medics for the guerrillas. They looked at the communal land ownership and saw red. They burned it all to ash: hospital, school, store, church, every single house. They left behind a psychological mark, too. When residents on the river refer to El Arbolito, you can hear a dirge behind the words, that community progress is short-lived, perhaps even dangerous. The new attitude on the river is not like the old one. Since the burnings, say the old farmers, they don't take life by the horns.

———

The morning we were to continue downriver dawned foggy. I heard the soft sound of women at the fire, rhythmically patting cornmeal into tortillas. I dressed quickly. From the doorstep, I saw Serafino descending the hill. He must have been sleeping in the ruins of the old chapel. By the time I caught up he was down by the shore, sitting on a boulder near the boat, looking at the river, his back to El Arbolito. A woven shoulder bag rested packed at his feet, ready to go. He was *desanimado*, he said, dispirited.

I sat alongside. I had to ask: Did the armed men kill a dream?

"Yes," he said, without hesitation. "We had a vision of achieving something, as much for ourselves as for our country. But we became demoralized when this violence happened. Now people live here just to pass their lives. They plant only to eat and sell a little, not like before when we planted to better ourselves, to better everything."

The river was running clear because a brisk morning wind meant no one risked burning fields. Serafino said he would never live at El Arbolito again.

I did not look his way but stared at the river, too. In my mind, however, I addressed the old man as if I were looking right into his eyes.

The army knew what it was doing, didn't it? You had your own road. There was no city hall around, no representatives of the state to bother you, only as much church as you wanted. And you called your system cooperativism or whatever; but all the army saw was that people on the river were acting deliberately, according to plans, and that you aspired to escape from the rule that had prevailed for the life of the country, that peasants exist to work for others and never get ahead themselves.

You threatened the old system, and that threatened the army. It didn't discriminate between the enemy that was the guerrilla and the enemy that was the river communities. They saw both of you as organized, suspicious, outside their control.

Serafino murmured, "All my youth went into this, and it was in vain, because in the end nothing was achieved."

It was a sizing-up voice, and it shook.

"Lost. Into the garbage. Because of the bad minds of people who interpreted us badly. All the effort one put out to *superarse*, to become more than what one had been. It ended, in a little bit of time."

His grief enveloped me. If someone had suggested that there was an alternative truth on the river, I would have found it hard to believe. But there was. And I would hear it from, of all people, the man they killed.

As we floated farther down the evaporating stream, Jaime worked the tiller intently, aiming the silver prow of the little boat at the deepest-looking channels. In a week or two, the rains that had already started upriver would arrive and raise this treacherous sluice to its safer, customary heights. At that moment, however, the Usumacinta must have been reduced to the minimum flow a body of water might maintain and still be called a great river.

The Yucatán peninsula, the Mexican part and Guatemala's Petén, rests on limestone karst, skeletons of marine animals that sank to the bottom of the great sea that once covered these jungles. Parts of the karst skeleton were visible now, rocky islands in the river like bumps on a twisted spine. Whenever the water went shallow, Jaime expertly yanked up the engine. Despite its low level, the river still gave a feeling it could take your life, that it was boss. Swirls and eddies appeared out of nowhere. Some looked capable of gulping a small boat like ours whole, swallowing it down through some sink in the bed.

On calm stretches, I saw even more kinds of plants per glance than on the Pasión, as if the Usumacinta had been less touched by human hands, retaining the botanical mix that marked primal forest. Trees bearing soft, yellow *tamborillo* flowers. Bromeliads, tiny bursts of intensely blue and purple orchids. The fanning *xate* palms with fronds that florists at home import for the most elegant arrangements, growing here wild. The trunks of the biggest trees looked like columns on Greek and Roman temples, massive enough to bear the weight of centuries.

Jaime said we would soon reach our turn-around destination, the settlement called Bethel, and that the two of them would go no farther. He was, I think, concerned about his father. They would be heading back to Sayaxche, with me or without me.

"Have I already met the man they killed?" I asked Jaime.

"No," he said. "Must you?"

"I want to," I said.

I would have to go to another cooperative, beyond Bethel, alone, he said. I should look for a man called Juan Ramirez.

Low waterfalls spilled white and frothing into the river. Fed by underground streams, they felt icy where their waters reached us, like the temperature in Xibalba, realm of the Lords of Death. Lifeless trees lay submerged. Bare branches reached up and out of the water like petrified arms.

Jaime had warned that if I reached the cooperative called La Tecnica, to look for the man they killed, I should not sleep overnight, because it was too remote, too underpopulated, with no army post. "You have talked with many people on the river," he said when we parted at Bethel. "Who knows who was listening and what they think?"

I paid a fisherman to drop me off at La Tecnica. When he motored away, I looked around cautiously. A pig turned dirt with her snout, eight piglets fighting to reach her teats. No other life at the docking beach. I threw water from the river on my face and sat to get my bearings.

When Maler finished work at the Maya city of Yaxchilan in April 1900, he hid his extra luggage, photographic equipment, and paper molds of stelae in an abandoned temple, rowing to reconnoiter the area just north of where I sat. He took a tributary of the Usumacinta called the Little Yaxchilan River. Maler, in love with Maya ruins and a genius in documenting them with the budding art of photography, left a stunning body of work on which much early archaeology depended. He had an erratic, obstreperous personality, however, and some of his theories about the ancient Maya, or Atlantis, for that matter, might kindly be termed eccentric. But I liked the man because he was an adventurer in spirit, with no false modesty about assessing every person he met, every landscape he saw.

The Petén would develop, Maler believed, if only "some American company" would blast away obstructions and make the Usumacinta navigable for deep-draft ships its full length to the sea, much like the Amazon is naturally deep for hundreds of miles. This would bring "intercourse with the world," an opening to business, and a boon for research in nature and archaeology.

"It would become the fashion to travel on this famous river, which my publications have in a measure made known to the European and American world," he wrote.

A century later, in the 1990s, the only traffic I saw was an occasional canoe or a flat-bottomed boat clandestinely taking corn from the Guatemalan side of the river, where there were still almost no roads, to the Mexican side, where rough roads might move a crop to market. Except for the most determined travelers, others stayed away.

In Maler's time, Lacandón Indians still lived on Guatemala's Little Yaxchilan. A woman served him a dozen small fish hung on a vine and roasted bananas for dinner. Another Lacandón sent her oldest son to guide him to a mountain cave, where he found human faces carved onto stalactites, "perhaps by people of a long vanished race." Maler climbed a rise and wrote that from the point where he stood to Lake Petén Itzá, some 150 miles west, was "boundless wilderness . . . nothing but a vast, uninhabited and unexplored tract of country." Sometimes I felt that if people disappeared, the Petén would revert quickly to that uninterrupted jungle, where animals roam safely and great trees fall only to lightning and hurricanes.

After the June attacks upriver, rebel flyers had appeared in La Tecnica warning residents the army wanted to "repress" them. Locals burned the notes so soldiers wouldn't find them, or used them for toilet paper. Army troops arrived to warn, "Don't get mixed up in *babosadas*," the sentimentality that rebels would use to recruit them.

I learned these details from a woman named Magdalena, whom I asked for directions as she sat on a porch with her husband. Jaime's warning concerned me, but what else was I to do if I wanted to talk to this man with the eerie sobriquet? I was careful to use his proper name.

"Do you know where Señor Juan Ramirez lives?" I asked.

"The man they killed," said Magdalena.

He would not yet be home, she said, but she called a small girl from inside the house and sent her away with the message that Don Juan had a visitor. Both Magdalena and her husband, who spoke little, seemed astonished to hear I had visited El Arbolito, Bonanza, and the other cooperatives. When I mentioned the name of the *presidente* of one settlement, she told me without surprise that he was an uncle and asked me to sit with them. Of course she knew Donaldo Martinez, too. The small world of the long river worked to my advantage, permitting conversation as if I were *conocida*, someone known to others in their wider circle.

Rebels arrived openly at one time in La Tecnica, Magdalena said, in groups of three to ten, men and women, to buy supplies, sometimes to call a meeting about what they would do if they won the war. Each time, they returned to the jungle. Army troops, however, occupied the village for days. "Five minutes after the *chafas* [soldiers] left, *los muchachos* [the boys, rebels] came back." In late 1981, the army forbade townspeople to sell to anyone in military garb.

"Even to soldiers, although they did not like the idea," Magdalena said.

When guerrillas came through, they told locals the army had massacred entire villages in the highlands. Leave if you can, they advised.

Magdalena said, "But we had nothing to hide. He who owes nothing has nothing to fear."

Around three o'clock, a boy and a girl, about ages four and six, ran toward us in a state of high excitement. "His children," Magdalena said. "Don Juan's." I bid the couple good-bye and followed the jumping, clapping kids uphill to a small house with chickens running in the yard.

"Papa, papa!" the children called, presenting me like a stone found on the beach.

I stood before the man they killed, and for a moment I couldn't speak. He looked fit, if thin, in his late thirties, with dark-circled eyes and a gently ironic smile.

"*Mi casa*," he said quietly, and invited me inside.

We sat on either side of a narrow table in the one-room house. Ramirez's wife, named Lupe, stirred a blackened pot on a wood-fire stove. Sticks lashed with vine made the walls. Sunshine fell through them, slim rods of light crossing Juan Ramirez's shirtless body, a blue tablecloth, my notebook, my hand. The children lost interest. They took up a game of marbles at their father's feet.

"It was the day after Christmas, 1981, late afternoon," Ramirez began. "Five of us sat in a patio, just in from the cornfield, still wearing boots."

Two dozen armed men burst into town, he said, acting irritated, belligerent, *enojados*, as if they had just gone through a rough time in the jungle, perhaps been ambushed or thrashed in combat. "Maybe they were looking for someone to blame, to give air to their anger," he said.

"'You are guerrillas,' they said, but they knew we were not guerrillas. We carried only our machetes. We said we were simple farmers. Anyone could see we had been working. Then they said *they* were guerrillas."

Three more armed men brought Jorge Careto, a nineteen-year-old storekeeper, to the patio. "He looked afraid," Ramirez said.

"Were you afraid?" I asked. He took a moment.

"I wasn't afraid, I was afraid," he said.

Outside the open window, birdsong grew louder, so I bent closer to him. "They shackled our hands, piled packs on our backs. 'Walk, you sons of bitches,' they said. I am sorry, but that is what they said."

"Yes, it's OK, I understand," I said. "I have come a long way to hear what you have to say. They call you 'the man they killed.'"

Lupe looked up at us across the pot. She continued to pour a spoonful of beans into her hand, glancing down again to taste them.

"Yes, 'the man they killed,'" said Ramirez.

When they reached the fields outside town, the armed men murdered the oldest farmer, who was walking too slowly. He was "a bachelor," Ramirez said, who had never found a woman on the river to marry, a founder of the cooperative. It was he who had baptized the settlement with its original name, Light of Souls.

"We walked about an hour, through jungle, when we came to a cow paddock," Ramirez said. The armed men set up a communications radio.

"That was where they showed for certain they were the army. One of them was near me, elevating the antenna, when another came over and said, 'Hey, one of the soldiers is missing.'"

"'Shut up, you son of a bitch,' said the other. 'Don't say we are soldiers.'"

In the dark, patrol and captives walked five more hours, until the lieutenant in charge called another halt. He lifted his chin in a silent order. A pair of soldiers grabbed Jorge Careto, the storekeeper, and pushed him into the bush. Careto once had angered straggling troops in uniform by refusing them merchandise, following army orders. Now the men accused him of selling to guerrillas. Ramirez heard the young man struggle. Shots cracked. Quiet.

Then it was his turn.

"'So you know we're soldiers?' the lieutenant said to me. Then he told two other men, 'Take this son of a bitch away and kill him.'"

Ramirez said he felt a rifle in his back as he walked. They told him to lie down on his stomach.

"One took out his machete. I was thinking, kind of calmly, 'It is now that they're going to kill me.'"

He lay facedown in the dirt. A soldier lifted his head by the hair, exposing the neck.

"He sliced across from here," Ramirez said, drawing two fingers from his left ear to the center of his throat. "Then here." Turning his head, he moved the fingers cleanly across toward the middle from the other side. "I didn't feel cut—it only felt like a string was passing across my neck," he said.

But in the next moment blood flowed so thick, and his head tilted so unnaturally into the dirt, that Juan Ramirez said even he thought he had been decapitated.

Lupe served the children, who sat in miniature chairs and ate from plates on their laps. A man in weathered pants and shirt dropped in, consulted with Ramirez about the co-op's new corn husker, and left. I kept my eyes on the man they killed. I felt as if I were talking to a balladeer or a ghost.

I believe he sensed this. "Look," he said.

Ramirez lifted his chin. Slowly, he rotated his head left to right. His lean, muscular torso shone with sweat. I did not touch the scar but felt as if I had.

"I don't know why it did not occur to them to shoot me," Ramirez said. "It's the pure work of God I'm alive."

After they cut his throat, the soldiers unlocked the cuffs behind Ramirez's back. He dropped his hands like a dead man's.

"Imagine what you can do to defend yourself when you have to," he said. "The one who cut my neck, kicked me in the back. 'The son of a bitch is dead,' he said."

Ramirez heard the soldiers walk away and report to the lieutenant. He concentrated hard, he said, to gag without making noise, swallowing blood and vomiting it up again.

"'What time is it?' I heard the lieutenant ask. 'Three twenty-five,' someone said. 'Good,' he said. 'We will reach the highway before light.'"

The captive neighbors, Ramirez said, later were found shot dead at a settlement called Betania.

Ramirez said he lay still, facedown, for what seemed a long time. Slowly he crawled to a tree, lifting himself to lean against its trunk. "I took off my shirt and wrapped it around my neck, like this."

He waited for dawn. He heard branches snap, then silence. He began to believe he had not been fated to die at the hands of the army but by the jaguar, drawn by the smell of blood.

"When I saw the first light, I took off my boots," Ramirez said, because dry leaves make noise. He reached a village called Sinai, where residents already knew of the kidnapping, and some had heard shots in the night.

"I could see it in their eyes," he said. "They thought I was a ghost."

He pushed on toward the water, where he saw a canoe with an oar. "I robbed it. I went downstream, home. But the houses were empty." The inhabitants of La Tecnica had fled overnight across the river to Mexico. Ramirez rowed across the Usumacinta, too. He found his neighbors in a refugee camp.

Lupe served us coffee. Ramirez looked down at his hands. He took a deep breath. I prepared myself for wisdom, some lesson to be taken from his experience. Instead, he looked up with the eyes of a man asking forgiveness.

"I *had* to steal that canoe, don't you see?" he said.

We finished our cups of coffee in silence. Ramirez asked, "Do you want to see the corn husker?"

"Of course," I said. We walked.

"The love one has for where one comes from never ends," he said. "I was anxious to work our own land." In 1991, he and others returned to the cooperative, and by 1994 some twenty-four of the original seventy-five member families were living again in La Technica. Ramirez became the cooperative's *presidente*.

Inside a boxy cement structure with a tin roof stood a new generator, providing electricity for the first time in La Tecnica's history, four hours in the evening. Nearby was the new husker, a simple machine that cut the time spent separating kernels from the cobs by 50 percent.

It was hard to believe anyone who had been through an experience like that of Ramirez might be talking calmly about corn huskers. I thought he should be out of his mind with vestigial fear. At least show a nervous tic.

"Have you considered vengeance?" I asked.

"Soldiers aren't the ones to blame," he said. "As they say, 'so it is written, so it must come to pass.'"

"But someone must be at fault for violence against those who don't deserve it, right?"

"Yes," he said. The gentleness went from his voice. "The ones who sent them, their chiefs."

River farmers were unlikely to see satisfaction from the "chiefs." No Guatemalan officer ever has been cited for excess, none brought to trial for a war crime. Perhaps Juan Ramirez was correct to guard his memories, to move on with life as much as he could. When it came time to exchange names on paper, I saw he could hardly write.

"I tell the *compañeros* here that we always should treat each other very carefully, to discuss things and not offend," he said. "Because sometimes one doesn't measure words well. Maybe one offends another, and that person feels bothered, and that is where the contradictions and feuds come from, and maybe that can lead to a bigger disaster."

For Ramirez, living where two armed forces fought meant neighbors might turn against one another under pressure or in order to survive. Things are better now, he said, the plate set correctly on the table.

But before we said good-bye, Juan Ramirez quoted a Guatemalan saying: "You never know when the plate will turn over again."

At dusk I hired a boatman for the short trip back upriver to Bethel. When the late-night bus came, I grabbed a front seat for the legroom and for the wide view out the front window. We bumped continuously on the dirt road, but the night was superbly clear, with a thin new moon and stars bright as Christmas.

The river journey came back to me in images, as if I could see them reflected on the window, beginning with old Serafino's boatloads of peasants arriving at their promised land, ending with Juan Ramirez twelve years later, hand on his neck to staunch the blood, overcoming repugnance at robbing a boat to escape to Mexico. Serafino had said he would never live on the Usumacinta again. Juan Ramirez, despite what he had been through, looked at the future with something like hope.

I felt as if I had been seeing a microcosm of all Guatemala, of all post-war Central America: there was no choice but to continue, to recognize that the roots of war have not been eliminated, but to hope violence would not break out again soon.

Outside, a hundred fires lit the blackness. The rainforest was going up in blazes, the work of hungry settlers anxious to plant corn. They would farm independently, isolated from one another. Cooperatives, and the future of Petén, would be the last things on their minds. Juan Ramirez was out there, too, figuring how to increase his village's corn profits next year with the help of the new husker.

I wondered which of those two forces would prevail, the desperate newcomers or the experienced but still poor farmers like the resurrected Ramirez, working with neighbors. I wondered if there would be any forest left to cut down in twenty years. I pressed my face to the glass. Because it was still so dark, sometimes it was hard to tell where the sky stopped and the ground began. It looked as if fires peppered the air, or stars burned on earth.

3

The Skulls of San José Itzá

SEEN FROM AFAR AT MIDDAY, WHEN THE SUN BLEACHES THE sky, the island of Flores floats on Lake Petén Itzá like a mirage. Thick-walled pastel houses lose their density, shimmering like gossamer. The cathedral's slender towers and dome look transported from a desert kingdom, calling more for the muezzin's voice than a church bell.

Crossing the causeway from the mainland to the island, a walk of less than half a mile, I felt faint from the heat. I had been away from Petén for almost a year, on assignment in Europe and visiting family in California, and was not yet reaccustomed to the sultry air. Nothing to do for it but find the *posada*, shower, and lie under a ceiling fan through the worst of the afternoon.

That evening, strolling the lee of the island, I heard bullfrogs calling from the water hyacinths, promising rain. Clumps of the plants, pur-ple or white, broken off from the central mass, floated like miniature

91

islands. The Maya glyph for water hyacinth can represent the name of a god of the Underworld. The flowers were as shapely and delicate as orchids, except they feed not on air but on water, the medium of travel after death.

When possible, I used Flores as my base in Petén. It was only a mile square, and the memory of the Itzá Maya, the kingdom that held out longest against the conquerors, was everywhere. The cathedral stood upon the ruins of the most sacred Itzá temple. Children played in a park among carved stelae. Stone steps leading to porches of small houses looked like blocks recycled from pyramids.

The Spanish captured the last Itzá king, Canek, in 1697, carrying him away in chains to Antigua, then capital of the viceroyalty. Most Itzá who were left behind fled into the jungle. Over years, friars lured the displaced from their hideaways, a few at a time, settling them in a town on the lake's far shore, Ixtutz, whose name was changed to San José Itzá. It has always been a purely Indian town, where an unwritten rule said outsiders were not welcome to live.

From my hotel that night, I looked across dark waters in the direction of San José and imagined its faces would be different from those of the island. On Flores, the surname Canek, the name of Itzá kings, remains prominent, and older residents use Maya household words, for kitchen implements, for instance. To my eye, however, Flores was an island of ladinos, descendants of colonists, not Indians. I wanted to cross the lake to visit the Maya whose grandparents a dozen generations ago made a last stand for independence. No foreheads purposely sloped, of course, or teeth shaped to sharp points, but otherwise visages that mirrored those of the last free indigenous kingdom on the continent.

The next morning, I walked the causeway back to the mainland, to a dock used by passenger boats from San José Itzá. In a shoreline field, two children flew triangles of blue plastic. The Day of the Dead, November 1, was not far off. Kites helped souls fly up to heaven, even if they must travel on found plastic and old string.

When the boat arrived, high school students from San José spilled onto shore and headed for classes in San Benito. I boarded with two teachers going to work at the elementary school in San José. The pilot steered the boat north, and we passed saplings floating near shore, uprooted by the overnight rain. A canvas roof shielded us from the sun. Around midpoint in the lake, tule reeds rose above the surface, bending gently in the faint breeze.

Hernán Cortés, the Spanish soldier and explorer, stopped briefly at Lake Petén Itzá in 1525 on his way to subdue a recalcitrant officer in what is now Honduras. Cortés left behind a favorite horse gone lame, which the Itzá fed a diet of flowers, befitting a creature with a touch of the divine, the first they had seen who ran like wind and made the sound of thunder with its hooves. When the horse soon died, the Itzá tried to make amends, giving birth to the kind of spiraling misunderstanding that characterized so much of the period of first contact.

Itzá sculptors created a stone statue of the animal, which they named Tziminichac after the thunder god, so they might present Cortés with at least a likeness of his horse. Cortés never returned. Almost a century later, however, in 1618, two missionaries sent by the bishop of Yucatán to evangelize the Indians saw the statue at an altar and flew into a rage, assuming it was an object of pagan worship. They smashed the stone horse to bits. The Itzá king, also named Canek, barely managed to save the missionaries' lives from a furious population. (Back in the Yucatán the bishop was also displeased. "Before destroying the Indians' idols," he told the friars, "you should have destroyed the beliefs they held for adoring them.")

The Itzá carved another Tziminichac, which fell overboard when they tried to float it from the mainland to the island. I looked over the side, hoping to see an animal form, even briefly, through the gray-blue water. Older residents of Flores have told me that when they were children (always when they were children), once, when the water was very low (always only once), they saw a wavering image of the stone horse, looking up wide-eyed from the bottom of the lake.

When we reached San José Itzá, the teachers said good-bye and walked diagonally to the school while I headed straight up the steep main street, drawing a glance or two. When I said *Buenos días* and *Mucho gusto*, however, passersby readily returned the greetings. Yes, faces were different, skin ruddier, cheekbones more prominent. I saw no cars. I knew the town had no telephones. Some houses were built with cement blocks, but more seemed in the old style of wattle and daub with thick palm thatch roofs, materials that would have been familiar to the Itzá refugees from the conquered island.

A church tower rose about two blocks away, stucco painted pale lemon. I walked over and saw the letters on the bell were large enough to read: "1718," it said, just twenty-one years after the fall of Tayasal, as Canek's kingdom was called. Inside the small church, plastic flowers, the only kind that last in the heat, stood in glass jars. Filmy white curtains blew lightly through open doors and windows, a trick of the tropics, to give an illusion of coolness. To the right of the altar, looking out through transparent glass from inside a wooden box, stared three skulls. Whatever worship took place in this church was linked with a much earlier age. On the floor burned a single candle whose smoke rose and curled at the level of the hollow eyes.

A man approached, carrying what looked like a cleaning rag in one hand. "The candle burns for those who have no living relatives to remember them," he said.

"Thank you," I said. *"Mucho gusto."*

He introduced himself as the sacristan and turned to dust the pews, a still-young man lame in one leg, his head leaning to one side, as if he had been born with a condition that destined him to walk always at an angle. When he finished one side of the church, he returned, shuffling, to the altar.

"Do you see the *Cristo Negro*?" he asked.

It would have been difficult not to see, a crucifix above the altar bearing a dark-skinned Christ, more Indian than European. The *Cristo Negro* of Esquipulas, about 250 miles east, has drawn Central American pilgrims for years, as the Kaaba draws Muslims to Mecca. Other Black Christs appear in Petén, many with miraculous tales about how they came to arrive. I wondered why the sacristan would be pointing the visitor to a crucifix when three human skulls sat nearby.

"Who are they?" I asked.

"No one knows," he said. "They have been here a long time."

"I imagine so."

"I must finish the work," he said. He walked down the other side of the church, flicking his rag at the pews. When he approached me for the third time, his work apparently finished, I thought he was going to ask me to leave.

"My uncle was the *prioste* once," the man said kindly, naming a traditional community position with responsibility for ritual traditions. "He carried the skull when he was young. Perhaps he will receive you."

The uncle's name was Domingo Chayax, his house an old-style one in the middle of town, and he wasn't home. Chayax's wife, Teresa, invited me inside. Deer skulls and unpainted gourds hung from nails in wood slat walls. Radiant *guacamaya* parrot feathers had been stuck here and there around the room like mood lighting.

Teresa served powdered instant coffee, unfortunately . considered more special for a guest than the drink brewed from beans. She said she was sixty-two but looked much older, with gray hair pulled back from her lined face, wearing a tissue-thin flowered dress.

"I have fifteen children," she said, "six alive."

We talked easily, reminding me of those suddenly deep conversations one can have on a train between strangers who have no reason to think they will ever meet again. "Conversation" is not an accurate term for Teresa's running monologue, but I didn't mind. It felt comfortable, even marvelous, to sit in this room waiting for an old man who knew about skulls, looking out occasionally through the open front door, its rectangle framing the barely moving, dark blue lake. Looking at that lake gave you a detached and peaceful feeling, confirmation that there were places in the world that remained much as they had been created.

"It was just like today," Teresa said. "My mother and father left in their boat at dawn to fish. The lake as calm as you see it now, calm with the shine of a mirror."

No one knew whether a freak wave had overturned their canoe or if the dog, excited at a turtle or jumping fish, tipped over the thin wooden vessel. Teresa described the discovery of her dead mother as if she had recently redreamed it.

"There she was, her body held by the silt, her arm stretched out looking so long, and two fingers above the surface of the water . . ."

There was no stopping Teresa, intent on "just filling the time" before her husband came home. It seemed stories were the stuff of life for her, a natural storyteller with a sense of how a story moved and how it should end, unshaped by the formulas of television. She recounted the passing of a daughter, age three and a half, of "a fever." No moral, no explanation, no wrath, no villain, no continuation. Just an account of raging, unquenchable, unforgiving fever burning life out of the girl. In the mid-1990s, San José Itzá still had no clinic.

Teresa rose and stepped out a door at the back of the room, returning with a clay jug of hot water. She poured it onto coffee crystals that sat undissolved in the bottoms of our cups. "Now my grandson," she said, taking a seat once more and placing the jug on a small table. "I don't know if that was an accident, or *envidia*," jealousy that generates a curse. He was nineteen when a tractor clearing forest killed him. She didn't know exactly how.

Teresa's style was documentary, not self-absorbed or tragic. She described a village where death might come suddenly, even in peacetime. A neighbor, she said, died "like so many," harvesting chicle. High on a *sapodilla* tree, hacking for sap, he chopped the rope that held him, by mistake, and fell to the forest floor.

Beginning to feel overwhelmed by Teresa's tales, I felt glad when Domingo Chayax walked in the door. He looked about eighty years old, with a taut body that seemed spring-loaded, suggesting he never stopped working. He settled immediately into a frayed string hammock that hung across the small room in a way that let him look past me, through the door to the lake. He spoke with Teresa in Maya Itzá, to find out who I was, no doubt, and who had brought me.

It was a choppy-sounding language, said to be related to Lacandón Maya, and I did not understand a word. But I enjoyed listening, because Teresa and Domingo Chayax were two of only about fifty surviving speakers of the tongue, the language of the last free lords of Petén. In the 1930s and 1940s, when dictator Jorge Ubico ordered the country's twenty-three Maya ethnicities, each with its own tongue, to speak only Spanish, the dictum hardly affected most groups. But the Itzá were few in number—perhaps only two thousand—and they lived almost entirely in this single town, where they could be controlled. The government teachers sent out from Flores beat schoolchildren caught speaking Itzá; their parents were fined.

The population of San José Itzá had remained about the same, but now, every time an Itzá speaker died, one of the world's few rainforest languages drifted closer to extinction. Its intimacy with a unique corner of the world, built into the tongue over centuries, disappeared. How do you find the local vine with sap that cures if you cannot say precisely between which trees and under what conditions to find it, and how to prepare its poultice? How can you sing of harvesting food and shelter plants, with all the information old songs carry, when you no longer understand the meaning of the words? And the animals! How much knowledge of the other kingdom is embedded in the subtleties of the tongue?

Domingo switched to Spanish. Teresa evidently had appreciated a good listener and approved me for her husband. Yes, he said, as *prioste* he had for many years accompanied one of the three skulls for hours around town on the Day of the Dead.

"Once you start, you must finish," he said.

That is why he no longer walked in procession, he said. If he failed to complete the long night because of his age, some misfortune might befall him. Walking with the skull, the *calavera*, was a sacred duty, which ensured the world might go on for another year. If only a few persons completed the procession, he said, that was all right, too, because they were doing the job for the others.

How did they know which skull should be walked through the night? Each year after the procession, the *prioste* melted wax in the shape of a cross onto the forehead of the returning skull. The *calavera* with the faintest wax cross was next in line. Thus, every three years, each had its turn. Domingo Chayax spoke of the skulls as if they were powerful friends. I would be welcome to return the next day, he told me. He looked tired.

Returning to Flores by boat, I saw the peninsula between San José and the island flung across the lake, as I imagined the arm of Teresa's drowned mother had lain in the shallow water. Thoughts of death and finishing things ran through my mind. I would never forget certain pictures from the last few years I had spent reporting in Central America, no matter how much I traveled, no matter how much I tried to replace them with the beauty of creation. It was too late now to wonder whether I had done a good enough job, told enough of the story, taken enough risks, stayed up late enough times. I supposed I would wrestle with all that when the time came.

A turtle riding the wake alongside the boat abruptly dove, stubby limbs sticking out from the four corners of its shell. Seeing it this way, I realized what Maya scribes had in mind when they depicted the animal as a sacred image: its round back the earth itself, its limbs the four directions that, with the center, make the five cardinal points of the Maya world. Even standing before the famous stone turtle at Copan, or studying drawings on Maya vases in books, I had only accepted that the creature had something to do with the shape of the world and its winds because others said so. But looking down upon on its living form plunging expansively, round, hard, and green, limbs aligned, I felt I understood the turtle–earth connection the way the Maya, who were immersed in nature, not statues or books, understood it.

The next day Domingo Chayax told me that besides being a *prioste* at the Catholic church he was also a Maya *ajq'ij*, a spiritual guide charged with giving thanks to the Creator lords, keeping the sacred calendar, and performing Maya ceremonies. I wondered aloud if there weren't a contradiction between the two roles. Chayax regarded me sympathetically, as if I were having language difficulty, my words meaningless to his ears.

Chayax said much of Maya ritual still practiced in San José Itzá honored *antepasados*, literally "those who passed through before." The fields, the very earth had to be remembered.

"Every year at the harvest we make a sacrifice, burning copal incense, and pray," he said. "We can't end this practice because the earth gives us life."

I had seen Maya ceremonies in the highlands. A chicken head ripped off, blood spurting into the air and dropping onto the fire like rain. Sheep sliced down the breast, the heart extracted still pulsing while raised to the gods, then tossed upon the sacred flames.

"That is no longer the Itzá way," Domingo said. For him, the word "sacrifice" meant "a sacred oath."

"We burn incense," he said, not animals.

While Teresa served coffee, the sacristan from the day before appeared at the door. Another family had signed up to receive the skull in its house, he said, during the procession scheduled for the next night. "That makes nine," he told his uncle.

"Good, then there are enough," said Chayax. "Just right."

The *Popol Vuh* named Nine Lords of the Underworld. Nine is the number of death. I guessed that was why Don Domingo said nine houses were "just right."

"No, it's just a number," he said. It could be more or fewer houses. But indeed it was "often" nine. I should have known the reply would not be definitive.

The nephew left. Domingo reminded Teresa that their house was going to be the third on the next night's procession route. Families needing a special favor, a cure, or safe return of a loved one could pledge in their prayers to receive the skull, giving those prayers more edge. Or they might ask to host the skull as insurance, anticipating the need for spiritual capital. The commitment was a serious one: those in the household had to be at peace with one another and with neighbors, abstain from sexual relations for days before the visit, prepare food and drink for all those walking with the skull. Domingo had signed up during the month his wife was bedridden with dengue fever.

Teresa left to sweep the entryway outside with a dry palm frond. My conversation with Domingo meandered pleasantly. Somehow we arrived at the question of whether the word "Ek," the root of the last Itzá king's name, meant "darkness," as it could in some instances.

"They say the Christ of Esquipulas liked the Petén so very much he did not want to leave," Domingo said. "Because here lived the King Canek, of the Maya Itzá. And that is how the Black Christ stayed."

"Excuse me, Don," I said. "What does Christ have to do with Canek?"

All the accounts I knew said the first of the Black Christs in Petén arrived decades after the fall of Tayasal. Domingo spoke deliberately, like a teacher.

"Canek governed Petén. Christ was passing through. According to what the old ones recount, Canek became resurrected in the *Cristo Negro*."

So, I thought, for Domingo, Canek had never died.

"And that's the story," he said.

Teresa returned to the room, standing the palm broom in a corner. Domingo took a pair of macaw feathers from a crack in the door lintel and presented them to me as a gift. I had nothing to offer, so I pulled back my hair and removed earrings Teresa had admired, a gold turtle and a tiny eagle effigy, placing them in her hands. The feathers they gave me are fiery orange-red on one side and peaceful dark blue on the other. I have them before me now as I write.

My third and last day with Domingo and Teresa was the Day of the Dead. Teresa made special *bollos de ixpelon*, corn dough filled with delicate, small dark beans harvested just once annually, not two or three times like other beans. She worked in a kitchen detached from the rest of the house, hung with smoke-blackened pots and drying herbs. We washed down some sweet, chewy *ixpelon* with *atol*, a corn drink, in clay cups.

"Come help with the candles," she said.

In the main room we took down Domingo's hammock, placing chairs and stools against the walls to prepare for their visitors. The candles looked slightly darker than ordinary white ones. They emanated a deep, syrupy scent. She had made them, Teresa said, from wax gathered directly from the combs of forest bees. She showed me how to place them on an altar prepared in the living room for the skull, which would be arriving in a few hours.

Teresa slipped into the kitchen and returned with plastic plates and cups she arranged on the table. "Too bad we must use these," she said. "For three years we have not made our true plates." Traditionally, women offered food for the skull in ceramics they crafted anew each year from pale clay collected across the lake at the mouth of a stream.

"It's the *tek-sako*," she said.

"The what?" I assumed the word was Itzá.

"*Tek-sako, tek-sako*," she said, and gave more location details.

The place she described was that of a big Texaco gas station on the highway that skirted Santa Elena, built on land that probably had been the women's source of clay for generations. The art of handmade ceramics for the Day of the Dead had itself died.

"*Eso es,*" said Teresa. "That's it."

In the evening as San José's church filled, the sacristan removed all three skulls from their cabinet, carrying them individually, carefully, almost tenderly, up the aisle, and placed them on a table in the back of the church. White flowers—real ones—stood in vases: chrysanthemums and a bloom with white pods I had never seen before, airy and delicate like something found on a vine wrapped around a jungle tree. Every electric light in the church was lit. The priest wore white vestments, and two dozen youngsters who had made their First Communions the night before wore their new clothes again, the girls in snowy dresses and veils.

At the offertory of the Mass, when parishioners bring bread and wine from the back of the church, three congregants brought the skulls forward, too, placing them directly upon the altar. Later, during the part of the rite known as the kiss of peace, when those attending turn to embrace one another or touch fingertips in greeting, several of the faithful also left their pews and approached the altar. Gently, they touched the tops of the skulls. Candles burned, stuck to the floor with their own wax.

If the Mass was jarring to a Catholic from anywhere else, the consecration—that most solemn moment when the host is raised high and is transformed into the body of Christ—was downright eerie. Facing the congregation, flanked by the angelic children whose faces shone in the light of the candles they held, the priest lifted high the round wafer, directly over the three skulls, whose empty eyes stared into the church. That night, the skulls were not called *calaveras* but *Las Animas*, the term for souls suffering in Purgatory, who in the end will see Paradise.

After Mass the tower bell rang, and the procession went forth from the church, led by a boy of about thirteen in the white garb of an acolyte, carrying an antique wooden cross, black and dark brown. Two other boys the same age, one tall, the other quite short, bore enormous wooden candlesticks. In a few weeks, the taller of the candlestick boys would drown in the lake near his home. Accidentally, as in one of Teresa's stories. But tonight the youth looked handsome, his gown starched and hair slicked back, taking responsibility.

A single skull came out of the bright church, into the night. I recognized the man who carried it as a fellow I had noticed around town and assumed had some sort of mental handicap. He could not speak clearly, tripped often and unaccountably, and burst into laughter at nothing at all. Leading the procession, however, he was the picture of dignity, walking slowly, cradling the skull in the crook of his arm, protecting it from falling with the palm of his other hand, as you might carry an infant.

The *prioste*, a man of about fifty, walked behind him, and then came the *rezadora*, the one who prays. Rosary beads in hand, Doña Monica recited the first half of each Our Father or Hail Mary, to which the faithful responded as they walked. Domingo's nephew, the sacristan, occasionally rang a small brass bell. At the beginning, when we were about three hundred persons, its sound was one among many; as the evening wore on, the number of those walking dwindled and the bell became more noticeable, a lonelier sound marking the path, ringing out over the silent lake.

The procession wound back and forth across town following the order in which households had signed up, not how close they were to one another. Thus, the first house stood across town from the second, and the third house—Domingo and Teresa's—was literally next door to where the first had been located. Crisscrossing the village that way, north to south, east to west and back again, the skull and its attendants wove an invisible web, connecting houses and neighborhoods.

Up one path and down the next, each ascent seemed more difficult than the last. It took two people at times to balance Doña Monica, who looked overweight and unfit, dressed in a long black skirt with a trim white sweater, occasionally favoring someone with a sweet smile. Doña Monica's murmuring was like glue, holding together the procession and its nine vigils. She nodded off only once, about 3:00 A.M., perhaps because it was the first time during the night she sat in a chair with a back.

There seemed to be not a single sofa in town, just hard wood slat benches, hammocks, and stools. Eventually, you saw how discreetly wealth was displayed, the chair with the back, for instance. Or a wall made of cement instead of bound sticks, perhaps a roof of corrugated tin instead of thatch. A house might have a low-watt electric bulb dangling from the ceiling, not squat bottles of oil and wicks. In each house, however, altars looked the same, a table covered with embroidered white cloth, bearing a plain wooden cross. To feed the skull, a bowl of cooked chicken in its broth stood before the cross, another of *atol*, a glass of water. Most bowls were simply gourds, set on circles of yellow and black maize kernels so they would not tip over.

In the poorest house of all, the only food passed around was sugary bread in bite-size pieces. At that moment, we might have been standing before the skull at any time in the last thousand years: reddish mud walls, a thatch palm roof of ancient design, illuminated only by the jumping light from tiny bowls of burning oil.

Domingo and Teresa Chayax received the skull together with their unmarried son. Teresa wore her Itzá dress, white, with black geometric designs and birds embroidered around a square collar, the once-typical costume few women wore daily anymore. Domingo had donned the red head kerchief and red sash that marked him as a Maya *ajq'iq*. He sprinkled powdered copal incense on a plate of coals to send the prayers up with the smoke, addressing the *Dios poderoso*, the all-powerful God. He asked Doña Monica to kindly be quiet while he prayed aloud. She continued anyway, apparently not out of defiance but rather because she was already on a kind of automatic pilot.

Everyone in the procession became tired, especially after midnight, but each time the skull arrived at a new house the response was as emotional as the first. The boys placed the big crucifix before the altar, the giant candlesticks on either side, and a family member would step forward gravely, sometimes trembling, to receive the skull, placing it on the center of the cloth. In one house, a man holding a sleeping infant received the skull; in another, a middle-aged housewife. Once, it was received by a couple and returned by their four-year old, under her mother's supervision. Another family displayed the graduation certificate (in Accounting) of their young man, praying for his safety away from home. His picture as an army recruit, holding a rifle, hung nearby.

At each house, the sacristan signaled the time to leave by ringing the brass bell. The families looked grief-stricken, or regretful, removing the skull from their altar, delivering it into the hands of the man who cradled it again and moved on. Once, the *prioste* adjusted the skull so its hollow eyes stared straight ahead. The fellow carrying it never slipped, as everyone else did from time to time. He seemed protected.

Very late, when many were practically sleepwalking, the parade inadvertently split. The cross and candlestick boys solemnly took one fork, while the skull and the rest of us took another. Someone noticed, and the two parts of the procession reunited by calling out to each other in the silent streets. Walking was patrolling, too: some needed to stay awake and watchful, covering the village, because this was the night when troubled souls wandered unappeased or looking to cause harm. There was a pilgrimage feel to it all, a sense of being united in religious journey.

The town drunk caught up, moving along the procession line, chanting *mucha cuesta*, what a steep hill, which everyone felt but no one else would say. Sometimes the drunk mimed the *rezadora*'s prayers or bent his elbow in unbalanced attempts to copy the man carrying the skull. No one tried to quiet him, and households fed him at each vigil as they fed everyone else. If he were missing for too long, having disappeared to urinate behind a bush or nap on a door stoop, someone would say, *Y el bolo?* "And that drunk guy?" When he reappeared, the procession felt complete.

In the first hours of the evening, there had been much good-natured, mutual inquiry: "Will you make it?" *Aguantas?* "Are you bearing up?" Later, when only a few dozen remained, communication became reduced to nods exchanged, an outstretched hand to help the next person over a high threshold. Once, in a small house that felt overly warm, I thought I would pass out if I didn't escape the flickering candles, the mesmerizing voice of the *rezadora*. I took a brief walk in the cool air. When I returned, the *prioste* looked up in surprise and seemed to say with his eyes, "Welcome back." A woman bent over to whisper, "We thought you had given up."

It wasn't only climbing in the cold, then squatting on floors of hot, smoky houses, that addled body and mind. It was the obligation to eat at each vigil: *bollos*, chicken tamales, hot sausage. Caffeine in endless coffee and hot chocolate did not clear the head but befuddled it, making the heart flutter. An atmosphere of hallucination grew. The stars disappeared. Clouds muffled the moon, rendering the lake a deep gray mirror, reflecting nothing. Murmured prayers, the bell in the dark. Sleeplessness. Keep your eye on the skull, the skull.

I never examined why I was accompanying this cool, hard symbol of no more chances. I did try to make connections. Christ, whose death Christians say redeemed them from human weakness, from the consequences of an original sin, enabling them to attain heaven, was crucified on a hill called Golgotha, the Place of the Skull. In the *Popol Vuh*, the talking skull of One Hunahpu lures Blood Maiden, then spits, impregnating her with the Hero Twins, who eventually overcome the Lords of Death. Most of the night, however, did not lend itself to thinking. Anyway, as Domingo said, once you start, you shouldn't stop.

The sun rose after we left the last house, just thirty persons at the end. When we reached the church, the bell in its tower rang contentedly, the skull, cross, and candlesticks headed back to their places. The procession atomized into individuals departing along separate paths, the job done. A woman touched my arm in good-bye, saying that word for rising in the morning I have always liked in Spanish.

"*Amanecemos*," she said. "We brought the dawn."

I took the first boat out, postponing a final visit to Teresa and Domingo Chayax for another day, when I would be more awake. The Maya Itzá had been well and finally conquered those three hundred years ago, losing their trade routes, esteem, and, according to counts, about 90 percent of their population, mostly to disease. Now even their distinctive dress and language were waning. The Maya who live on with the blood of the ultimate fighters running through their veins rest quietly at the end of the road on a radiant lake.

Motoring slowly across the waters, glassy at the early hour, it came to me that the Maya term for death resonated with no finality. Its glyph is a combination of two signs, *och*, to enter, and *be*, the road. *To die. To take the road.* I cannot say that walking with the skull gave me a deeper understanding of death, but it did leave a sense that those who pay attention to its proximity, its ubiquity, may be more at ease in life than those who deny its existence until the end.

4

Equal Day, Equal Night

There is not yet one person, one animal, bird, fish, crab, tree, rock,
hollow, canyon, meadow, forest. Only the sky alone is there. . . .
Only the sea alone is pooled under all the sky . . .

—*Popol Vuh*

IN THE BEGINNING, THE EARTH WE KNOW SLEPT UNDER
watery darkness, like the view before dawn from the island of Flores.
Standing on the balcony of my hotel, I saw the Petén sky rippling down
to the horizon on all sides. The lake slept, however, unmoving as the
firmament. Still lake, rippling sky. This brought a feeling of standing on
one's head or reeling. When Cortés came upon Lake Petén Itzá in 1525,
he thought he had reached the sea. The waters can still appear rimless
at times, especially in the dark.

The hieroglyph for "island," *pet*, is a circle with a small circle at its
very center. Add a flourish to its side and the glyph reads *Petén*—Petén,
the old name of the island, which gave its name in turn to the entire rainforest region. The island and its people, encircled by their sea, remained

sovereign until the eve of our eighteenth century, the last independent Maya kingdom.

Imagine. As Samuel Pepys tracked the ebb and flow of a recognizably modern London, a Maya king in Petén kept track of a trade network, with rest houses, that spanned hundreds of square miles. He compared obsidian prices from suppliers and maintained cacao plantations where the Rio Dulce met the Caribbean Sea. He danced before his people wearing jaguar hides, shells, and feathers until he entered a trance, crossing over for a while to the Underworld, then dancing himself back again.

In Europe, John Locke had just published his *Essay Concerning Human Understanding* when the last Maya king, Canek, fell in 1697, despite sending a canoe of topless maidens early in the battle to distract the attacking Spanish. I could imagine regal Canek, standing in a wooden tower, watching the enemy craft with guns blasting overcome his warriors' canoes. I could see arrows floating like dead birds on the surface of the lake, as Canek recognized the end of a world, gone on his watch.

A horn like a klaxon ripped through the air. I scrambled down two flights, groped for my pack in the dark lobby, stepped out to a waiting shuttle and into the front seat, next to the driver. In the rearview mirror, I saw other bleary-eyed passengers. Maybe they, too, had trouble sleeping on this island, not from noise but the quiet. The mind wants to stay awake, to experience the feel of floating atop an earth yet uncreated.

The driver turned from the island onto the causeway that connects to the mainland. "The floating flowers are still out there," I said, forgetting the word for water hyacinths. Their whiteness under a setting moon sparked the still-dark lake, like the *Popol Vuh* says the Begetter gods glittered in the sea.

"A mess," the driver said. "They choke the lake, more each year."

He took both hands from the steering wheel and strangled an imaginary neck. He had grown up on the lake, he said, and missed the way it once ebbed and flowed without entanglements.

My eyes jerked to the left. *Ay dios!* A new Burger King and a Pollo Campero, a fast-food chicken restaurant like KFC, rose side by side where the causeway met the mainland. I had missed them the night before, asleep in a taxi.

"How can that be?" I asked.

"Good, eh?" said the driver, without irony.

We were heading toward Tikal, the huge kingdom once conquered by Dos Pilas. The autumnal equinox was not far off, and I wanted to know where I should be when light broke that day. There was someone I might ask at Tikal. I wanted to pay my respects to Maya cosmology, which began three thousand years ago and continues among modern Maya.

Yet I felt sad as we drove. A few weeks before, I had returned to San José Itzá after fifteen years, for the first time since the night I had walked with the skull, on a Day of the Dead. Now in 2009, I wanted to put the question about the equinox, and other things on my mind, to Don Domingo Chayax, from whom I had learned much in the days I spent with him and his wife, Teresa. Stepping off the boat this time at San José, I had looked up at the place the wonderful old house had been and knew something out of joint had occurred. In place of the wooden house stood a bright, whitewashed police post manned with officers who did not look local.

"Don Domingo died three years ago," said the first person I asked.

"Doña Teresa died a few weeks after Don Domingo," said the second.

That meant only eight Itzá speakers remained. A project to rescue the language by teaching it to children occupied a large house surrounded by trees, a twenty-minute hike from town. The head of the program gave me a list of words they taught, including terms created for "airplane" and "Internet." I remembered what a linguist had told me, that once a language reaches the point of "rescue," it is finished.

Relatives said Domingo's nephew, Gilberto, was among the Itzá speakers. They said he too was an *ajq'ij*, a Maya spiritual guide, as Domingo had been. Gilberto Chayax, they said, might be at the old Maya city of Tikal, where he performed ceremonies. If I found him, I wondered if he would advise me to stay or tell me to leave Tikal before the equinox and push farther into the rainforest to Uaxactun, where a famous ancient observatory stood. I hoped he was there.

The shuttle driver and I watched the sun come up on land shorn of trees. Occasional grassy mounds rose on either side of the road, perhaps unexcavated temples. From the speedy van, they looked like natural features in a pasture. Cows roamed. An hour after sunrise, heat waves undulated on the paved highway.

Once into the precincts of Tikal, the air became cooler. Trees grew thick on both sides of the road, which narrowed. The shuttle slowed, and my ear became attuned to a new landscape of sound: cries of spider monkeys, cawing toucans. We were solidly inside the Maya Biosphere Reserve, where the government forbade hunting and cutting trees all the way to the border with Mexico.

I saw the tail of a snake disappear into the trees. There are more jaguars now than there were in 1959 when Tikal, 222 square miles, was declared a park. In a couple of generations, jaguars had learned that within this territory they might be particularly safe. In 1990 the government declared an area of 11,016 square miles, virtually the entire northern jungle, a protected biosphere reserve. The protection keeps settlers at bay, discouraging hunters and relic thieves.

The shuttle dropped passengers on a stretch of concrete that was still a working airstrip when I first came to Tikal in 1972. Propeller planes severely shook up the ancient structures, however, and soon after, take-offs and landings stopped. Few tourists came then, anyway. Today six hundred arrive daily, by bus and car.

At the entrance gate, freelance guides sent me in the direction of a trail that led to the abode of Don Gilberto Chayax. I walked for less than an hour on quiet paths to the Great Plaza, turning east into a passage between the towering Jaguar Temple and the Southern Acropolis.

The last part of the trail ran through a maze of full-grown trees, vines, enormous surface roots. I recognized a thin trunk, spiny as a Goth choker. Fishermen used its thorns to make hooks. The forest sounded with the buzz of unseen bees. Insects the size of a pencil eraser, and nearly the same shape, lifted and dipped in a single cloud ahead of me, making no sound at all.

In the mulch of the path lay the hard brown fruits of the lifesaver tree, the white ramón. Maya who fled from their homes to the jungle in the 1970s and 1980s, to hide from a murdering army, ground the nuts and shaped the mass to cook and eat like tortillas. The fruit held little water, lasting a long time. Archaeologists find ramón trees entwined with the fallen stones of ruins, leading some to believe the ancient Maya used them, too, when food was scarce. Others say the ramón grows all over the rainforest anyway, why not among ruins?

A flash of orange appeared in a breach in the canopy. Soon another followed, two flames crossing the blueness of the sky. Standing still, watching to see if more birds might pass, I heard a sound like a crack. The forest buzz hushed. Nothing moved. Then sounds of crackle and whoosh followed each other quickly, like branches breaking. I looked up in time to spot a black spider monkey with infinitely long arms coming toward me overhead. I jumped aside, out of its path. It might not have happened there, but I have seen the gracile monkeys defecate on astonished humans, near the Great Acropolis.

I saw light ahead and figured the trail was ending. But instead it was an island in the forest ruled by palms—huge, unusual palms with widespread fingers inviting sunlight. Rays fell brightly on the tallest, fell dappled on young palms close to the earth. A fading wooden sign said: IN THIS PLACE EXISTED A LACANDÓN MAYA ALDEA.

Lacandón, the magic name that first drew me to the rainforest. In the early 1970s the Lacandón Maya lived only in Metzabok, Naha, and a couple of other jungle villages on the Mexican side of the Usumacinta, so deep in the jungle few ever saw them. But as recently as the early 1900s the Lacandón lived so widely dispersed, mostly in Guatemala's western Petén, that they were not found at all unless they wished to be. A large, extended family might settle in a place like this, among palms, self-sufficient, needing only water and good hunting.

Perhaps those who lived in this secret spot felt close to their ancestors, who once lived among the nearby temples and palaces. The longer the Lacandón are known to the world, the more scholars and other researchers challenge their direct descent from the pre-Collapse Maya who occupied the rainforest city-states. Some say they are Yucatecos who fled the peninsula north of Guatemala to avoid being herded into colonial settlements, lying low in the steaming jungle, which was of little interest to the Spanish. Or that Lacandón ancestors were individuals of various Maya ethnicities who resisted harsh colonizers and escaped them; today, goes this theory, after twenty generations in the forest, the progeny of early rebels have given birth to the new Maya group ("ethnogenesis"), distinct from its many forbearers.

Personally, I like imagining the Lacandón as survivors of the Great Collapse, too resilient to die out. The population of Europe did not disappear, after all, during the Dark Ages. Lacandón stories retold by outsiders speak of two brothers as ancestors, much like the *Popol Vuh* revolves around the Hero Twins, whose adventures resound in images carved into stone more than a thousand years ago. The Lacandón have no migration myth, which says to me they have always lived in the Mesoamerican rainforest.

Past the Lacandón grove, the path became straight. I saw a sprite of a man striding toward me, wearing a baseball hat and floppy pants. A woven cloth bag hung from one shoulder, the kind an *ajq'iq* might carry to hold ceremonial objects.

I took off my sunglasses so he could see my eyes.

"Good morning," I said.

"Good morning."

He stopped, as if to let me pass. He seemed the right age, about seventy.

"Don Gilberto?"

"Yes, I am," he said.

He wore a T-shirt bearing the logo of a defunct environmental organization, with a message that advised caution when using fire. His faded dark pants were rolled at the bottom above worn black shoes.

"I am looking for you," I said. "For a visit."

"Of course," he said, without surprise. He turned and headed back up the trail in the direction from which he had come. "We will go," I heard him say, already several paces ahead of me.

We came to a corrugated metal building carved into tiny single rooms, far inferior to the archaeologists' freestanding cabins on the other side of the ruins. Gilberto Chayax lived with maintenance men and gardeners, he told me, each cooking for himself, sharing the fire.

It seemed an *ajq'iq*, kin to the Maya priests who once read the skies and interceded for rulers and populace, might merit better housing.

But that was not the case. Chayax brought me a molded-plastic chair grained with cracks, the good seat, and for himself a three-legged stool. Sheltered under a patio roof of tin, we sat for a while and watched the rain.

Already I could feel that Gilberto Chayax did not have the fuller presence his uncle, Domingo, possessed in life. Not only was Gilberto slighter in build, his eyes did not command as Domingo's had. It might have been difficult to live, I thought, even as a spiritual guide, in Domingo's shadow. Gilberto told me that, since his uncle died, he was the only remaining priest who might invoke Maya Itzá ancestors in their own tongue.

"I have attended ceremony where some *ajq'ijab'* speak in Spanish, partly or entirely," I said.

"Yes, that is all right," he said, but seemed troubled. He did not like the idea of calling upon "our grandmothers, our grandfathers," violently vanquished and enslaved by the Spanish, in the language of the conquerors.

"I have thought a lot about this and carry great worry about the language," he said.

Chayax's age took over his face. I looked away. Drizzle fell like a shroud over the living forest before us, turning it shades of gray.

"The calendar," I said. "The Maya calendar. I want to go to Uaxactun, to see the equinox."

Gilberto Chayax adjusted the bill of his cap. He brightened. This was where he shone, where certainty replaced doubt, where the past flowed unbroken into the present, and the present into the future.

The 260-day Maya calendar, called the *tzolkin*, is the same used by his ancestors, Chayax said. Its year is made of thirteen months, each with twenty days. The days of the month have names, indicating which *nahual*, or powerful spiritual being, influences it, and have a number between one and thirteen. The *tzolkin* is a divinatory table, in which the Maya priest can read elements important to the psychic and spiritual well-being of individuals, beginning with the day and time of their birth. He knows which days are propitious, which call for caution. Often the *guia* may be illiterate, despite managing such a deep and complex system. The calendar is sacred, and thus the work holy. One of the spiritual guide's other names is Keeper of the Days.

Besides the sacred *tzolkin*, Maya use a 365-day calendar for planting, the *haab*, based on cycles of the sun. Dates inscribed on stelae and painted on vessels, however, are based on a third calendar, measured from the year zero of the Maya historical cycle in which we live, the fourth era. Commonly called the Long Count, the era cycle is 5,126 years long. In our counting, it began August 11, 3114 BC, and comes to an end on December 21, 2012. We know cycle endings are important events from evidence of glyphs describing the attention given to them by the rainforest Maya. The years and months before the end of an era, and after, may be charged with special significance.

Chayax drew from his pocket a datebook of the *tzolkin*. He showed me the glyphs for the current month and day. He placed the book on his lap and studied a page.

"Uaxactun," he said. "Yes, to be present for sunrise on that day."

"Uaxactun is good because an old observatory is there?" I asked.

"Uaxactun was the college, the house of studies when our ancestors studied the movement of the sun," Gilberto said. "They had to know the movements, so they could find the balance, to measure the time of planting, to measure time."

In other words, Uaxactun was the place the astronomer-priests, over centuries, worked out calculations of time marked by the movement of stars and planets that ruled lives all over the Maya world, even today. Chayax seemed to take my mulling for a struggle to understand.

"Balance," he said. "You have to weigh yourself to get on a plane, don't you? Because the plane must keep its balance so you can arrive."

Don Gilberto must have flown on small aircraft where the pilot noted the weight of both cargo and passengers to gauge the fuel requirement. If "balance," as Don Gilberto saw it, was so important for an ordinary mortal to arrive safely at his destination, how significant balance must be in the movement of the universe. How transcendental the work of the calendar keepers, like him, who know which spirit rules each day, who follow the way time operates in maintaining the balance on earth.

"It is a good place to be, Uaxactun," he said.

The rain stopped, becoming a wall of mist between the place we sat and the edge of the forest. As the wall thinned, the trees took on their palette of greens once more, moist and fresh.

In the *Popol Vuh*, when the Lords conversed about creating "the human work," they wanted beings capable of honoring their names, keeping their days. Otherwise there could be no praise for the creators, no appreciation. First attempts did not work out well. Mud men melted. Other creatures—deer, rabbits, foxes—turned out to be squawkers or barkers who could not voice praise or prayers. Wood mannequins looked and talked like humans, but they only thought about themselves, kept no memory of the Heart of the Sky, the designers and creators; they were crushed, ground down, and destroyed, only monkeys remaining in the forest to remind us of the failed attempt.

Listening to Gilberto Chayax speak, it occurred to me that the old book was saying that if it weren't for men and women like him, continuing to perform ceremonies, remembering the days and the spirits to which they belonged, the "human work" would not exist. Like the cloistered nuns and monks I heard about in my childhood, who spent their days praying for the rest of the world or working at baking or farming as a form of prayer, the *ajq'ijab'* were covering for the rest of us. His realm of knowledge was the "Short Count," Don Gilberto said, the 260-day round, the *tzolkin*.

"The other calendar, the long one, the one which is in its end, that is not the one we use in ceremony," he said.

"Many think there will be world war or that the world will disappear at the end of the long calendar." But his view was more complex, even puzzling.

"The earth will not bear the cold. We are going to suffer more heat than now."

"How can that be?" I asked. Heat and cold?

"The sun and moon will come in contact with the surface of the earth," he said. "We must see how the earth handles the lowering of the sun and the moon, the being out of balance."

This had "happened before, many years ago," his grandparents had told him, when water dried up and there was "a scarcity of sacred food."

"Like now," he said, and indeed newspapers had been full of stories of malnourished children, some dying, in the Guatemalan countryside. "It's not that God is not good," he said. "But now we've gone beyond the measure, gone overboard, become excessive. How many are killing each other? God is the parent, the former and creator. He wants his children to grow with obedience."

It didn't seem right for God—whether you saw him singular or plural, him or her—not to give second chances. But soft-spoken, humble-looking Don Gilberto sounded unequivocal.

"We have to revive what we have been killing," he said. "If not, everything is smashed."

I felt a chill in spite of the muggy air. Until now, everything I had read about the 2012 date spoke of astronomical phenomena, wondrously predicted by ancient Maya. Or of one mythological cycle ending and another beginning, like an odometer turning over. Perhaps because I felt afraid at the concreteness of his words, I asked him if feeling this way, knowing these things, did not make him fearful. He said no.

"Fear humiliates us," Don Gilberto said. "We can die thinking of it."

For the rest of the afternoon, I took Tikal's less beaten paths. No other visitors appeared that day on those trails through thick, dark forest. Birds and midsize mammals acted unafraid, especially toward sunset, when they grew in number and looked for food. Somewhere out of sight, I knew larger creatures might be roaming, like peccary that charge in branch-breaking herds, baring tusk-like canine teeth. Jaguars prowled, but almost always at night.

Sometimes the fullness of life is overwhelming. That day I saw a bright orange parrot flying past the sky-reaching arms of a giant ceiba tree, an oropendola, a pair of soaring, black-winged toucans with hard yellow beaks. At dusk, I walked among the structures archaeologists identify simply as Group G, amid a line of stelae lined up like an honor guard. The American archaeologist Sylvanus Morley, a contemporary of Maler, camped for weeks in the building behind the stone slabs, even signed a doorjamb, more than a hundred years ago. Puffy brown birds hopped around underfoot, miniature energy machines. When it was almost dark, I stood with my back to the ranked stelae, looking across a clearing to where the jungle began. A velvet-brown deer and a doe grazed peacefully in green shadows.

That night couples in khaki shorts, or threesomes and foursomes, filled the dining room at the inn and its outdoor tables. Thirty years before, when I first came to Tikal, the cook offered only beans and rice, beer or Coke. Now I heard myself ordering a Caesar salad with Gulf shrimp, dressing on the side. I shook my head, perhaps looking dismayed.

"Is something wrong?" asked the waiter. "You can have that with grilled chicken, if you prefer."

I could not explain that the sensation of time passing brought on an unexpected wave of nausea. "No, no, I'm fine," I said.

"May I offer you a drink? Margarita, mojito, something soft?"

I wanted the moment to be over. "Whiskey," I said.

"Glenfiddich? Johnny Walker?"

"Johnny Walker. Fine. That's it."

"Red Label, or Black?"

After dinner, I asked a couple from Mumbai if they wanted to go with me to see the equinox at Uaxactun. Had they known about it they would have loved to, they said, but they were booked on a tour of Yaxha.

"They take tourists there?" I asked.

I had been the only outsider during my own sojourn to the site, on a lake in eastern Petén, during excavation. An archaeologist came across a flower no one had seen before and suggested that if it were new to science, he'd see they named it after me. "It's one of the things you can do when you're the first to find something," he said. I'd slept on a cot in a row with team members and bathed in the river.

"Well, enjoy it," I told the couple. "And be sure to see Topoxte, on an island in the same lake. The palaces—everything there is miniature, a small-scale, ancient Maya city. Amazing."

"It's not on the tour," the husband said.

I also proposed the equinox to a cosmetics company representative from Lima, who had seen all the important Inca sites in Peru. She, too, would have gone, she said, but had already paid for a Tikal canopy tour, to see the jungle from the air.

That night in bed, I considered that the solitary traveler evaluates experience at length, sometimes writing in a journal, blogging to the ether, reviewing photographs at night, or reliving moments, before sleep comes. The accompanied traveler's experience, however, is inextricably linked to the fellow traveler. That argument on the boat ride. Those memories of a certain bridge, tied to words of tenderness. That hot walk back from the mountain shrine, the welcome shade in a niche of the mountain wall, the unexpected passion. Neither solitary nor accompanied travel is inherently better or worse; it's just how I experience the difference between them.

When the music in the dining room stopped, laughter and footfalls sounded for a while outside on the stone paths to the other cabins. Then rainforest silence, soft owl calls and droning insects, the kind that brings sleep.

A loud sound in the room startled me, a nearly indescribable *plop-suck*. I bolted upright in bed, grabbed my flashlight from the nightstand, directing the beam onto the floor, along the walls, into the ceiling corners. Something was in the room with me. Bending to the side, I swept the light under the bed. Nothing. No one to ask, "Did you hear that?"

On its second circuit, the flashlight found a green, black, and gold creature smashed against the door, legs extended, flattened on the wood like a frog run over by a truck. When it twitched, I realized the thing had flattened itself as maybe some kind of camouflage technique. And it had to possess a method of attaching high and sideways in defiance of gravity, like superglue, or a chest like a vacuum. I did not want to sleep in the room with the animal. I had no idea what it was. It could tire of the door and attach itself to me. Steadying the beam upon it, I rose from the bed.

Standing, however, I heard again *plop-suck, plop-suck*, less loud. There were more of them, I realized, maybe half a dozen on the porch, hitting my room from the other side. If I opened the door to push this one out, the others would come flying in. I returned to bed and slept with the sheet over my head. In the morning the creature was gone, the air quiet.

Once a day, at three o'clock in the afternoon, a local bus passes through Tikal on the way to Uaxactun twelve miles northeast, deeper into the jungle. There, a woman named Neria Herrera would tell me there had always been a trail where the road runs now, in her father's time and grandfathers' time, as far back as anyone could remember. If you left at dawn, she said, carrying a load on your back or balancing it on your head, "you didn't even need two days" to walk between Tikal and Uaxactun. Now the bus took less than two hours. The forest pressed in upon us from both sides. I had no trouble believing I traveled the path of an ancient *sacbe*, its packed white clay once cool to bare feet.

"Not so many animals, now," said the driver. Nevertheless, he said, recently he had sighted deer and—he was sure—a diurnal jaguar. I saw only a couple of roadrunners and a single, harmless-looking snake slithering in the sun.

The jungle became corn plots, and we entered the limits of Uaxactun. I got off the bus, started to walk, and realized I was in a town unlike any I had seen in Central America.

The Spanish traditionally laid out the central square as a communal space, a plaza, bordered on four sides by the powers that ruled colonial life: church, government, authority like military or police, and the commercial sector, ranging from a roofed corridor with multiple shops to—in small towns—a single stall selling oranges and avocados.

Instead of the familiar pattern, however, today's Uaxactun, founded in the 1930s by the Wrigley Chewing Gum Company, is strung along two sides of a runway. From the 1920s to the 1970s, and briefly again in the 1990s when the Japanese had a taste for real gum, residents called *chicleros* searched out *sapodilla* trees in the forest, the same hardwood tree the ancient Maya carved into storied lintels for their temples.

For weeks at a time *chicleros* tapped trees, boiling and molding the pale sap into blocks, each the size of about a dozen phone books, packing the blocks on burros and taking them to Uaxactun. The blocks were weighed and loaded onto DC-3s, which flew them to the Wrigley factory in Chicago. *Itz*, the old Maya word used for *chicle*, or sap, can also mean blood or other bodily excretions, semen, sweat, milk. The *chicleros* bled the trees, bringing in cash, giving new life to the ancient city.

More planes than ever came and went during World War II, when GIs carried packs of Spearmint or Juicy Fruit and a European child's first English words could be "Hey Joe, gimme gum."

In the 1980s, vinyl resins replaced *chicle*. Unkempt grass sprouted from the landing strip at Uaxactun. Horses grazed.

I walked into town along the north side of the runway, passing white nursery sheds where men worked behind wraparound screens, counting bright green *xate* leaves. Others tied bundles at the stems with strips of soft bark. Florists abroad value *xate* for bouquets and exotic arrangements because the leaf can live for up to forty-five days after it is cut. But only the forest men know which to harvest without killing the wild plant, just as once they knew the depth and angle of every cut they could safely make on the *sapodilla* tree. *Xate* moves out on trucks to the international airport in Flores. The brave *chiclero*, famous in lore with his ropes, boiling pots, and showdowns with snakes and big cats, is being replaced by the *xatero*, just as brave. While the jungle survives, the forest people will live from it one way or another.

In Guatemala City, an archaeologist told me where to look for a room if I got this far. "Only you?" asked a woman standing at the widest gate along the old runway. She looked unusual for these parts, short-cropped hair instead of long, wearing pants instead of a dress. Over her head, a sign spanned the width of the entrance to a small ranch with concrete buildings: CAMPO CHICLERO.

"Only me," I said.

"Well, welcome to Uaxactun," she said, introducing herself as Neria Herrera, proprietor. "This way," she said.

Campo Chiclero spread over more than an acre of land. Facing the runway was a large, screened space in which I saw a few tables and an attached kitchen. Opposite was another, smaller building with two doors. Six rooms for rent stood in a row on a raised porch, doors open, apparently empty. Under a persimmon tree stood a Maya stela.

I stopped to admire the carved stone with its ancient glyphs and image of a Night Lord with a beaked nose. The monument stood about two feet wide and four feet high, decorating the dirt yard as if it were part of a Maya site.

"I suppose this entire area was part of the ancient city," I said, swinging my arm to take in houses and the runway. The ruins, I knew from the map, lay less than a mile away, both north and south of town. The land on which Campo Chiclero stood certainly must have been part of the ancient city.

"I suppose it was," said Neria. "But this stone came through the door."

A *chiclero* showed up with the thing "years ago," having ripped it out of an even more remote jungle site. He set himself up to cut the monument into pieces, easier for smuggling. The Herreras put together a modest sum.

"We took it off his hands," she said.

We climbed a narrow porch that ran along the row of windowless rooms with the open doors. She showed me to one on the far left, which at least possessed a screen to the outside.

"It's the best room, the corner," she said. "The others, you have to open the door for air."

There was only a bed, covered with a sheet. Nails studded the wall to suspend anything that should be raised above the concrete floor. Given the certainty of night-crawling spiders and ants, I hung my pack.

We walked about twenty feet away to a concrete structure where an outdoor communal washbasin stood with a single spigot. Inside, Neria showed me two toilets "with seats" in their cubicles and two showers where she indicated curtains "just brought up" from Santa Elena. All that was missing, days would show, was dependable running water.

"I'm surprised more people haven't come to witness the equinox," I said. We walked back toward the main building with the large, screened-in space.

"We still have three days," Neria said.

In the high-ceilinged common room, a scale hung from the rafters. A kettle steamed on a wood-burning stove in the kitchen, open to the room with the tables. Sitting comfortably together, we spooned instant coffee from a jar and drank it sweet. Through the screens, I saw the pale runway broken with tufts of grass.

"Of course this was a camp, just like the sign says," Neria answered when I asked. "My husband and I weighed the blocks and helped load the plane. We fed the *chicleros* who didn't live nearby, and they could sleep here, too."

She knew all the ruins around, Neria said, satellites of Uaxactun reached only on foot. She had sold a generations-old family residence on the island of Flores to continue living in Uaxactun.

We talked through one cup of coffee and half of another. I liked this woman, who had sold a house in "town" rather than leave the jungle. Her husband had died of a heart attack ten years before, she said, their kids were gone. She had no place in the new *xate* leaf production, which anyway brought less work than chewing gum sap once did. But she had her nearness to innumerable old Maya settlements, where she roamed and which she knew as well as anyone. And she had the old camp.

"Yes, yes, come in," Neria said to a boy peering through the screen.

He bent as if to pick something up and then entered carrying a toddler with fine, wispy hair. A big-eyed girl of about four followed. Neria rose and went into the kitchen. I asked the children their names and how old they were, but they only stared at me.

Just as well, I thought. Foreign women traveling alone could still fall under suspicion, as they had in the early 1990s, accused of stealing children for adoption or to traffic in body parts. I spoke Spanish too well for misunderstanding to spark the hysteria, I told myself, but traveled aware that anything can happen. Central Americans see their children taken off by white people to faraway countries in adoptions. They hear that in rich countries, organs are transplanted into living humans from the dead. In some corners, under the right circumstances, the jump from suspicion to action is fast and has been fatal.

"Sit, eat," said Neria to the youngsters, handing them tin plates of sliced chicken. The boy held the baby while the girl tore the slices even smaller and fed the youngest with her fingers. Satisfied, the toddler crawled about quietly while the other children ate.

Neria explained that the boy left his nearby house with the girls when their parents were too drunk to feed them. As she spoke, two men in frayed pants and patched shirts walked through the door, looking worried.

"The land?" Neria asked them.

"*Sí*," one answered.

"They could cut down trees," said the other. "They set the meeting for next week."

Neria waved the men to a table at the far end of the room, excused herself, then left to huddle with them. I thought back to Flores, where an officer of a Petén environmental organization also had mentioned Neria's name. "She understands what we're doing," he had said.

"Go. Go to the *ruinas*," she called over. "You still have a few hours before dark."

To me, Uaxactun will always be dressed in mist. I crossed the runway and turned left at a path that passed some of the oldest houses I have seen in Petén. They were made of adobe and wood planks, hardly big enough to hold more than a few beds or hammocks. Barking dogs came out of the fog. Even the fences were alive, sprouting leaves. The houses petered out, the dogs retreated, and the trail became narrower.

The first pyramid rose dream-like to the east, unpruned of grass and trees that grew upon it. On the right, mounds appeared farther away than they might have been, seen through wet, heavy air. I walked slowly, as through a cloud.

In the middle of the main plaza I looked up a stone staircase on one of the ancient buildings. I was startled to see on top a replica of the very houses I had passed. The typical old Petén abode looks like a cottage in size, its thick walls plastered smooth and white, with few windows. Its thatch roof can last twenty to forty years, so intricately woven it makes a stunning ceiling design seen from underneath, inside the house. On the platform atop the old palace building stood just such a house, as if petrified twelve hundred years ago. Dark stones made the peaked roof, which fell over white walls exactly like thatch roofs fall on Petén houses seen to the present day.

To the right of the pyramid, I looked through the mist and saw three structures in a perfect line, evenly spaced. This must be Uaxactun's observatory, I thought, what Don Gilberto had called "the house of studies when our ancestors studied the movement of the sun." A circular altar lay before the triad. It was not old, but made of cement.

When I had interviewed Nobel Peace Prize winner Rigoberta Menchú in 1992, the same day the prize was announced in Oslo, she said something I did not understand well at the time. It resonated now. We had met at the offices of a war widows' organization, so full of well-wishers we could not hear each other talk. Someone brought her a beer, welcome in the heat, and we climbed to the building's flat roof.

"We must reclaim our sacred sites," said Menchú, a K'iche Maya from the highlands. She did not want to go into detail. I had visions of indigenous groups occupying Iximche or Tikal. Perhaps she wanted to control how millions visited the ruins or reserve income for today's Maya from the country's number one industry, tourism, which includes their "sacred sites."

Permanent altars now rested before temples in Maya cities such as Iximche, Tikal, and here, at Uaxactun. Perhaps this is what Menchú had wanted, or part of it. Congress member Otilia Lux ordered them installed when she was minister of culture and sports from 2000 to 2004. Lux is K'iche Maya, like Menchú. The laureate placed Lux on the board of directors of a new political party she formed in 2009. *Ajq'iqab'* like Gilberto Chayax at Tikal offer ceremony at the new cement altars, reclaiming the sacred places, burning colored candles, chocolate, pine-wood sticks, and incense, sending prayers up with the smoke.

For Maya, time is sacred. An altar before the Uaxactun observatory makes sense. Only if one understands holy time—knows the day, its number, where it fits in the cycle of the moon, the year, the era, who its patron spirit is—only then is prognostication and divination possible. This is how understanding comes of human action and of *Madre Tierra*, Mother Earth. To be guided by the sacred calendar is to be in synchronization with the movement of the stars. Most important, ceremony dictated by the calendar is occasion to remember the Creator Gods, to praise them for the natural world, of which human life is a part. Without remembering, awareness, the Design falls apart.

In the morning, Neria served breakfast of black beans, fried banana, white cheese, and eggs covered with piquant red sauce. My legs ached from the day before. After exploring the observatory side of the ruins, I had recrossed the runway and walked to the less-visited eastern side of the site, encircled by big-leafed trees dripping in the heavy mist. I climbed up half a dozen structures and down again, the descent harder on the legs.

One curiosity caught my attention on the ground. Within the rubble of a ball court wall, only half excavated, stood an upright stela. Had

someone fallen out of favor, his image on the stone relegated to invis-
ibility? For whatever reason they trashed it, using the stela as wall-fill
showed the Maya were early recyclers.

"You covered in one day what you should have done in two," said
Neria.

"Yes," I said, rubbing my right leg.

"Well, you'll want to sleep early tonight anyway, so we can rise at
four tomorrow for the equinox."

"You're going?"

"Of course," she said. "I cannot let you walk alone in the dark to the
temples."

I had prepared two flashlights for myself, one that turns into a lantern with a twist and a sleek L. L. Bean in metallic blue. But it was a
relief to hear Neria say we would walk in together. I pushed back from
the table and told her I would spend the day writing and reading.

"And the museum?" she said.

The thought of a proper museum in this place jarred the mind.

"I have errands," she said. "Here's the key." She pointed through the
screen to a door across the yard, which I had mistakenly assumed led to
her living quarters. "Just lock it again when you leave," she said.

I procrastinated until afternoon. What waited behind the door to the
"museum" had to be a private collection, I feared, of stolen or purchased
artifacts. Out of context, unassociated with other pieces or material,
whatever was inside had been robbed of the richer history it might have
carried in situ, properly documented. Maybe the room held only plain,
broken ceramics, the kind your boot kicks up sometimes on a new road
cut in the forest. Perhaps I should not enter at all. I liked Neria; what I
did not see could not trouble me.

I passed the door a couple of times without going in, walked back to
my room for a water bottle, returned. The key fit smoothly.

Inside, hundreds of vessels, plates, skulls, necklaces, and figurines
rested on blue shelves set against pale green walls. The room was about
thirty feet long, with a table nearly its length, painted the same soft
green as the walls, holding more pieces. I flipped a switch to turn on a
bare overhead bulb and stood struck for some moments by the colors

alone: cinnamon red, bringing dancers to life on vessels and plates; creamy white like the surface of ancient Maya roads, *sacbe*; the pale of human bone; black, gone charcoal with age; here and there a trace of turquoise; burnt orange.

Like other imperfect mortals enamored of certain art and left alone with it, I went around touching things. I did so lightly, on their reverse sides, as if fingerprints might deface or be discovered. I felt guilty, sinning against the rule that said one only looked at such irreplaceable pieces. Yet it was a thrill to feel their coolness, imagine their age. I skipped the skulls but ran my fingertips along the rims of plates. When a circular design ran to the back of a bowl, I turned it around and around, watching the story told by its figures like an animated film. As surely as venial sin turns to mortal, soon I was lifting pots and figurines, feeling their weight, possessing them. I raised a beaker until it almost touched my lips, looking through half-closed eyes to see inside, the way a noble lady might once have done. I inhaled its soft ceramic smell.

The door was closed. I set the key in the lock so it could not be opened from the outside.

The dancers attracted me most. I approached a handsome young maize god inside two circles of glyphs, on a plate with only a small piece missing from the edge. He was the picture of masculine grace, lifting the left leg so one bare foot touched the ground with heel raised, thighs big and strong, both arms fully extended with palms facing downward, open. I held out the plate and moved my legs the same way.

I don't know who the other man was, but his forehead sloped up and back unnaturally, so his skull, like that of my first partner, had been shaped with a board worn as an infant, to give him the look nobles must have. He was fiercer than the maize god, eyes rimmed black as if with kohl, black lips, mouth slightly open, promising a wilder dance as I held out the plate.

Someone was knocking at the door. I had lost track of time.

"*Voy*," I said, replacing the plate on the table. "I'm coming."

I took a breath and composed myself but rammed the side of my hip as I rounded the table corner on the way to the door. "Oh, is it locked?" I called, almost in tears from the pain.

When Neria walked into the *museo*, she laughed and said, "Don't worry. I do the same thing myself sometimes." I presumed she meant accidentally locking the door from the inside. I handed her the key.

That night, after a chicken dinner with rice, she asked, "What do you think?"

She had brought a Lipton tea bag to the table, with two cups and a pot of hot water.

"Delicious," I said.

"I meant the museum," she said.

I had loved it but couldn't be too effusive since I suspected that such a collection of pre-Colombian artifacts had to be illicit. Yet Neria had been very gracious with me, and I did not want to seem rude.

"I liked the plates," I said. I knew it sounded feeble.

"Oh," she said, looking disappointed. "You know my husband and I put a lot of work into collecting all that."

"I expect you did," I said.

"And the archaeologists say I have done quite a good thing."

Archaeologists?

"They've seen it? The ones from the government ministry?"

Of course, Neria said. She recently had named the *museo* after the head of the excavation project with whom she sometimes worked, she said, although the sign wasn't up yet. The man turned out to be someone I knew, Juan Antonio Valdés from Dos Pilas, the architect-archaeologist accompanying Arthur Demarest the first time I descended to Ruler 2's tomb with him. Valdés had risen to the post of vice minister of culture and sports. Each piece in the *museo*, Neria said, was registered at the ministry in the capital.

"For years my husband and I watched the *huecheros* come through," she said. *Huecheros* chip holes (*huecos*) in structures or tunnel into temple burials and palaces to rob them. Some work full time; others supplement meager earnings as farmers or fishermen. Hundreds of ancient Maya sites remain unprotected in deep jungle, open to the tomb robbers, who sell what they find to collectors or middlemen.

"We convinced them some pieces weren't worth carrying out," she said. "We knew the pots and plates should stay in Petén."

Neria said they had been unsuccessful separating *huecheros* from jade and jewelry, but sometimes *chicleros* or robbers themselves gave tips about where other pieces lay abandoned. If the *museo* held the crooks' castoffs, I marveled at the haul they succeed placing into traffic. And Uaxactun was on just one of hundreds of jungle smuggling routes.

I finished the coffee, relieved that this resourceful person, making a life for herself on the rough frontier, was not a criminal. Neria cleared the table, and I waited for the miracle of electricity, which came only between 6:00 and 8:30 P.M. I did not want to watch television with Neria but to read. And I wanted to shower under a light bulb, without worry about what lurked in dark corners of the bathroom beyond a candle's flickering flame. Also, the TV program was rotten, a salacious account of sex trafficking presented as documentary.

Nevertheless, I sat by Neria's side from beginning to end. In my mind, I owed her something for suspecting her of bad behavior. She clucked at the evil liars on the screen who trapped young women, and I nodded. The two men from the day before entered, sat before the set without ordering food, and the three railed against corrupt authority. Neighbors drifted in, pulled up chairs. No eyes left the screen, but everyone talked, soon about general lawlessness, a topic inexhaustible.

Later, the moon had not yet risen when I took a sputtering candle to the shower room, pushing open the door with my foot. The flame illuminated hardly any of its darkness, not the ceiling, no corners. I turned away and walked to the outdoor spigot. Washing my face would be enough.

By 4:00 A.M., stars pricked the sky by the millions. The firmament shone so densely, unchallenged by electric light, that the path past the stela in the yard was clear. Neria was closing the door to her room next to the *museo*. We nodded to each other and walked together in silence out the gate of Campo Chiclero.

Just past the cavernous Evangelical church, which had been over-flowing with singing and clapping worshippers the night I arrived, we crossed the old airstrip. It seemed to stretch straight into oblivion in both directions. A few horses fed on the grass, occasionally swishing their tails and snorting. I passed so close to one he lifted his head, catching me for a moment in a big, round eye. We were the only creatures about.

The roads of Petén can shine white at night for the color of their clay, providing their own illumination. I didn't need my flashlights. We passed the Catholic church, a homely, lopsided structure marked simply with a painted cross on its wooden front and the words *Iglesia Catolica*. It had no bell, only a tire rim hanging from a tree, sounded with a metal bar to call the faithful. Neria shook her head sadly.

"It's about to fall down," she said. "We have no money." I had attended Mass Sunday night in the church lit only by a few candles, in the company of a catechist, seven women, two children, and a dog that walked up and down the aisle. A Catholic priest with many other parishes on his route came only occasionally. The livelier Evangelical church, which could name its preachers when it liked, independent of a hierarchy, and forbade alcohol, attracting those cursed with family drunks, drew a much larger congregation.

Turning from the runway and climbing in the night, Neria and I brought on a wave of barking and rooster crows from the yards of sleeping houses, a wave that ebbed as we entered the forest beyond. The canopy cut out even starlight. Neria knew the path and wore a white shirt, which I followed closely instead of breaking out the flashlight, which might have been disorienting. Soon the stone mountains, as the Maya saw them, the temples, loomed in the plaza. We made our way to the oldest of all, directly across from the three observatory structures.

Ascending, I used my hands sometimes, feeling like the *taquazin* that famously scales the steep staircase of Tikal's Jaguar Temple. Neria climbed more slowly. On the first platform, I stood, shook my arms, and paused to look up the final flight. There at the top of the pyramid, like Lords of the Night, two figures waited. Neria reached the place I stood, and followed my eyes.

"*Buenos días,*" she said weakly, although day was still far away.

"*Buenos días,*" came the reply.

"We didn't think anyone was here," she said.

"We didn't think anyone else was coming," said a male voice.

We climbed to sit below them. They were young men from the capital, come to Petén to visit relatives, who insisted they witness the equinox at Uaxactun. As often happens in Guatemala, Neria and they quickly discovered they were distantly related, through cousins and in-laws. Then talk was over. The young men sat silently behind and just above us, like court attendants on Maya vases, handsome, mute.

"Yes, Uaxactun," Don Gilberto had said when I asked him where I should go. The breeze blew cooler atop the pyramid than it had on the ground, and I pulled my nylon jacket tighter around me. But I felt satisfied, not wishing I were anywhere else on the planet but this crumbling stone palace, the observatory complex, Don Gilberto's "college" of the ancestors, where Maya learned to follow the stars, the beginning of timekeeping.

We watched the structures across the grassy plaza, just as the astronomer-priests once did from this point. Designed purposefully to show the solar journey, the three small temples shared a stepped platform, and each, in turn, stood on its own dais, perfect in their symmetry, the middle one larger but otherwise a mirror of the other two, with rectangular throughways cut into their precise centers, front and back. This was architecture as observatory, observatory as architecture.

On the winter solstice, the sun would dawn over the left corner of the northernmost temple, throwing light in a perfect diagonal across platforms and plaza to the observation point where Neria and I sat. On the summer solstice, the sun rose above the right-hand corner of the southern building, throwing light perfectly from the other direction. On the equinox, less than an hour away, the sun was supposed to rise directly above the building in the middle, its roof now sprouting with bushes. Sensing the shapes of the stone structures in the dark rather than seeing them, I wondered at the marriage of science and grace. I felt close to fellow curious beings far in the past, who created such art for the purpose of understanding the universe in which they lived.

Owls, opossums, and other nocturnal animals had gone quiet, and the earliest birds were not yet singing. In perfect peace, we waited. There are places on earth that exude age and venerability, where you can feel the weight and richness of what has gone before. Uaxactun, I think, dating from 1000 BC, perhaps the longest continuously inhabited Maya metropolis, is one of these. On all sides were temples of its classic period—about AD 300 to 900—where explorers have found even earlier sacred buildings nestled inside. Their unearthed masks and paintings sometimes show influence from the shadowy Olmec civilization, which preceded the Maya, perhaps died absorbed by it.

The sky was becoming lighter. I felt by now we should have seen that red streak that announces true dawn. Neria adjusted herself on the stone, looking uncomfortable, but said nothing. Below on our temple, invisible from where we sat, giant stucco masks of animals sacred to the Maya kept watch from the walls. At least we waited in good company, I thought, with jaguar, parrots, turtles.

And then, unbelievably, it began to rain.

Drops fell on our heads, our feet. I reached into my pack for a contraption I had purchased on Canal Street in New York, "The Smallest Umbrella in the World." It was, even extended, but Neria and I huddled together underneath and kept fairly dry, except for her right arm and my left. I glanced over my shoulder and up at the young court attendants, who had already pulled up their jacket hoods. They nodded in tandem, the points of the hoods above their heads bobbing forward.

Above the three structures, the eastern sky had become so fully light it was clear the sun had risen, unseen. I could hear the fellows above us rearranging themselves wordlessly. Neria made herself smaller under the umbrella, as if preparing to wait for the next equinox if she had to, six months off, to see what she had come to see. Neither did I feel any desire to move, even though the water was pooling on the uneven steps, soaking through my jeans and chilling my bottom and the backs of my legs. Instead of leaving, as logic would dictate, each of us on the pyramid stayed in place.

I do not know how much time passed until I could fold the umbrella. The hidden sun was testing us. Eventually it broke through the grayness, yellow as a yolk and perfectly round, already two fingers into the sky above the roofs across the plaza. That the bright orb had first appeared exactly at the center of the top of the central temple, we took on faith.

5

Voices from the Well

*The hand of the Lord came upon me . . . and he set me down in the
midst of the valley that was full of bones. . . . And behold, there
were very many, and lo, they were very dry. And behold a shaking,
and the bones came together, bone to his bone, and the skin covered
them above. . . . And the Lord said, come from the four winds, O
breath, and breathe upon these slain, that they may live.*

—*Ezekiel 37*

WHEN I MOVED TO ANTIGUA IN 1989, EVERYONE TOLD ME THE
civil war had never reached Petén. Like the western United States in the
American mind a century ago, the Guatemalan jungle region remained
vast and mostly unknown, possibly beautiful, undoubtedly heathen.
Certainly outside history.

On the Usumacinta in the 1990s, however, a cooperative member
who had stayed in place after the violence said, "Skulls explode in the

fields when farmers burn near Dos Erres." He recalled shocked-looking peasants emerging from the jungle over several weeks in early 1983. "They were in a mad hurry" to cross the border into Mexico, he said.

"I offered one man food, but he only wanted to push on, saying a village by that name, Dos Erres, *ya no existe*, no longer exists."

In Antigua, even among those who followed the war, no one I asked had heard of it. The name Dos Erres, the "r's" rolled Spanish-style, appeared on no map, not even in the library where I once read the leather-bound memoirs of Teobert Maler.

At the library one day in 1993, I mentioned the name to a friend, a University of Illinois professor who regularly visited Antigua to use historical archives. He didn't recognize it either but said the janitor at a Guatemala City hotel where he once lived, to whom he brought old clothes each visit, had confided he had lost a son to violence in Petén.

By this time the press of daily reporting had waned with the quieting of the wars in Nicaragua, El Salvador, and Guatemala, and I took on magazine reporting assignments, which had more flexible deadlines. Between a story for *Vogue* (on the growing pattern of male-to-female HIV infection already evident in Central America) and one for *Sierra* (on national parks in Costa Rica and El Salvador), curiosity led me to follow up on the mystery of Dos Erres with a quick trip to Guatemala City. I did not know I would be so taken by its story that I would still be following it more than fifteen years later.

On New Year's Day, 1994, I climbed the winding road out of Antigua's valley and drove another half hour along the Pan American highway, descending into the valley of the capital. I went to the hotel and found the janitor in a corner of the lobby, sweeping up bits of dirt around the flowerpots. His name was Anacleto Garcia, and he was dressed in overalls, unusual for a Guatemalan, perhaps a gift from my friend. When I mentioned Dos Erres, his face paled.

He looked around nervously. Except for us, the lobby was empty. He grasped the broom and stared at me. His dark hair was slightly gray, shoulders slightly bent.

"Yes," Anacleto Garcia said. "You are a friend of my friend." Still he did not move, until he lifted the broom, murmuring, "And it is time."

We climbed a labyrinth of back stairs, sitting on steps near a trash drop. Occasionally a rush of garbage fell down the chute on its way to the basement.

"It is early morning," he said. Sometimes Garcia spoke in the present tense, reliving moments three armed men came to his isolated farm outside the village of Dos Erres, near the Petén market town of Las Cruces.

"The men say, 'We are the guerrillas, and we have come to take you with us, and if not we'll kill you.' But they aren't guerrillas. They are the army. The army had been circling our village for days. They even carried a camp kitchen."

Garcia said the men wore old clothes but hadn't bothered to change their distinctive army boots or backpacks. They carried Galil rifles, the Israeli brand issued by the army. Garcia stood on the step, puffed out his chest, and gripped an imaginary rifle, one hand on the barrel, the other on the trigger.

Taking the part of Rosa, his wife, he seemed to pat down an apron and then placed his hands on his hips. Rosa had played along with the armed men's story that they were guerrillas.

"How could I go with you to the mountains with my small children, to suffer hunger and thirst, where mosquitoes and flies and every other animal can bite them?" Garcia said in a high-pitched voice, apparently meant to be his wife's.

The armed men asked the family for guns, which it did not have, and money. They ordered everyone to lie facedown, wives, daughters, sons-in-law, eight children. Garcia said he alone remained standing. Without warning, he lifted his arms before me and spoke what I thought was gibberish. His voice rose, the sounds still unintelligible.

Oh shit, I thought, my mouth going dry. Unpredictable. A trickster, mad, a fool.

I looked around to see how I might leave quickly, if I needed to do so.

But Garcia's upraised eyes looked sage and clear. Soon he spoke in words I could understand.

"I prayed, 'I commend my spirit and those of all your small children here. You will know what to do with us, Lord.'" Garcia was an evangelical Christian and said he had reckoned he would die that morning and had begun to speak in "angelic tongues."

Perhaps the soldiers had been taken off guard or frightened. They were young, and there may have been the God-fearing among them in whom the outburst struck a chord. Whatever the reason, the drama changed course, and the armed men turned to leave. Over his shoulder, one warned the Garcias not to go in a certain direction "because our companions are there, and they'll kill you."

"At that moment, inside the village, my son was living his last, with the others," Garcia said. "And my other son was escaping death."

This was unexpected news, that there might be a surviving eyewitness to whatever had happened in Dos Erres. Anacleto Garcia's son Federico had been eleven at the time, his father said, and now lived as a caretaker on a ranch outside the city. At the possibility of interviewing Federico Garcia, my heart started beating fast, a throwback to war-reporting days when the mission was to quickly discover the facts of a battle or behind an assassination. There was no such urgency now, but habit popped adrenalin from its gland and sent it rushing into the blood.

"Return next Sunday and I will take you to him," Anacleto Garcia said.

A week later Federico Garcia, the janitor's son, told me a story he had kept secret from those outside the family for thirteen years.

"It is time," said his father when he introduced us.

There were only two beds in young Federico Garcia's one-room house. His pregnant wife went to an outside kitchen, returning with a small table and two stools, a way of giving importance to the moment.

"That day we took a shortcut home from Las Cruces and didn't pass anyone in the road," Federico began, returning in memory to December 1982. "My brother and I asked each other, 'What could be happening?'"

I listened for two hours to Federico's clear and detailed rendering of events. How could this story have remained invisible for thirteen years? The more time I spent in Maya realms, the less I believed time only moves forward inexorably, but instead sometimes must loop back on itself to complete the present, to shape the future. Part of the reporter's job is to serve as witness to history; I knew Dos Erres would not end for me in this small ranch house.

———————

Six weeks after I heard Federico's story, I boarded a bus in the Santa Elena market, carrying sunscreen and a rain poncho. Falling between the jungle's only two seasons, rainy and less rainy, February days may begin sunny, tricking the traveler into dressing light, but end in crippling rains. "Never marry in February," Peteneros say, because unpredictability rules the month. At 7:00 A.M., the sun already burned hot through the roof of the bus as we passengers waited inside.

An inebriated newspaper peddler bumped his way up the aisle. "Woman Cuts Off His Penis with a Chainsaw!" said the headlines. With one hand the peddler obscured a front-page photo, not too drunk to forget the cash value of curiosity. Some who could read whispered to others. Women blushed. Men's eyes widened. Babies suffering from the heat complained, refusing to be nursed into silence.

The driver gunned the motor. The peddler and other vendors, of mangos, photocopied books, and a Complete Course of the English, jumped from the bus. In the slow crawl out of the crowded market, one last hawker leapt aboard, gold neck chains flying.

"Who has not failed in his duty as a man at night, after a hard day in the fields?" he asked. "What mother has not yearned for the medicine to calm the tormented newborn?"

I imagined myself at a stagecoach stop in the old American West, listening in wonder to a patent medicine man. This one wore short leather boots with side zippers, stylish but useless for real walking in these muddy parts. He carried a canvas shoulder bag so clean it could only command respect. Slowly he slipped a hand into the bag, withdrawing it empty, teasing.

"And what father has not wished for a miracle, to stimulate the appetite of the wasting child, who refuses yet one more meal of tortillas and beans?"

Eyes dropped.

"Imagine the special offer I am authorized to present you—only ten quetzales! But wait . . ." He held the prize close to his chest, and passengers looked up once more. "I must speak of more, as a man of medicine.

Taken regularly, the contents of this flask combat the sorrows and pain of that quiet disease which comes to even the most beautiful of women, that sickness which arrives in cities and countryside alike to cut down the proudest of them, that scourge that touches each family in time, that sad fate."

He seemed to look each passenger in the eye and then closed his own.

"No one dares say its name," he said, then practically breathed it: *Menopausia*.

When the bus finally quit town, gaining speed on the road, the breeze from open windows caressed a dozen crying babies into tranquility. At a military checkpoint, we stopped. I felt around at the bottom of my bag until I grasped my notebook. I had taken the precaution of scattering through its pages the names given to me by Anacleto Garcia and his son Federico, written on purpose in messy script. I felt nervous anyway. But the soldiers seemed interested only in the male passengers, frisking two youths before they allowed them to reboard, and waved the bus on.

Two hours later, I stepped out into the air at La Libertad, a venerable settlement still marked on some maps with its Maya name, Sacnicte. Walking the quiet road through town led me to the remains of a cenote, a round break in the Petén's karstic crust, almost surely once a sacred Maya well. Nearby was the low, square white building I was looking for, shaded by palms.

The local *padre* greeted me warmly when I gave him the name of a mutual friend, an American priest who told me the man had served the Central Petén parish for years. "Come, come into my office," he said.

The *padre* offered me a cigarette, which I smoked a little, out of politeness. We drank coffee, despite the heat. His short stature, dark skin, and last name told me he was Maya. He dressed in khakis and a *guayabera* shirt, loose and smarter for the heat than traditional black cassock and tight collar.

"Call me Huicho," he said, beaming at the sight of a new face in what surely must be a lonely post. Our banter didn't last long.

When I broached the subject of Dos Erres, a curtain of seriousness and formality fell between us. Padre Huicho slowly crushed his cigarette in a tin ashtray. He coughed. He rose from his desk, closed the office door, returned, and took his chair once more.

"We are aware of this; people have been coming to us," he said.

I don't know who was more surprised, I, to hear that Huicho was already involved somehow with Dos Erres and looking jangled about it, or Huicho, to hear that the secret of Dos Erres was an object of interest to an American woman he had never seen before. I believe I recovered more quickly than he.

"Where can I find the place? How do I get there?"

He offered another cigarette from his Payasos, the red pack with the clown on the front. I declined. He lit one for himself, took a drag, and sighed, blowing out smoke.

"I am going to ask you not to try," he said.

Investigators in the guise of hunters were reconnoitering the site as we spoke, he said, for the purposes of a legal exhumation. The appearance of a *gringa* in the area, asking questions, could alert those who wanted the crime to remain hidden.

I must have looked upset.

"I didn't say 'don't go,'" Huicho said, smiling. "What I am saying is don't go yet."

He took a small, lined notebook from his *guayabera* pocket. "Now, tell me," he said. "What do you know?"

We compared my list of officers' names and the dead with information he had. He jotted notes. He examined a map the Garcias had drawn for me showing houses, school, church, a dry well, and places where bodies might be found. He copied the sketch by hand.

"This will help," he said, tucking the notebook away.

Huicho was a frail man, about thirty-five, wracked by emphysema. We walked from the parish office to the rectory. There we ate a simple lunch of beans, tortillas, and fried fish, talking of poetry (he himself wrote, he said) and the progress of the Dos Erres investigation. Events had been "converging," he said, to lift the silence about the village. For four years, since 1991, rebels and government had been fitfully negotiating to end the war. Closer to home, the army had abandoned its camouflage-painted, cement box buildings in the garrison at Las Cruces, a busy cattle-trading town just four miles from Dos Erres.

Meanwhile, the Petén's Roman Catholic bishop had opened a legal assistance office to help illiterate peasants navigate government bureaucracy, to obtain birth certificates required for enrolling children in school, for instance. Unexpectedly, survivors of Dos Erres showed up for help with their own paperwork. Municipal authorities issued no death certificates in the massacre. Survivors could not reclaim their old farmland and work it again without proof of the demise of the registered owners—husbands, fathers, sisters. Indeed, living relatives asked, how could they prove anyone had died at all, since the bodies were hidden at the bottom of a dry well or their remains mixed with one another in gullies and groves?

Huicho and a fellow local priest had heard of an investigation team in Argentina that looked for burials of the "disappeared" in their country. In 1992, this forensic anthropology team had worked at a village called El Mozote in El Salvador, where 767 residents died at the hands of the Salvadoran army in 1981. Salvadoran authorities and US government supporters denied the El Mozote massacre had taken place until the Argentine team exhumed the common graves. Quietly, the *padres* in Petén contacted the Argentine team, for the sake of the living.

Huicho told me that once the "hunters" had fixed a place to begin, the forensic anthropologists would go to work. He considered aloud whether I should come. "An international presence might not be such a bad idea," he said.

This was code: when a Central American invited "international" presence, it meant he or she was going to do something legal but nevertheless certain to displease authorities. A foreigner's presence made it less likely thugs might crack heads. The assumption does not always hold, but it works often enough. I have always accepted such invitations.

"You want to come along, don't you?" Huicho asked.

"I want to finish something I started," I said.

———

Several weeks later, in Antigua, I received a call from a woman I did not know, saying that if I wished "to make that tour in Petén," I should come to a house outside La Libertad in three days. I flew to Flores and took the bus again from Santa Elena. The place outside La Libertad turned out to be the residence and clinic of a team of medics from a Spanish humanitarian agency. About 7:00 P.M., a rotund, dark young man came through the screen door without knocking. It seemed everyone knew him but me.

"Just call me Paco," he said, shaking my hand vigorously. "Francisco Romero. But Paco, Paco."

This was the other *padre*, who had worked with Father Huicho to organize the exhumation. He didn't look like the priests of my childhood, Irishmen imported to Southern California who wore black cassocks with a thousand tiny buttons down the front and stiff white collars. Paco wore a T-shirt, shorts, blue baseball cap, and sandals.

One of the doctors set spoons and paper napkins on the table. The conversation turned to infiltrators, spies working for the military in the guise of local journalists or curious observers. They might watch for who participated in the work of exhumation, who helped.

"We have to keep a sharp eye for strangers," Paco said, for the safety of local people. Wasn't he worried about retribution?

He tipped back his chair and laughed largely. "No," he replied, quoting Ezekiel, the passage about the bones that had no hope of resurrection but found themselves nevertheless called back to life.

"Do you realize that was one of the readings in yesterday's Mass?" he asked. The coincidence was like a miracle, said the look in his eyes. It meant a greater hand was directing whatever happened in these days, so why worry about his fate?

One Spanish medic asked in a sardonic voice, "Do you think the army is worried about all this, that they even care?" His handsome face nodded to a fellow across the table, who passed a bottle of Marqués de Riscal. Filling glasses, the medic spoke in the tone of one who liked argument for its own sake, more appropriate to a Madrid café than this plain house a world away from Europe, surrounded by screaming cicadas.

"The army knows that neither soldiers nor officers are punished, no matter what they do," said the medic. "Any means they use is justified, to keep guerrillas from taking over the country. Right?"

Paco sniffed the air elaborately. He would not be drawn into polemic. The pleasant aroma of instant packaged noodle soup and garden vegetables cooked with sweet onions filled the air. A nurse on the Spanish team set the food before us on the Formica table, smiling at each of half a dozen faces as she performed the elegant gesture.

"Shall we eat?" Paco said.

We squeezed fresh lemon into the bowls, sprinkled chopped cilantro on top. Another bottle of the wine appeared. Paco and the two medics confirmed details in the hidden history of Dos Erres that I had taken from Anacleto Garcia and from two other Guatemala City residents who once had owned land near Las Cruces.

Beginning in 1978, forty-three families cleared virgin jungle near Las Cruces, planting three hundred acres of corn, beans, and squash. They named the place Dos Erres, Two Rs, for the Reyes and Ruano families, the first to arrive. Together the pioneers cleared a two-kilometer road to connect to the Las Cruces road—by machete, because no one could afford a chain saw. They built their own houses, a one-room schoolhouse, and two churches, Catholic and evangelical Protestant. They forbade liquor sales in three house-front shops. Most inhabitants of Dos Erres owned land for the first time in their lives.

Men and teenage boys declined to participate in the army's "volunteer" civilian patrol system. When they heard rumors of the attacks on the Usumacinta River cooperatives, residents spoke among themselves about leaving Petén but then dropped the subject. Like a protective mantra, they repeated *Nada debe, nada teme.* "He who owes nothing—is unbeholden to either side—has nothing to fear."

War came first to Dos Erres's neighbor, Las Cruces. It came as war often does to a small place, beginning quietly but building inexorably, because even a provincial town is connected to wider events. It started with tins and boxes.

In 1979, Mexican products smuggled across the Usumacinta and English products from Belize, next door, flooded the town. The contraband underpriced Las Cruces merchants, who were paying dearly to bring goods overland from distant Guatemala City. When local authorities requested help, the government sent some thirty treasury guards to patrol streets and shops, to keep out the contraband.

At first, the arrangement worked "like honey on pancakes," as they say in Petén. Within months, however, the underpaid, unsupervised guards overstepped the bounds of the job. They dragged suspects into their blue wooden barracks on the strength of an accusation from someone with a personal score to settle or in exchange for a bribe. With leather strips, they whipped backs until they bled.

In 1980, Guatemala City answered complaints by sending regular soldiers to replace the treasury guards. Eventually the soldiers committed excesses, too, but the larger picture had changed, and now the town's complaints met silence. Guerrillas had arrived in this corner of Petén. No one would agree to move the soldiers away, no matter how badly behaved.

At 11:00 P.M. on September 1, 1981, a moonless, rainy night, guerrillas silently surrounded the small Las Cruces garrison, attacking from all sides. Soldiers answered fire until ammunition ran out. Rebel machine guns prevented them from escaping. Terrified townspeople spent that night facedown under their beds while stray bullets pierced the wood planks of their houses.

At dawn, the rebels left. Residents cautiously left cover and found the garrison a heap of planks and blown concrete blocks. No soldier had survived. As neighbors stood around in small groups, wondering how to report the incident (there were no phones), a truck arrived carrying inhabitants from settlements farther up the road.

"Where is the garrison?" asked those who arrived in the truck. They wanted to report that guerrillas had attacked their towns, called Joséfinos, Palestina, and Los Chorros, killing the mayors.

At midday, helicopters landed near the ruined Las Cruces garrison. As the men and women watched, wondering what the incident would mean for them, the army removed its dead. In the remoter towns, however, no one dared come to certify the executions of civilian authorities. After two days, the residents of Joséfinos, Palestina, and Los Chorros considered their Christian mandate to bury the dead, and, although it was illegal to do this without death certificates, they interred the mayors' corpses on the side of the road. The guerrillas had announced themselves in a big way; the army prepared to respond.

Eight days later, at a crossroads called Subin, eight miles east of Las Cruces, a line of trucks and jeeps spilled forth artillery, provisions, and twenty-five hundred soldiers. They billeted in tents while they built a permanent base. Now no one coming from points north, or to or from the Usumacinta or Pasión Rivers, traveled by road without being detained and, if soldiers wished, searched to the skin. Soon the Subin garrison earned a reputation for being a house of horrors, where villagers, named as rebel sympathizers by local spies for the army, were interrogated and sometimes disappeared.

Bars and prostitution sprouted like evil flowers; families feared for the safety of their young girls. When satellite garrisons went up in surrounding small towns, guerrillas attacked them. More soldiers arrived.

The greater the army felt the heat from the guerrillas, the more it tightened the screws on the civilian population. At checkpoints, troops limited the amount of food any individual could carry, making life miserable for those who had to walk hours to reach a store. Pharmacists became suspect because they might be supplying the rebels; soon few medicines of any kind were available. Soldiers closely watched those who left town for medical care or to buy supplies in Santa Elena. If they did not return, the soldiers knew where their families lived.

One day hundreds of rebels appeared at the central park in Las Cruces. They called a public meeting, collected people from nearby houses. They read a list of "commissioners," civilians licensed by the army to carry guns. Their leader said local commissioners, expected to turn in neighbors suspected of supporting rebels, were responsible for many deaths. Rebels left behind copies of the names when they marched out of town, flying a banner of red and black.

The army called a public meeting in the same park the guerrillas had used. "We know some may look like peasants by day but turn into guerrillas by night," a lieutenant said, taking his time, peering at expressionless faces in the crowd.

An army intelligence unit officer stood nearby. His camouflage uniform looked starched and pressed, the way an officer at headquarters in the capital might wear it. He, too, examined the crowd but did not speak.

"The terrorists have come to take the crops you work so hard to plant," the lieutenant said. "They trick you, with words."

Guerrillas were entering outlying *ranchos* to explain their cause and to eat. Usually they paid or requested food to carry. They did not rudely demand to be fed, as soldiers might. Yet rebel visits were not necessarily welcome, either. They drew attention from the army. Sometimes they asked the residents to plant a second crop to help feed them. And guerrillas might order the population to witness the execution of a neighbor charged with spying. When rebels came to Dos Erres, residents listened with respect, provided tortillas and other food at hand.

"We are your only hope," a guerrilla cadre told them. He promised rebels would protect peasants from landowners and from authorities who treated them badly.

In the end, the guerrillas could not protect a single village from the army's response to their presence. The Las Cruces garrison sent soldiers disguised as rebels to Dos Erres. They dressed in faded camouflage or patched cotton pants and rubber boots, but their haircuts were regulation neat, and anyway, they could not fool the locals. Residents treated the ersatz guerrillas with customary politeness. The garrison communicated its suspicions that Dos Erres favored the guerrilla, maybe even *were* guerrillas, to the Special Forces base at La Polvera (Gunpowder), two hundred miles east, headquarters for the jungle region.

Well north of Dos Erres, in the kind of skirmish with rebels not unusual at the time, the army lost men. Base 23, home to the fearsome special forces called Kaibiles, sent word to the lieutenant at Las Cruces: Encircle Dos Erres. Forbid entry or exit for a certain day. Base 23 ordered in the Kaibiles, about sixty men who traveled with personal knives and guns and a camp kitchen.

While Kaibiles were inside Dos Erres, the perimeter of local soldiers did its job, refusing entry anyone who came to the village by the main path, offering no reason. A farmer who was turned back proceeded to the garrison at Las Cruces for information.

"What's happening is a cleansing operation," an officer there told him. "Like the Bible says, those who are judged filthy shall die, and those clean shall live. The filthy to the fire."

Three hundred seventy-six persons died on December 6, 7, and 8, 1982, at Dos Erres. Besides villagers, the number includes about forty day laborers hired by residents during harvest time. Soldiers raped young girls before they cut their throats.

Thirteen years later, our motley group walked single file through the place Dos Erres once had stood, led by the men who had posed as hunters to reconnoiter the site. Behind them followed a long line: three Argentine forensic anthropologists; the local *padres*, Paco and Huicho; a dozen former villagers, men and women, looking stern, carrying machetes and digging tools; three members of a human rights organization from the capital, Families of the Detained and Disappeared (Asociación de Familiares de Detenidos-Desaparecidos de Guatemala); a church lawyer; and a judge. Two policemen, who proceeded lackadaisically, brought up the rear. They were charged with keeping track of any evidence that might be found.

I had expected to see the remains of buildings, but from the path we took the place looked simply like a stretch of brush with a few stunted trees. Two shallow watering holes stood dry, their bottoms just cracked, red-colored clay. We plodded in silence for half an hour. The sun burned my hands. I believe each person in the straggling line who knew the history of Dos Erres was thinking of the last march of some who died here.

"They brought in more people we knew, our neighbors, about thirty men and thirty women, in separate columns, herding them like cattle," young Federico Garcia had told me.

"That's not counting the children, who were walking behind their mothers, weeping. The men with guns had surrounded them, grabbing the women by the hair; they directed the men more carefully, cursing, but not hitting them as they hit the women. They took my cousin Rosita and another young girl from their mothers and made them stay behind. They took the women and the children to the Protestant church and told the rest of us, 'We are taking you to the school. Don't worry.'"

As I walked in the line at Dos Erres, the living village described by Federico Garcia seemed to have disappeared, absorbed into tall grass bending in hot wind. The fields of his youth, he said, had been covered with corn, squash, bananas, twisting bean plants, and chilis; some houses then still had roofs of palm thatch gathered from the jungle, but more families each year were installing safer, more fireproof tin sheeting. He worked in the fields alongside his older brothers but also joined youngsters his age to watch progress on the well a neighbor, Juan Arevalo, was digging.

"He used to give us pineapple slices or sugar cane," Federico said. "We whispered to each other, 'He'll dig all the way to China!'"

When my part of the line reached the site of Juan Arevalo's well, I saw senior anthropologist Patricia Bernardi standing at its rim, gloved hands on hips, a blue bandanna around her neck. "This may call for digging a trench to come in from the side," she said.

In her midthirties, tall and slim, Bernardi possessed the grace of a high-fashion model and might have looked like one had she allowed her cropped blond hair to grow out, used makeup, and worn anything but baggy cotton pants. Her teammates, a dark-haired novice still in her twenties and a burly, urbane professor of forensic anthropology from Buenos Aires, requested villagers who had come along to find saplings. Soon the three "forensics," as they were beginning to be called, were kneeling in the dirt, lashing the young wood together with vines. They built a kind of sawhorse, six feet tall, spanning the six-foot diameter of the well.

Villagers had come in hopes of finding remains of wives, brothers, children, and to work alongside the professionals. "We'll use it to hang a bucket," Bernardi said, explaining the sawhorse to them. "Someone on the bottom will shout when it's full, and we'll pull up the . . ." She searched for a word, a term. "The excavated material," she said.

The two *padres* wielded machetes to clear brush, hefty Paco sweating profusely, thin Father Huicho coughing constantly. The professor flung a rope over the crosspiece of the sawhorse, attaching the bucket. A lone farmer climbed seven feet down the well, hacking away at invading tree roots so the dig could begin. He worked intently, a man who had lost neighbors.

When the farmer came up, Bernardi descended with a trowel. A local woman named Carmen Perez arrived with a basket of tortillas and a covered blue pot of refried beans. She distributed the food. When the pot was empty, she claimed a place next to the well.

"They're down there, the children and the old men, they are there," Carmen Perez said, each time Bernardi sent up a bucket with nothing but dirt. In time the well produced the first items, shreds of badly disintegrated cloth.

The district attorney stood apart from the others, a neatly turned out man in his thirties wearing a baseball cap. On the walk to the site, he had told me he doubted bones would be discovered. Men in his position were threatened and shot at, their houses firebombed, for signing off on investigations like this one. Three hours after it began, the district attorney announced he was suspending the dig.

"You can't do that," said the church lawyer, quoting chapter and verse from a new penal code she carried in hand.

The professor said, "We came four thousand miles, and you've come barely one hundred. Can't you wait a little longer?"

Eventually the district attorney relented. "Twenty-four hours. I cannot permit the expense for no reason," he said, gesturing toward the pair of mute policemen.

Later, he said to me, "Look, everyone knows it was the military, but this was all years ago. I have sixteen cases on my desk right now that need tending."

In early afternoon, one of the Spanish doctors I had met the night before beckoned from a distance and then disappeared from sight. Soon I was part of a search party, six or seven of us loosely following at a distance the large figure of Carmen Perez and the diminutive young woman anthropologist. We advanced quietly in the direction of a thicket about a mile in the distance, keeping far apart from one another. Spies called *orejas*, ears, might be in the growing crowd at the well. The searchers did not want to draw attention lest evidence disappear.

Bushes gave way to edible *chipilin* weeds and tall grass called *golondrina*, the name for the swallow, the bird that symbolizes return. Some became edgy and called out in low voices when they strayed too far out of sight of another.

When we reached the copse we reunited, breaking branches to use as walking sticks and protection against snakes. In the dim light under the tree cover, we used the sticks to probe dead leaves, uncovering bits of clothing and footwear, partially mulched into the forest floor. We used our boots to turn over soil and found bones. The young woman anthropologist scanned with a more practiced eye, stooping to the ground to examine small objects. She noted that the remains were dispersed in a wide area, probably because they had been exposed to animals and the elements over years.

"Animals carry away the long bones early, while they still bear flesh," she said.

Thus clothing and other clues to identification, and clues to the cause of death like bullet fragments or casings, could not necessarily be "associated" with particular skeletal remains. As a scientist, she was saying this wooded site was not worth the time and expenditure of scarce resources.

Carmen Perez did not need a scientific investigation to know this was a killing field. She sat upon a boulder, and I next to her, on another. When the soldiers came to Dos Erres, she said, she was sharing a house with her sister's family outside the settlement. Her brother-in-law left to help a neighbor, who believed his seven children were there. The sisters heard shooting. Two days later, when neither men nor children returned, the women went to look for them. They found bloody desks at the school, pieces of looped rope, ripped clothing.

"We walked through the fields of Juan Arevalo," Perez said. "Like everyone, we know Don Juan has been digging month after month, even thirty feet into the earth, finding no water."

When the sisters looked into the shaft and saw it newly filled in with dirt, they fled home to huddle with their own children. From there, Perez said, they could see vultures flocking over these woods.

"It took us a month to get the courage. Then we came here together," she said.

"There were many decapitated bodies. Heads were piled among the roots of the trees. They were our friends and neighbors. We could see the dogs had been eating them. We felt afraid, because of what happened in this place." Recognizing individuals was not easy because during the month "a kind of green stuff" had grown over the remains.

The others in the thicket where we spoke began to drift away, returning to the well site. I wondered why this timid-looking, aging peasant mother of six exposed herself by appearing at the well, leading others to this open tomb in the woods.

"I was amazed when I saw them digging out the well today," she said. "Because we thought our lives had been worth nothing to anyone. We had told no one what we saw, because we felt that for others, for those whose lives are worth something, we were like animals, who could be killed even for speaking."

Seeing our caravan had been a shock, she said. The last time so many vehicles had entered the village was after the massacre, when soldiers in trucks took away what the dead had left behind: corn, pigs, calves, chickens, furniture, anything that could be moved before they burned the place down.

By quitting time in late afternoon, Carmen Perez and I had rejoined the others at the well. Two unearthed objects rested on the ground: makeshift shovels, crafted from yellow plastic cooking oil containers and rebar. Whoever covered the bodies with dirt probably jerry-rigged the tools on the spot. They would have tossed them down last.

"We will find bones tomorrow," said Patricia Bernardi. "That much is certain."

I slept at the rectory in La Libertad, in the temporarily vacant room of a priest I had never met who was out ministering in the jungle parish. The bedroom was a cell made by partitioning part of the living room with a fabric-covered screen, its door a curtain of the same vivid, dark blue cotton cloth, the kind found by the bolt in open markets. Its weft remained undyed, forming abstract humanoid shapes, elongated white figures that looked like ghosts against a night sky.

I blew out the candle. The sleeping cot creaked, a wood frame covered with a thin sheet of foam and a woven mat of dry grass, a bed kind only to a body dog tired, like mine. Yet I could not sleep.

I thought of that scrubbed table in the house outside Guatemala City where I had listened to Federico Garcia, his dark eyes strangely unlit. He remembered sitting close to his older brother in the one-room schoolhouse where the Kaibiles had taken the men, until the soldiers sent youngsters Federico's age to the church with the women and children.

"Let's escape," Federico whispered to another eleven-year-old, who was carrying his infant brother.

The other boy shook his head no. "I have to stay with the baby," he said. Then the moment to flee was gone.

"Inside the church some women prayed, and others sang, thinking that would change the hearts of the soldiers," Federico said. "Instead, the troops mocked them. One soldier played the guitar they used for services. Another put on the pastor's necktie." Some women nursed babies; many just gazed at their children. "Everyone knew what was going to happen."

Soldiers marched the men from the schoolhouse past the church, and, through a window, Federico saw his brother, Ernesto. "I ran to the door. I was yelling, 'I want to go with him!' But the door was locked."

The men looked "sad, composed," Federico had said. I asked him why he thought they did not resist, even unarmed, since they outnumbered the soldiers.

"Those were not the kind of people who opposed authorities," he said. "They were afraid of anyone with guns. Maybe if they had had more time, they might have thought of a plan to defend themselves."

When his brother went by, he looked "dignified." Bursts from machine guns sounded, then individual shots.

The troops returned to take the women and children from the church, trying to lead them in the other direction from which they had taken the men. But many refused.

"The women cried out that the soldiers should kill them there, in the patio of the church, and not in the woods, that they wanted to die in a clean and open place."

One of the Kaibiles had been guarding Federico, clearing a path at the same time. He muttered back at the women, "I'll beat them into walking." He warned the boy, "Don't even think about moving."

"But instead of freezing, when he turned his back I jumped into the woods and rolled behind a fallen tree," Federico said. The soldier entered the woods and fired extended bursts from an automatic weapon on all sides. "He thought I was dead in there, but I was alive, right near the edge of the path," said Federico.

The boy heard the Kaibiles order their charges into a line. Rapid fire, screams, children crying. Then the finishing off, *tiros de gracia*, shots of grace, single shots.

When the soldiers walked away, Federico lifted his head above the fallen trunk and saw the women and children "heaped over like bundles on the ground." He lay on the ground, "hardly breathing," he said. After sunset, he began to crawl toward his family's house on the outskirts of the settlement, colliding in darkness with more bundles. These were the dead of the night before, the other half of the hamlet, who had been killed first, silently so as not to raise the alarm, by cutting their throats.

I had stopped writing notes at times in the small house on the ranch, listening to Federico, stunned by his face, the mask of a youth hung upon the skull of an anxious old man. I wondered whether by sharing his memory of Dos Erres he might be freeing his spirit, permitting himself relief. Or whether someday he might regret an afternoon of talk with a stranger. I believe that Federico Garcia often returned to exist within those hours, and that was the reason his eyes could look flat, because they were so used to looking in, not out. No wonder he could still describe the experience in such detail.

Inching through the night toward his house, Federico said he lay quiet whenever troops passed. Once, hidden in tall grass, he watched a soldier wearing his brother's hat, riding his brother's mule. Crawling, he approached the house of a neighbor called Jeronimo, stopping when he heard soldiers' voices inside.

"They were laughing," he said. "'We finished them off,' they said. 'Now we've cleaned it up. And we're going to keep going until there's not one left of those, those . . .' and here they used ugly words. I heard them talking about violating young girls and joking about that and about other things they did."

Instead of feeling relief at his escape, Federico said he wanted to die after what he had seen, thinking he was the only one left in the village. He had only known life in a small community and could not imagine living without relatives and neighbors. At the same time, if his family were somehow alive, he needed to survive.

"It was my responsibility," he said, to reach home, "and tell my parents what happened."

"Any bad dreams?" an old peasant farmer asked mischievously at the well the next morning.

Patricia Bernardi said she was feeling pressure to find remains quickly. "Witnesses have exposed themselves," she said.

Interviews and court orders already had taken weeks. The district attorney had to be mollified. Other government officials could call off the project, too, at any moment.

Forensic anthropologists begin with the maxim that it is hard to commit violent homicide without marking a bone. But they must collect more than just a few of the 206 bones in a human body to find those that speak mayhem: a cranium with the beveled entrance and larger exit wounds of a bullet, broken forearms, commonly seen in someone trying to ward off blows, congruent breaks in consecutive ribs of a chest crushed by a rifle butt. Eventually the well would produce such evidence, but not on the second long day of exhumation.

I spread my plastic poncho on the ground, taking a seat near a pile of dirt from the bucket. Alongside others, I sifted by bits with sieves and fingertips. A widower in the circle bid me welcome with a smile lacking several teeth. Concentrating in a manner that seemed meditative, Padre Paco fingered dirt that already had been examined by others. He found tiny bones.

"These are human but really too small and dissociated to be of use at the moment," the young anthropologist said.

"I don't care how small they are," the *padre* replied gently. He continued to extract fragments, placing them on a clean, blue kerchief, a pile of ivory shards.

By now, I already had taken hours of testimony from the Garcia father and son and from Carmen Perez, had read several church reports, and had reviewed lists of the dead. But it was not until the moment I blew dirt from a small object, like blowing sand from a shell, and watched an upper vertebra appear in my hand, the top one that connects the spine to the neck, that I heard the voice of the massacre in my own ears.

At the well, fathers, widows, and siblings of the dead kept watch. How sacred life is, I thought, so that even its remnants carry meaning, so it cannot pass without being noted, honored. A lock of hair, a bone, ashes. The living must have something with which to remain, to touch, to guard. We must be able to say, "This belonged to someone I loved, someone with a place in this world, someone with life."

As a journalist covering the Central American wars, I had kept a list titled "#s Dead," continuously updated on an end page in my notebook, for quick reference: *El Salvador, 50,000; Guatemala, 200,000; Nicaragua, 11,000* . . . Reporting by the numbers had given no hint of the holiness of human life, not an inkling of the tears shed for each soul.

At seventeen feet, the well began to speak. The bucket yielded a rubber boot and a pair of women's underwear. The next time it descended and rose again, Bernardi, now working on the surface, delicately lifted out a child's red T-shirt with decorative patterns at the shoulders.

"A boy's," volunteered Carmen Perez.

"For a child of what age?" Bernardi asked.

"Six."

The anthropology professor took the shirt from Bernardi. He measured and photographed it, placing it in a brown paper bag numbered to correspond with a form noting the depth at which the item was found, time, associated material. Villagers wear the same clothes for so long, a shirt or housedress can be a clue to identity.

The appearance of the first object changed the atmosphere around the well. Paco continued to sift at a mound of dirt but looked determined, no longer meditative. The farmers and women in aprons seemed careful not to meet each other's eyes. No one spoke except to say, *Calorcito.* Or *Que calor.* Or *Calor, verdad?* It's a little warm. What heat! It's hot, isn't it?

Some looked as if they could bear the wait no more when a clear call from deep in the earth rippled to the surface and burst in the air, proclaiming like a clarion. *Huesooo!* A long bone.

Paco rose. Farmers stepped to the well. Bernardi bent over the rim. "Are you sure it's not just a root?" she asked. "What color is the surrounding dirt?"

In a few hours the scene resembled the digs at Dos Pilas, with multiple dirt mounds and bags of findings, bones, and clothing. The suspense of waiting had dissipated, replaced by an atmosphere more complex.

Joy, because remains were surfacing. Sounds of weeping, catches in throats. Foreboding about what might appear next.

The forensic anthropologists fretted over the same dilemmas as Arthur Demarest's team at Dos Pilas: how to light an ever-deepening hole, how to prevent rainwater from seeping in, how to rig a sling to work in the tight, practically airless underground circle, exposing the site without standing upon it. The team worried about the sturdiness of the shaft's walls; it would be terrible to lose another life to Dos Erres.

"I have to get down there," Bernardi said. "How long can a person work at twenty-five feet?" she asked a farmer.

"An hour," he said.

"Maybe you who are used to it," she said, frowning.

There was no money to do it right, with parallel shafts and proper roofing, and there was little time anyway, with the rainy season coming. Bernardi walked to a madrone bush that cast a dappled shadow, sat on a poncho, and drew up her knees. We could never slake our thirst, but every couple of hours we were forced to find even partial shade and drink water, a little at a time, to slow the heart and clear the eyes.

Bernardi was a twenty-one-year-old anthropology major when the American physical anthropologist Clyde Snow, a former FAA crash investigator, came to Buenos Aires to train the first Argentine forensic team in 1982. Snow would one day identify the skull of Dr. Josef Mengele, the Nazi "Angel of Death," buried under a pseudonym in a Brazilian tomb.

When Bernardi first met Snow, she had been spending her time "studying the question of when man's ancestors began using this thorn, or that stick, for tools," she said. "A friend asked if I wanted to help solve the mystery of Argentina's 'disappeared.' It seemed so much more real than what I was doing."

Bernardi rose, brushing dirt from her khaki pants. "I didn't realize it would become my life."

After quitting time on the third day, Bernardi, the other two anthropologists, and three members of the human rights group retired to their quarters on church grounds in Las Cruces. During the night, someone threw rocks on the roof. Someone fired guns nearby.

The following week, peasants reported roaming army patrols. Strangers showed up at the well. Bernardi suggested caution, and Carmen Perez stayed home. Soldiers stopped cars traveling to the dig and searched them at gunpoint. Parishioners warned Paco that his life was in danger.

"I do not feel very threatened," he said. "I haven't yet received any of the notes or other warnings you usually get in such situations."

Bernardi told me, "I sleep like a rock."

When the rains finally came, everyone around the well began to look alike: tired, bathed in a layer of red-brown mud, a democratic patina of clay covering police, *padres*, scientists, survivors. The rain began seeping into the earth, each drop threatening to loosen the walls of the shaft and bury anyone working inside. When tracks from the main road became impassable, the forensic team called off the first phase of the exhumation. They took the remains to a Las Cruces clinic, accompanied by the bored-looking policemen to control the chain of custody.

There the scientists washed the bones, laying them out on flat surfaces. They looked for answers to cause of death, such as a bullet in the head, and for manner of death—homicide, suicide, accident, or natural causes. They measured leg bones to extrapolate stature, determined left- or right-handedness by observing the beveling of the scapula and length of the humerus. They calculated how many remains belonged to children and adolescents by checking the degree to which epiphyses— the rounded ends that ossify at determined ages—had fused.

At the end of a week, sniffling from mildew, Bernardi packaged the remains of seven adult males and three young boys in the best material available, cartons used for importing cornflakes. She stacked the boxes in the clinic's unused broom closet, sealing its door with a chain and bicycle lock.

The scientists returned to Guatemala City, where they sent a report to the judge responsible for determining whether a crime had been committed at Dos Erres. From an archaeological point of view, the report said, the well was "a primary, synchronous common grave." Primary, because bones were found articulated and in proper anatomical positions, as if individuals had died in place or just before burial, and bodies decomposed in the well; synchronous because skeletons were super-imposed one upon another, even intertwined, indicating burial at the same time; common, the single grave of at least several persons. The site revealed evidence consistent in time with witness reports, because coins and even a 1982 calendar remained in pockets.

Persons "died violently," the report concluded. A fragment of metal "compatible with the projectile of a firearm" was found embedded in a lower jawbone. A green mark, typically left by the copper coating of a high velocity bullet, stained a cranium. "Ribs broken at death" . . . "bullet fragment attached to shirt". . ." "spent cartridges". . . "cleanly cut neck . . ."

Remains of ten persons were discovered five feet down. Bernardi termed them "a token" of what the well contained.

"There are undoubtedly meters more of bones," she said.

In 1995 relatives of twenty identified persons found in the well walked in a procession from the Las Cruces town hall, carrying the remains of their dead in tiny coffins—they needed to be only the length of a femur, the body's longest bone. They buried them at the cemetery in a single grave. That weekend I met Patricia Bernardi in Guatemala City's airport. Poor health was obliging her to return home to Buenos Aires ahead of the other scientists. She looked wan but seemed anxious to talk.

"Can you have a coffee?" she asked.

They had excavated the shaft down to rock, she said. She swore never to exhume in a well again. Once, she said, she shook a fer-de-lance from her shoulder. Vandals stole the life belts, measuring devices, and, eventually, all the ropes. Bernardi reached into her purse and took out a handful of snapshots. She pushed them across the table.

"It looks like a little Grand Canyon, no?" she said, pointing to a vale between mounds of dirt.

After the first group of men, the forensic team found the bodies of twenty-four women killed by blunt instrument trauma and from gunshot wounds, almost all from the kind of Israeli Galil rifles used by soldiers. The next seven feet produced remains of sixty-seven children, average age eleven, their small craniums filled with milk teeth.

Examination revealed few bullets had been wasted on the youngest, who had been battered to death or died from fractured skulls.

I drove to the outskirts of the capital to find Federico Garcia once more. I wanted to tell him the latest news and say good-bye, because I thought it was unlikely I would see him again. I wanted to show him a newspaper photo of the dig I had been carrying around. On the way, I collected his father, Anacleto, and his mother, Rosa, from their home, a one-room bungalow in the parking lot of the hotel where Anacleto still worked as a janitor.

In his tiny house on the ranch outside the city, Federico Garcia stared at the picture, his flat eyes momentarily filled with wonder. He said he felt emboldened to give testimony to Families of the Detained and Disappeared and to the Catholic church, which was collecting eyewitness history of the war years.

"My aunt had a gold tooth," Federico said. "Do you think that will help people tell which one is her? I might go there to help them find my brother's bones among the others. It is hard to say that, because the last screams are still with me."

The grainy newspaper photo I gave them showed mostly a pile of dirt. But Federico and his parents pointed as if they could see more in it.

"Look! Your brother is there!" said Anacleto. "Your aunt Feli and the girls! Rosita! Carmen! The little ones, too! Cristobal's brother is there!"

Federico Garcia adjusted his lap to accommodate a three-year-old, named Ernesto after his dead brother, and examined the clipping. He spoke to his father, who stood amazed, and to his mother, who sat on a bed folding and refolding a thin blanket, looking as if she would weep. I cannot say what Federico was seeing in his mind, but he lifted his eyes in the direction of the tall buildings that marked the beginning of the capital.

"They will believe us now," he said.

———

In 2001, seven years after the first exhumation, I befriended two of the army special forces Kaibiles involved in the Dos Erres massacre. I chatted with them, talked to their wives, played with their children, moved around with them for days in Guatemala and in another country. With my presence, I participated in protecting them. I spoke with them on four occasions after that by telephone. To say the experience generated moral confusion is an understatement.

After the exhumation, a woman from Guatemala City who had attended every day on behalf of Families of the Detained and Disappeared heard that one of the Kaibiles said he was willing to testify in a legal case. Aura Elena Farfan traveled to the ex-soldier's house in a Petén town near the border with Belize.

"I spent five hours with him," Farfan told me. "I had to find out his motive, if he would tell the truth. Near his feet, his small boy was playing with toy cars, and a little girl with a pretty doll. The Kaibil told me, 'Every time I look at them, the children of Dos Erres come back to me. I see them. They did not deserve to die. I cannot stand it any longer.' That is when I began to believe him."

Later, another former Kaibil present at the massacre came forward. With two witnesses willing to talk, Farfan and young allies in the law community quietly prepared a legal case. The Guatemalan Justice Department finally agreed to pursue it.

On a muggy morning, Farfan, a colleague of hers named Lily, three of their rights group supporters, and I waited for the two ex-military witnesses at a courthouse on a buff clay road in Santa Elena, about fifty miles from where Dos Erres had stood. The men were scheduled to testify in secret to a judge, the first time soldiers who had participated would describe one of the hundreds of killing events in Guatemala, swearing to the truth, using their own real names and those of their officers. During the night, guards had spirited the Kaibiles' wives and children from a safe house in the capital, escorting them out of the country.

By now, all hoped, the families were untouchable by anyone who would blackmail the men or influence their testimony. It had taken months for Families of the Detained and Disappeared to arrange a country of asylum, despite the witnesses' value for strengthening the Guatemalan justice system. California senators Dianne Feinstein and Barbara Boxer and congressional representatives Nancy Pelosi and Vic Fazio wrote letters recommending visas for the ex-soldiers in the interest of "significant public benefit" for US policy. The State Department said no.

An ordinary sedan pulled up to the courthouse. Public Ministry guards stepped out of the car in knit shirts, carrying no visible weapons, and briefly looked around. The two Kaibiles emerged. One stood spindly and pale, the other short with dark skin and Indian features. They looked frightened, silently nodding to Farfan, walking into the commotion of a rural courthouse among drug suspects and drunks handcuffed together in threes. The judge took their testimonies separately, behind closed doors. Whichever of the two was free at the moment came out to sit with us, ate chips, and talked.

When tears came to the eyes of the thin, pale witness, Farfan looked aghast. "My daughter is only seventeen," he said. "I cannot leave her behind."

His daughter's boyfriend would not sign off on a passport for their infant, the Kaibil said, and his daughter would not leave without the baby. Farfan's face showed no sympathy. If the witness did not continue, the entire train would leave the tracks. Uncorroborated testimony of a single Kaibil was worthless. Eventually, the tears stopped. The sad Kaibil talked little after the episode, appearing to understand there was no turning back.

Lily, Farfan's colleague, a middle-aged grandmother normally unflappable, jumped unexpectedly from the outdoor bench where we sat to stand with her back to the others near a bush of flowering red hibiscus.

When I caught up to her, she said in a low voice, "It has cost us to work with murderers. I hope their repentance is true."

After seven hours of testimony, the Kaibiles left with the Guatemalan Justice Department marshals while the rest of us hurried to grab the last plane to the capital. Petén flights ended at sunset because the runway had no lights.

I don't know who arrived at Guatemala City's international airport first, but we spotted the witnesses in the large, crowded waiting room. They looked unremarkable in sports shirts, with cheap in-flight bags and vacant gazes. Near them stood the federal prosecutor in charge of the case. He was also in charge of the country's new witness protection effort, the Kaibiles its first subjects. A fresh set of black-vested guards were scattered in the waiting area.

"They often take them from airports," Farfan warned, speaking of forced disappearances by the army and police. The guards were present to protect the prosecutor, they said, not the witnesses. Certainly not us.

Farfan's brother had been kidnapped on a Guatemala City street in 1984; Lily's son left her house to buy milk and never returned. The women wore the same kind of flowered dresses, carrying the little handbags I had seen them use at the exhumation site. They appeared to be middle-aged housewives, but their eyes combed the overhead balcony with the honed skill of those who recognize threat.

When we arrived at our destination airport late that night, the witnesses vanished from our sight. Farfan and Lily looked shaken. Officials shuttled us through customs and immigration apart from other passengers. We could have disappeared into a side room or a back corner without anyone noticing, so confusing was the process, so involved with passports and their own concerns were the passengers around us. Once in the terminal, Lily glimpsed the Kaibiles surrounded by men in dark clothing, followed by the prosecutor, all moving like a single unit through the terminal. We reached a door just in time to see them slip into three cars and drive away.

Families of the Detained and Disappeared had pledged safety and accompaniment to the witnesses. Nevertheless, in their first days outside Guatemala, the Kaibiles looked back toward Farfan and Lily anxiously whenever their new guards began to walk quickly or made a sharp turn in the car. The women had discovered the men willing to talk and had built the Dos Erres case over years. Now they had to hand over control to government agents.

The next day we took a local bus, to keep a low profile, to the house where the men had been reunited with their families. The neighborhood was not poor, but modest enough that a car would draw attention. We carried bags of groceries "paid for by the Sisters," as Farfan put it. While some dickered about moral equivalency in helping massacre participants, a convent of Roman Catholic sisters in Southern California had donated $25,000 to make the project happen. It was the only way to bring the generals to justice, said the nun who entrusted the funds to a go-between. "It's the only kind of testimony that will hold water."

Inside the house where the witnesses' families would live, a security officer gave the Kaibiles and their wives simple cover stories. "Remember, one small thing could mean you would have to leave all this behind and go somewhere else," he said.

When the briefing officer left, one of the witnesses and the Kaibiles' wives went to the lawn to play with their children. The huskier witness quickly closed the door.

"I feel something is going to happen," he said. "Please don't let this case hang like something in the water."

He had torn his wife from her parents, their children from cousins and friends, and now he feared the prosecution might be dropped, hit a dead end, come to nothing. "I didn't leave the country because I am a traitor, but for something else," he said. He knew he would never go home.

"Be assured . . . be assured," Farfan said. "We won't take a step backward. We are not going to cede."

———

In 2009, Aura Elena Farfan's unmarked office in Guatemala City looked much as I remembered, walls covered with outsized black and white photos of people missing since the 1970s and 1980s. "We are not living in the past," said Farfan. "Most exhumations provide evidence sufficient for legal cases, but families are afraid."

More than eighty exhumations have taken place since the first one at Dos Erres. Six attributed responsibility to guerrillas, a handful to the army-created civil patrols, the vast majority to the army. After the Kaibiles testified in Petén in 2001, the judge issued capture orders for seventeen officers. Since then other judges, arguably weaker, had approved injunctions, and no officer been arrested.

Evidence about Dos Erres continues to surface. Soldiers forced four women to make tortillas so they could have hot food; after eating, they killed the women. Each of two Kaibiles took home a small boy. Farfan discovered one of them, by then a young man. He added testimony to the case and gained asylum in Canada. Dos Erres is "paradigmatic" of

1980s atrocities, Farfan said, "emblematic" of the impunity perpetrators enjoy. For her, the well and the woods continue to speak for two hundred thousand dead and disappeared between 1976 and 1992, almost all unarmed civilians killed by the army.

Federico Garcia, however, whose crystalline account of the massacre had put me on the road to Dos Erres, may have done enough speaking. He did go to church investigators and Families of the Detained and Disappeared in the months after we talked, as he said he might. His original testimony was "invaluable," said Farfan. Lawyers also took him to Washington, D.C., to testify at the Inter-American Commission on Human Rights. A lawyer on the trip said when it came time to go home, Federico Garcia disappeared for days and "didn't look well" when he reappeared.

When I visited Farfan she told me Anacleto Garcia had died and his son Federico recently had come to the office. She asked him to testify at the most important venue of all, the Organization of American States' Inter-American Court of Human Rights, based in San José, Costa Rica. The court's judgment is binding on OAS member states such as Guatemala.

"The Lord has illuminated me," said Federico. "He told me no."

In January 2010, without Federico Garcia's testimony, the OAS court found Guatemala had failed to comply with its obligation to investigate and punish the killers, a monumental decision for those who would correct history and bring healing to survivors. The US State Department Office of Special Investigations, established to hunt Nazis who had committed crimes against humanity, turned its attention to Central America in 2007, leading to the 2010 Florida arrest of two former Kaibiles who killed at Dos Erres. Another Kaibil, who had been teaching martial arts openly in California, was captured in 2011 in Alberta, Canada. In a sign of confidence in his new life, the former officer appears in a YouTube video dressed in karate uniform with black belt, demonstrating a Tae Kwan Do kata.

A few weeks after my visit with Farfan, I took a bus from Santa Elena toward the Usumacinta River. From the road, I tried to spot the place Dos Erres once had stood, but all I could see was the grass.

6

Dead Birds, or,
The Return to Naha

FOR THE RAINFOREST MAYA, WRITING AND DRAWING WERE not separate arts. The same person did both. We cannot know everything pre-Columbian Maya wrote about because when Catholic priests arrived they burned every book they found, conscious of the subversive power of words.

What remains, on stone, on ceramics, and in five codices, preserves the memory of royal lineages, a kingdom's roots, history, names of the gods, the movement of time. So important was the work of sustaining memory that for the Maya, "Scribe" was a royal title. As he (probably always he) repeatedly sculpted and painted certain images and combinations of sounds—serpent, jaguar, water lily, the calendar glyphs—the Scribe attempted to keep account of the world, to keep it in order.

The classic Maya term for "the act of writing" has always resonated with me:

That is: tz'i   +   b'i   =   tz'i-b'i

(verb) to write, paint + (noun) the road = to paint the road

I am no longer the young woman who first fell in love with the Maya tropical forest. The rainforest is not the same one, or not only the same, with which I fell in love. The only way I can make order of this is to paint its roads, those I have taken.

For many years, even as I traveled elsewhere in Chiapas as a reporter, or as an aficionado of the old sites, I wrestled with myself over returning to the Lacandón rainforest itself, a setup for disappointment. The air, the light, nothing could match the loop of memory that had played in my head for so long.

Yet by the 1990s, when I reached my forties, I had been shaped by the other path, too: journalism, investigation, the curiosity that asks, what exactly is happening? This is the opposite of the sensuous lens.

I have had fundamental life experiences I did not have before. I have known a love that wasn't meant to be. And one that is. I've given birth and watch the child growing into a young woman with a good heart.

What can there be to be afraid of? I mean, *really* afraid?

I decided to go back to Metzabok and Naha, the villages I first stumbled into with the sweet and unexpectedly stalwart Etcher, whom I never saw again. I could tack the trip onto something else—a visit to a Maya site I had never seen—lest the journey of return seem too much like closing a circle, the destination loom too large in the planning.

The westward-heading bus from Santa Elena made its final stop at the pair of piers on the Usumacinta. Authorities on both sides of the river had gone home. For an exit stamp from Guatemala and a Mexican entrance stamp, I would have to wait until morning.

After an airless night sleeping in a room in the only *posada*, more like a modified shipping container, I threw some water on my face and found a border agent. The inkpad he used was so dry the faint stamp hardly seemed worth having endured the rotten night. A fisherman charged about ten dollars to motor me across the river in his red-painted wooden boat, the water a low chop, smooth to traverse. On the Mexican side, unfortunately, the immigration kiosk stood empty.

"Just hang around and he'll find you," said a middle-aged man with a half-full burlap sack at his feet, sitting on a tree trunk with about a quarter of it sliced out to make a bench. He looked as comfortable as if he were waiting for a bus.

"Sit. Wait," he said, making room.

I wanted to continue on my way, official stamp or not, but there was a war going on in Chiapas. I might have to show proof of legal entry to some jittery teenage soldier. Resigned, I sat. So much of traveling is waiting.

We watched porters with very short black hair shuffling single file into a building of corrugated tin, empty sacks tied around their heads and falling down their backs like cloaks of a brotherhood. Another line of men filed out a side door, bent under heavy-looking bags from which sometimes dropped kernels of corn. In and out they went in continuous lines, cloaked in, burdened out. They looked short, even for Maya.

"Chol," my seatmate said.

Of thirty Mayan languages in Mexico and Guatemala, Chol is closest to the language heard in the streets of the ancient rainforest cities. It isn't exactly the same, but close enough so that if you speak Chol, study the glyphs and phonemes for years, and have a photographic memory, your chance of deciphering Maya code is better than someone who speaks only English.

I listened to their shouts and apparently humorous barbs, imagining the men carrying corn a thousand years ago in Tikal or Palenque, calling out, "Make way!" Around them would be children playing with hairless dogs, women bartering peanuts for tomatoes, men using chocolate beans as coin, hosts of other traders shouting, "Careful there!" From the crowded market, shoppers and sellers can look up to see the bright red roof combs of temples, not far away in the sacred plaza.

The customs and immigration agent arrived, dispatching my passport with celerity as if there had been a crush of travelers instead of just one. I thanked him, said good-bye to the man on the bench, and approached a Tzeltal Maya couple selling vegetables from their truck parked at the edge of the paved road. They looked as if they were packing up. Yes, they said, they could take me as far as Lacanjá ("Serpent Water") Chan Sayab, a southern Lacandón village near Bonampak. I had always wanted to see the Maya site of painted walls.

We left behind the only other vehicle in sight, a dilapidated Blue Bird still painted schoolbus yellow next to a wooden board announcing departure next morning. Behind a cracked window, a canvas strip gave the destination: FRONTERA, U.S.A. I marveled that it was possible now, avoiding washouts, guerrillas, bandits, and corrupt police, to travel by road for twenty-five hundred miles from the shores of the Usumacinta to the lights of San Diego. This was the most recent Maya road, taken by young indigenous men emigrating to look for work in the United States.

In an hour the Tzeltal couple dropped me at a house with cement walls and metal roof, gratefully accepting money I gave them "for gas." The house allowed campers on its lawn for a fee, they said.

As the little vegetable truck drove away, a tall, fine-looking man, about forty, came out of the house. Wide cheekbones, with the long, loosely worn hair that sets Lacandón men apart from other present-day Maya, although shorter hair like bangs hung over his forehead, which differentiates men from southern villages from those in Metzabok and Naha. A rush of that rainforest memory came, mentally landing with a thud against the look of the sturdy house, clear-cut lawn, and pickup parked nearby.

"I'm looking for a place to stay overnight," I said. "I want to go to Bonampak."

"It's close," the Lacandón said. "Come inside."

We sat in a kitchen that was part of the house, not a separate structure. His name was Kin Bor, he said. His wife, Nuk, stood cooking on a gas—not wood—stove, the first one I had seen in such out-of-the-way jungle towns. On a wall hung a newspaper photo of masked fighters of the Zapatista National Liberation Army, who had led an uprising against the Mexican government on January 1, 1994.

"They have some good ideas, but the picture hangs there because it is a nice picture," Kin Bor said, before I even asked.

No crucifix or Bible was visible to say the family had finally succumbed to Christianity, but they were the exception in Lacanjá. "Most are evangelicals now," Kin Bor said, talking easily.

A "Protestant from America" had converted most of the village. But the northern settlement of Naha, deeper in the jungle, had remained loyal to Maya gods under a strong spiritual leader.

"Chan K'in?" I asked, naming the venerable shaman who had led the Etcher and me out of the jungle in 1973.

"Chan K'in," he said, looking unsurprised that I would know the name. By this time books had been written about the Lacandón featuring the old man.

"The father of my wife," he said, and Nuk nodded. They had both come from Naha, he said. A vague recollection came.

"As a young man, were you a very good hunter?" I asked.

Nuk glanced over with a smile that, to me, looked patronizing. I didn't remember meeting Kin Bor before, but the name rang, and I guessed it was he who had bagged the animals I had seen being brought into the village.

"It's a long time since most have switched to rifles," he said, his tone dismissive. Probably the switch had meant the end of appreciation for Kin Bor's special skill.

"Of course, now some are switching back to bows and arrows," he said.

The sound of gunfire scatters animals, who learned to run from it "in one generation." Anyway, these days he did not hunt much at all.

"There are few animals left."

I looked at Nuk, long hair braided, no dead birds, and guessed I must have known her on that visit, when she would have been a child, because I had played with every kid in Naha. If I told her and Kin Bor I had visited their home village so many years ago, I was certain it would be the first crack in the spell the period had cast upon me. Populating the dream with its original persons, grown and changed since then, would be the beginning of its end.

Truth, however, will out. I confessed.

Kin Bor at the table, Nuk sitting down, too, stared in disbelief. Slowly their expressions changed to reasonable doubt, through wonder, to something like approval. They seemed apologetic they did not remember.

"Don't worry," I said, "I don't exactly remember you, either."

I could sleep in the shell of a house under construction next door. Kin Bor said someday they wanted to run tourist lodging on the property.

Late in the afternoon, I bathed in a quiet, icy pool formed by boulders in the midst of a rushing stream, delicious. If I had simply packed up and left the next morning, I would have said that the Lacandón civilization in Chiapas no longer existed as something separate, homogenous, and truly linked to a rich past. Instead, after breakfast, I walked with Kin Bor through dense forest for half an hour toward his *milpa*.

The jungle opened onto a field that covered about a square city block, surrounded by trees. The place felt like a micro-ecosystem in the wider forest. Only about a quarter was planted; the rest had been allowed to go feral, covered with bushes and grasses in various stages of growth. Jungle land must rest three or four years after harvesting, Kin Bor said. Using just a quarter of the big square each season meant he destroyed no more rainforest to enlarge it.

Despite resting unplanted, the *milpa*'s fallow three-quarters provided food, too, drawing birds and game, protein. This wasn't a picture of the neat, trim rows of beans, corn, and squash marking highland *milpas*, or those of jungle settlers who brought old ways with them. Instead, the field mimicked the diversity and spontaneity of the jungle around us. The mind of the rainforest, benevolent chaos, was the governing principle of the Lacandón *milpa*.

When Kin Bor said, "There are a few beans," I counted four kinds. Corn, sacred and bountiful, grew everywhere. Two types of yucca, slim green onions, and fat white ones grew over and around one another. Red hibiscus for tea and cool drinks flowered amid sweet potatoes and three kinds of a vegetable that looked like yams but shone light pink, orange, yellow. There were sunset-toned papaya, maculis (like a potato), hard-shelled jicama, and jicara for its fruit and gourds. Green, leafy heads—they looked like chard and kale—sprouted from the earth amid red tomatoes and green tomatillos and a dozen kinds of chilis—waxy yellow, hot green, red—interspersed with squashes and purple flowers. Pumpkins grew, whose seed Kin Bor could sell for fifty cents a pound, near yellow-red fruit with an enormous seed that looked like its name, "monkey's head."

"And medicine plants?"

"*En la selva*," Kin Bor said. In the jungle. No need to plant what can be gathered wild.

Even what looked like fallen vine supports and uncleared branches had their purpose. "Wood is like feed for the soil, a kind of fertilizer," he said, twisting his machete into a piece of rotting stake that crumbled like chocolate cake.

A host of yellow flowers caught my eye. When I carefully asked, pencil poised, what qualities they possessed or purpose they served, Kin Bor regarded me curiously.

"They're pretty," he said.

I looked around at fruit trees and plants Kin Bor had not even named, keeping my mouth shut for a while. The place was a model of a secret of the ancient Maya. Imitating the rainforest's variety and spacing had been key to their survival. It protected food from epidemics that might vanquish closely planted species, as Maya themselves had been cut down by disease when the Spanish arrived and forced them to live close to one another, the better to be controlled and evangelized.

Seeing the *milpa*, which felt wild even though it was cultivated, made me want to walk farther into the forest. I asked if we could go into deeper jungle the next day, perhaps to see the archaeological site after which the settlement was named, Lacanjá.

"It's not Bonampak, with its famous painted walls, you know," Kin Bor said. "It's not Tikal or Palenque or Yaxchilan. It's a hard walk, and at the end it's just one small temple, overgrown with jungle."

We set off carrying tortillas and water. Some nocturnal animals had not yet turned in for the day. A *tepesquintle* dived on its short legs into a cradle of leafy plants. I watched for roots as Kin Bor strode ahead, sometimes slashing at branches with his machete.

Here is how the mysterious author B. Traven described what I was seeing in one volume (*March to the Monteria*, 1938) of his series known as the Jungle Novels:

> It went on for hours. It was as if an entirely new world had begun and the old, known world had sunk away. A new world had opened and this new world was nothing but a confused, intertwined, matted mass of something that grew. Grew and grew and grew. One lost the capacity of distinguishing the individual plants. Anything and everything around was green, thicket, abundance, confusion. Little golden dwarfs of sunlight were continually dancing from one feathery palm leaf to another. It was as though over this solid dense world of plants floated a call urging creation to beget a new planet, a fantastic one in which not man or beast would be the master but plants.

The rhythm of the path took over. The rest of the world peeled away, and I walked again in its living green heart. Kin Bor's long, straight black hair swung as we walked. I recalled the barefoot Lacandón youth who had led the Etcher and me from Metzabok to Naha, who had returned on the trail when I faced the viper as if he had a sixth sense.

"*Pica, muerto*," he had said. "Bite, death."

I wondered if middle-aged Kin Bor, dressed in T-shirt and rolled-up jeans, tennis shoes without socks, carrying no arrows, still possessed such a sense. In a few minutes he called back over his shoulder, "Don't worry, there are no poisonous snakes around here."

We heard the rushing sound before we saw the river. The water ran so clear that even as it tumbled, you could make out tiny fish shimmying among stones. I stood smiling in dumb admiration until I realized we had to cross it. The bridge was simply a fallen tree, about thirty feet long, suspended inches above the fast water. I bent to touch the flow. Freezing.

"Take off your shoes," Kin Bor said. I tied them together by the laces as I saw him do with his own, hanging them around my neck.

"Don't walk straight ahead."

He stepped onto the log with no apparent regard for how I would manage. I imitated his moves. Point the toes out in a kind of duck walk, find the moment of balance in each step, move quickly to the next. Don't pause, don't look down. With just a few heartbeats skipped, I was on the opposite bank.

Once among the trees again, Kin Bor kept a quick pace that almost left me behind a couple of times, when the trail seemed to peter out. "Kin Bor! Kin Bor!" I called then.

"Here!"

Following the sound, I nearly bumped into him, standing before a tree with gray-white bark. He pierced it with the machete's point. Out oozed an opaque white sap, innocent-looking as cream.

"You blind fish with just a few drops," he said.

The year before, clearing a path, Kin Bor accidentally brushed leaves of the *chenchen* tree, only in passing, but they left a terrible rash on the back of his thigh, he said. At home, the skin peeled off. Only after weeks of applying poultices from of the leaves of another tree did the wounds heal. When we set forth again, I walked forward with trepidation, afraid to come within inches of any green leaf.

"My friend was jealous of his wife," I heard Kin Bor calling back to me. "He went to a *chenchen* and cut four small pieces of bark, wrapped them in deerskin."

Of all times for the man to tell a story, I thought, straining to catch up. "At home he confronted his wife, but she claimed to be faithful. 'You don't love me,' he said to her. He unwrapped the four pieces of bark and ate them, before her eyes."

Without breaking pace, Kin Bor imitated the horrible convulsions of the fellow's last moments, walking and writhing at the same time. He emitted a curdling cry. "He was dead in half an hour," Kin Bor said.

Was the Lacandón recounting this story to shock? He didn't seem to care how I reacted. Probably the recollection just crossed his mind as we walked, a memory linked to a plant. As my sweaty shirt cooled, I shivered.

We met the looping river again and followed its bank. Boulders appeared in the stream as it widened and deepened. The water came to a cliff and fell twenty feet.

"Well, we have to cross somewhere," Kin Bor said, grinning.

We climbed down to a ledge that ran behind the falls. He placed his back to the cliff and I followed, inching along on the ledge behind the cascade. Tons of water rolled over our heads, falling in a curtain before us. At first I saw the precariousness of the situation, the danger, as if watching from outside the falls. Soon, however, the all-encompassing, wet, and wildly uneven continuous sound transported me, quelled thinking, leaving only the hearing sense. Water running heard from within the running. Rushing water roiling the air, mist hissing, sound primordial, harkening back to the first gurgling, pounding hours of creation when the earth was water and nothing but water, tumbling.

I walked in a daze, clothes damp and cooling, until we reached the temple. If Kin Bor had not stopped and pointed, I would have passed it without noticing. Little light permeated the canopy, and the mound looked like only a natural rise covered with vegetation. No wonder explorers could come within a few feet of ruins without discovering them.

Kin Bor had been right. It was small. A small stone palace on the verge of being devoured by vines and trees. Thin trunks and lianas grew from the hill underneath, crawled around its foundation, became one with its walls. Elephant-ear plants grew on the porch, peeked out of rooms, sprouted from the roof. I felt a catch in my throat. This was how seekers might find the remains of an ancient civilization, eyes looking for outlines through the forest's confusion. Standing amid the white noise of insects.

The building had risen in a world fully breathing, busy with human sounds. There was no way now to stand back and get a perspective, so much greenery stood in the way. The only manner of appreciating the palace was to climb, carefully working a way around it, using its walls for balance, touching the stone. Kin Bor confessed one of his in-laws had chipped pieces from the stucco facade for a buyer a few years before, and he couldn't remember what the figures on the face of the temple had been, but the building itself still emanated grace, an antique jewel set in jungle.

A breadfruit tree stretched its branches to embrace the decomposing walls from behind. The bark of its trunk seemed to glisten in fine strips. Kin Bor stared at the lines.

"Jaguar," he said.

Two sets of scratches, each nail perfectly delineated, stripped the bark from top to bottom. The tree's gold-red heart glinted where claws had peeled away its outer skin. In my mind, I saw the animal standing upon its hind legs, big paws moving slowly, top to bottom. The marks were fresh, the inner bark still moist.

"Jaguar," I repeated, whispering.

We began the return without speaking. I wanted to see the jaguar looking at us with green eyes, then turning back into the trees. I wanted to see it—briefly, of course—in its natural place, to understand, perhaps, why the ancient Maya imagined the spots of its coat symbolized the stars in the sky. At least I wanted to hear its voice, even from afar, a voice I knew would be unlike any other, although I had no idea how it might sound. Instead there were only birdsong and a few snorts from the kind of animals that walk on short legs, not the dead silence that would signal the presence of a stalking forest lord.

We reached the pool made by the waterfall again and sat upon stones. Kin Bor unwrapped a package made from a large leaf, holding tortillas. My bottled water was gone. I asked if the water from the pool was safe to drink.

"It will make you sick if you think it will," he said. I drank.

After we had passed the river, Kin Bor seemed to feel like talking again. He spoke of a certain man who liked to hunt monkeys.

"Everything in the jungle has its owner," he said as we walked. "The animals allow you to hunt them, but only until a certain point, and only when they are used in a moderate, respectful way."

But every time that hunter went out for monkeys, he threw the head away, didn't eat the meat, didn't bury the body or use the skull. He just liked to hunt.

"A frightening-looking man appeared. He told him no, that was enough of hunting and throwing parts away. A terrifying apparition."

"You're just throwing the head away," Kin Bor said several times, even raising his voice as if to someone in the distance, until he walked so fast I couldn't hear anymore. He seemed to become part of the story he told.

I took my time, recognizing parts of the trail. When I caught up to Kin Bor near the *milpa*, he seemed himself again. He pointed out orchids, his dark eyes relaxed. I felt tired but wanted to stay amid the abundant green confusion as long as I could. He seemed to sense it. Walking at a slower pace, we came upon a magnificent reddish mahogany tree. Kin Bor stopped at its base and turned around, facing me. He wore no shirt now, and his chest looked strong, red-brown in the soft light. He talked about the mahoganies as if they had a sex life and feelings.

"They are like us, they live in couples," he said. "This is the male, and nearby we will find his wife." And we did.

That night I sat before a television set inside the house with Kin Bor, his wife, their son, three young daughters, and a three-month-old baby. All the children possessed Lacandón names except the baby, who was called Paco. Electricity had arrived only three years before, but to look around the room, it seemed the family might never have spent an evening any other way.

About fifty VHS tapes, mostly action films and kid stuff, stood stacked in a tower alongside the set. Kin Bor and Nuk lounged on a bed with the mosquito net rolled up overhead. Their oldest son, Bor, who was twenty, played with baby Paco on another bed he shared with Rosilla, a non-Indian met in one of the towns who recently had become part of the household.

"I don't know where she came from—one day she was just here," Kin Bor said, feigning amazement, as if things happened around him that were out of his control. But he said it with affection, too. He launched into a soliloquy about where to find the cheapest videotapes in Chiapas.

Was this the same man who had led me through the jungle as if it were his primeval home? Who recognized the mark of a jaguar on the bark of one tree among thousands? Who carried inside him stories of relationships among animals, trees, and humans that made sense in a world I would never know?

"Quiet, everybody, we're showing the special tape for our guest," he said, aiming the remote.

Flickering before us in a European documentary came old Chan K'in, the Little Sun, the revered chief reduced in size for the television screen, smoking the ever-present hand-rolled cigar. He spoke of sacred drinking and of divine communication ceremonies only he and a few others still practiced.

The family watched Grandpa blow incense as if the program were on the Discovery Channel. The noise of horsing around rose.

"They are not too interested," Kin Bor said. He spoke like any father talking about kids who've seen the old family movies too often, full of scenes to which they felt little connection.

I asked for directions to Bonampak, in case the family was still asleep in the morning. On leaving the room, saying good night, I saw a clutch of arrows hanging on a wall above Kin Bor's bed. Their tips looked sharp, with feathers beautifully set. Next to them a bow, carved and bent from once-living wood, hung in an image of strength, a perfect arc.

———

The Lacandón, especially those in the south, hunted far into the rainforest and had always known about Bonampak, which they called merely *tun*, the heap of stones. So small is the site early explorers missed it, although rumors of its existence persisted, especially after 1900. In the 1940s, an American conscientious objector named Karl Frey, passing the war years in the jungle, came upon it with an American photographer, Giles Healey. The heap of stones became known as Bonampak, Maya for "painted walls," after the murals in three small rooms.

I left at dawn, trekking about an hour on a lonely but paved road, following Kin Bor's directions, turning onto a muddy but fairly well cleared jungle trail. In another half hour, I reached the mounds and temples. Two and a half miles was too formidable a trek for the casual traveler, and no planes had landed that day on the primitive airstrip, so the place was empty of other tourists. The warm air was still silent except for birdcalls and the rising hum of cicadas.

A lone workman sat resting under a palm frond roof on a stone platform, a water canteen at his side. I climbed the steps and saw that the roof also sheltered a seated stone figure about five feet high. She was called the Mother of the Moon, the workman said, found deep in the mound just a few months before. He was weaving more fronds into a wide, tight braid for a roof to keep rain off the silent image. There were still such massive finds out there as the Moon Mother, treasures that had escaped the grave robbers. And in the age of corrugated tin roofs, there were still craftsmen like this man, with an eye for just the right fronds and hands that could weave them watertight, an art as old as these crumbling platforms.

The Moon Mother looked as content as a Botero matron, round and nurturing in her bulk, none the worse for having held her breath down in the stony hiding place for a thousand years. A "cloth" of sculpted crosshatches rested easily on her thighs. Around the waist a wide belt still showed rich, clear traces of color, red and blue.

Across the grassy plaza, a much higher platform rose in white sunlight. The shells of several small houses or shrines glared bright and devoid of detail, without the painted stucco facades that once adorned them. I said farewell to the workman and crossed the plaza. Up close, I saw that colored moss climbing from the bases of the shrines broke their whiteness, thousands of tiny colored plants, rust-toned, flat green, cerulean blue. Between large blocks of hewn stone grew a dull green clover rooted to bits of soil. Kin Bor had described a similar plant as an antidote to snakebite. The Maya say, where there is danger in the forest, a cure grows nearby. These cool, dark crevasses between blocks would be a logical haunt of snakes. I stopped using my hands to climb.

From the high platform, I saw nothing but jungle, wide as the sea. The wind picked up, blowing over and through the trees, sounding a scale of pitches. The longer I listened, the easier it was to understand how Maya could believe in a Wind Lord, his voice detached from the corporeal but not from emotion and intelligence, barely audible at first, rising to a call stern and powerful, and back to whispering again.

At high noon, when the heat was becoming unbearable, the cool rooms that gave Bonampak its name beckoned. I climbed down from the height and walked toward the building that held the painted chambers. The pilgrim must bend through low doorways to enter so that the first glimpse of warriors and divine rulers is from a bowing position.

To be inside, amid the great figures and colors, cut off from the rest of the world, was to be part of the unfolding scenes. The entrance door became a mere rectangle of light in the fourth painted wall.

In the first of the three rooms I entered, a precise moment in the history of the city-state was unfolding, December 14, 790. A male child, the heir designate, is being presented to splendidly clothed nobles for their approbation. Looking around the room without pausing was like watching frames of a film: courtiers preparing costumes and dressing nobles, performers wearing carp and crayfish masks, others in deer and jaguar masks. Priests and royal family members stride in procession, features animated, some in conversation with one another.

I left the room for the light outside. Then I entered another a few feet away, a chamber whose interior gave none of the sense of movement and music of the first. Instead, in the second room I felt more as if I were entering one of those pre-Renaissance European churches where tableaux told stories of saints.

In the second room, three noblewomen sit cross-legged on a wide, green stone platform throne, piercing their tongues and lips with stingray spines, drawing thread or string through them. The blood drops fall onto paper, held in clay pots. Later, when the paper burns, its smoke will communicate the sacrifice to the Divine Lords. This is the noble's responsibility, man or woman, to cement the relationship with divine ancestors, to keep the world on its track and—on this occasion—to ensure acceptance of the young heir's ascent to the throne. Gentle-looking courtiers help the royal child with the piercing rite he tentatively performs, probably his first bloodletting.

In both rooms, where sunlight hit the walls along their lower quarters, painted figures had faded into shadings as if rendered by a cubist. Even the damaged places entranced, like the warm rose ceiling, where tones looked frosted with calcite, the white mineral that oozes from limestone walls where rainwater enters, and leaves a pale crust. If mold stained a picture, the flaw said these painted walls did not exist for today's traveler, touched up for the public, but that time was working its slow way with them, subject to the same forces of transformation as the surrounding rainforest.

I stepped outside once more—the rooms are not connected from the inside—and the sun hit my face. It felt pleasant now, coming as I was from the coolness. I closed my eyes, savoring again the colors of the first two rooms. White turbans on the heads of musicians who blew trumpets, or whistles the color of pale clay, or beat turtle-shell drums, solid figures emerging from a background blue as water. The skin of lords and warriors, big thighs and muscled arms, glowed rich terra-cotta, the tone of Kin Bor's skin. Their jaguar cloaks looked so thick a finger poked into the fur might sink to the knuckle. On the cloaks, the animal's head hung at the bottom, its tail dropping from behind the noble's neck like a tassel down his back, the spots on the hide that stood for the stars draping the men like constellations.

Between the two rooms I had already entered was a third, which I had saved for last, knowing it was the room depicting war and human sacrifice. I took one more look at the peaceful white clouds, the undulating green line where the forest began.

Bending and entering the third room was like falling down a hole, sucked down into circles of hell. Men painted on the walls held mean victory on their faces, still spearing the vanquished, the dead, and the dying, pulling up torn bodies by the hair of their heads, climbing among the fallen whose mouths are open and eyes starkly pale.

In the first two chambers the traveler had been required to step out of current time, to make sense of sacred lip piercing, the proud wearing of jaguar hides. However, the third room, the chamber of war, felt perfectly familiar, as up-to-date as a newspaper. Cruelty. Hubris. Chaos. Torture.

Warriors wore talismans, like shrunken head necklaces. They looked drugged or in trances, shared expressions that forbade individuality to shine through. Chance and surprise ruled, not tactics preplanned. Violence verged on the uncontrollable.

The pictures around me in the third room cut through the mendacious trappings used to disguise war as a noble effort since Maya times, when leaders said they fought to gather captives for sacrifice so the cosmos might continue to be reborn. Instead, the figures on the wall spelled out the base, unequivocal sense behind the Lacandón phrase for "war," *kinsik u bah solaw*, "soldiers killing each other." There was beauty in the trappings but no glory in the act.

I left the third painted room, and Bonampak, feeling gloomy, heading back to Lacanjá, where I would sleep one more night alongside Bor's house. I picked up a fallen branch to use as a walking stick. I remembered to thank local spirits for holding back the customary afternoon rains. A millennium ago, the trail I walked probably connected Bonampak with the great Usumacinta River city to which it was subject, Yaxchilan. They were only sixteen miles apart. Maya often built the white jungle pathways—*sacbe*—to join one such city to another.

I probed the ground and drew out a creamy mass. Later, Nuk told me the trail was a source for pale clay from which she still made figurines. The *sacbe* itself, if it still existed, must be somewhere under the mud. How convenient it must have been to have had those narrow, elevated limestone highways for jungle travel.

Upon the thought, my left foot sank to the top of my ankle-high boot. The more I struggled, the more the foot wanted to sink.

Stop, I told myself. Relax.

I drilled the sturdy stick into drier dirt a few inches away. Very slowly, placing weight on the branch, hoping it would not break, I extricated foot and leg, cursing my incapacity to eyeball the difference between shallow mud and deep.

The path had not dried under the canopy during the day, as I had expected it would, making the return slower than I had planned. I was walking overcarefully, too; those few moments of being stuck had shaken my stride. When I looked up from my feet and saw three men standing on the path, I yelped involuntarily.

They wore bush hats. Two of them waved and then returned to peering through equipment mounted on tripods.

"My name's Eddy," said the third, extending a hand. They were a surveying team and he was their chief, he said. They were building a road to Bonampak.

"A *road?*"

"Wide enough for two tour buses passing each other," Eddy said. "One coming, one going."

My jeans were mud-caked up to the knees. I wore a shirt limp from perspiration, a dusty backpack with flashlight and water bottle hanging from its loops. I gripped the makeshift walking stick.

"Yes," Eddy said, beaming. "If you'd just waited a few months, you could have driven."

"Imagine," I said.

Stepping around the legs of the tripods, I waved and mumbled about the coming dark. I tried to imagine an ancient pale clay road, perhaps buried only a few feet below my boots. After a thousand years, I would be one of the last wanderers to walk this jungle trail. If the old, white *sacbe* is still there, the new road will probably hide it forever.

———

Eddy came to Kin Bor's house in the morning to offer a lift to Palenque, where I could grab a bus to San Cristóbal and—I hoped—meet a Lacandón returning to Naha. I said good-bye to Kin Bor and bought from Nuk a white clay figure of a *hach winik*, a true human. That is, a Lacandón man, complete with woven plant fiber toga.

The road between Lacanjá and Palenque (about seventy-five miles) was smooth as a freeway, thanks to the fact that you cannot move tanks through thick jungle. Since the Zapatista uprising, the Mexican army had been building roads throughout eastern Chiapas to encircle the rebellious Indian zones.

We roared at fifty miles an hour along what had been only recently jungle floor. "This is progress," Eddy said.

Lumber merchants took advantage of the growing infrastructure, too, traveling in packs of two or three or more to discourage bandits. They carried massive planks or entire trunks.

Gone was the kind of lumbering B. Traven describes in his classic novels, where Indians enslaved by debt bondage, using chains and oxen, maneuvered magnificent felled cedars and mahoganies through fever-ridden swamps, where rising water carried even the hugest trees along ditches to streams and eventually to the Usumacinta. The trees' journeys took several months. Men died, hit by erratically falling branches, in swamps, on the fast river, riding the trunks, breaking logjams. The wood traveled downstream to Atlantic ports, eventually to adorn salons and boardrooms in Europe and America.

The premium price of fine hardwood has always been linked to the difficulty of transporting it. Now, loggers chainsawed trees where they fell, lifting them away like balsa. Most of what we saw was being sacked; even where permits existed, there were no authorities present where trucks hit the main road to monitor how much was being extracted from even licensed areas. The caravans with their newly dead cargo looked like flatcars in a long funeral train, passing through country empty of mourners, bearing cedars and mahogany so giant in life they had to be cut up in death. "It's the trunk of a felled *caoba*, a ton of mahogany," B. Traven would have said (*Trozas*, 1936). In the oncoming lane, empty trucks were hurtling back into the forest for more.

It looked from the road like plenty of jungle remained, but the truck hauls showed it was interrupted forest. The more that jungle fragments, the less its biggest animals—I think of the jaguar—have the extended tracts to roam, to claim territory, to reproduce without creating genetically monstrous versions of themselves. Destruction moves down the chain of forest life.

Kind Eddy dropped me off at the terminal in Palenque, where I caught the express bus, just six hours to San Cristóbal. There I went to NaBalom, once home of the Danish archaeologist Frans Blom and his Swiss wife, Trudy, the doughty photographer of the Lacandónes. Her pictures were among the dioramas in Mexico City's National Anthropology Museum that first attracted me to the rainforest. NaBalom continued to be a hostel for travelers. More important, it continued as a haven for Lacandónes who needed to come to the city.

On the third day at the Bloms' old house I was crossing the quiet courtyard, admiring the pink and white bougainvillea, when I noticed a young man on his knees, wrapping packages with string. I stopped to help. His name was Pepe Chan K'in, he said, from the Lacandón village of Naha. He would be returning the next morning with his wife, after a shopping trip.

"Of course," he said, tucking the end piece of string into the rest of the ball, I could travel with them. "We will take less than twenty-four hours." First, a shared van to the town of Ocosingo, and from there a daily bus that made a jungle road milk run.

"The bus from Ocosingo is kind of undependable, but I'm feeling lucky," he said.

Pepe Chan K'in knocked on the door at 3:45 A.M. He looked resplendent, short hair shiny with some kind of pomade, wearing a nifty, new-looking blue ranch shirt, creased jeans, and tooled leather boots with pointed toes.

While he looked for a taxi to take us to the bus, I waited on the curb outside NaBalom with Pepe's nineteen-year-old wife, also a Lacandón from Naha. She introduced herself as Margarita, a Spanish name like Pepe's.

She and I guarded boxes of stuff the couple had bought in San Cristóbal, including a long wall mirror in a wooden frame. The night watchman appeared smitten by Margarita.

"Do you have children?" she asked him.

"I'm a bachelor," he said.

"So why aren't you married, nice-looking fellow like you?"

Over our heads, the figure of a jaguar carved on a hanging sign creaked back and forth in the predawn breeze. Margarita wore silver lamé sandals with three-inch heels, snug pants, and a frilly white blouse. Her fingers with polished nails held a white handbag like Queen Elizabeth might use on a summer's day. Her pretty, round face was painted bright as a Kewpie doll, dark hair flipped at the shoulders, a silver plastic barrette for decoration. Not a feather. No mystery. Nothing on the body to connect to the forest home.

In the crowded van, Pepe and Margarita slept quickly. On every other turn of the snaking road, their combined dead weight fell upon me. Sometimes I could hardly breathe. I woke Pepe. He must have been dreaming about losing what he had bought in San Cristóbal, because he reached behind the seat to transfer the boxes to his lap and the mirror to Margarita's arms.

When they fell asleep again and leaned my way, they weighed even more. It seemed an eternity before the van belched its way into Ocosingo, emptying passengers stop by stop. Only Pepe, Margarita, and I remained. We headed for the central marketplace. The driver asked what language Pepe and Margarita were speaking.

"Pure Maya, from Naha," Margarita said. "We're married. But we Maya only marry for a year, and it's up tomorrow."

Pepe looked disgusted. This trip back to a remembered place of flamingos and misty lakes was becoming too complicated. It was none of my business that Pepe and Margarita bore no resemblance to the Lacandón of one *gringa*'s memory. But the disjunction jarred my brain anyway, a condition made worse by exhaust fumes and the sight of freshly cut beef hanging raw red from the sides of dirty, open trucks near the market.

The van parked before a long arcade I recognized from pictures a colleague took during the Zapatista uprising, after the army had regained control of the town. In the pictures, young men lie among the columns, facedown, hands tied with twine behind their backs. Not all had been killed in battle; some showed the wounds of *tiros de gracia*, summary execution.

"Well, it looks like our bus isn't leaving today after all," said Pepe, returning from a tour around the square.

I saw myself staying a night or two in rooms on this haunted plaza with Pepe, Margarita, and who knew, maybe the van driver, too. As delicately as possible, I jumped ship.

"See you there," Pepe said.

By nightfall I had checked into a hotel on the outskirts of Palenque, having hired a young man who drove a pickup to take me to the Lacandón villages the next day. There were roads now, a relatively quick trek compared to the 1970s.

"You realize it's just a drop-off—I'm not staying out there," the hired driver said.

In the room, I threw myself down on the bed, where I sweated and thrashed for hours. My body seemed to go through a purification of its own devising, helped by the sauna-like air. In clear moments, I realized returning to the Lacandón jungle was not a trip for pleasure but an obsession, after all, to close a circle.

The thinking part of me knew life could not be static, should not be, that you can never go back to a place and expect it to be the same. I knew Naha did not exist for my benefit, that lamenting change for others was romanticizing men and women, which takes their humanity away and can only lead to trouble. Around 4:00 A.M., my head cleared. The sheet was soaking from sweat, my hair felt damp on my face. I rose to look out a window at a small garden, where hibiscus barely showed red in the dark. I was mourning my own change, knowing I would never again be that young woman who first came here. It was absurd. But it was happening. I could do nothing but see it through.

Later, I watched the sun rise through the window of a cherry-colored pickup, sitting a few inches from a hired driver uninterested in conversation. We turned off the highway onto a track that looked newly carved from the bush. Settlers had given towns biblical names: Egypt, New Hope, River Jordan. We passed only two vehicles, flagging down each to inquire about road conditions, a truck driver carrying cattle and a Lacandón family in a pickup, en route to sell arrows to tourists outside the Palenque ruins.

Most of the time, the driver hauled at a speed I thought too fast for the road, and once I told him so, but he replied we must be wary of assaults. I think he was afraid because this was Zapatista country. We saw hand-lettered wooden signs at some turnoffs, often with the idiosyncratic orthography of writers barely, or newly, literate, but all boldly painted.

REVOLUTIONARY ZAPATISTA COMMUNITY
NO CULTIVATION OR USE OF MARIJUANA. NO DRUGS.
NO ALCOHOL. NO SOLDIERS.
PEACE, YES. CORN, YES. MUST ASK PERMISSION TO ENTER.

No Zapatista sign marked the road to Metzabok. What hit me first in the village was the new spread of proper houses, not galleries hung with hammocks outside stick-walled rooms. Lacandón here had come into money—perhaps modest amounts, but enough to make the place look and feel different. A fellow in his twenties, wearing jeans and a T-shirt, not the white tunic, leaned against a wall, too drunk to talk.

Electricity had arrived, too. The sound of a boom box came through the open door of the town *responsable*'s house, blasting a song that included the words "lucky to be born in America." Empty rum bottles and a half-empty Johnny Walker Black were visible on a table, and full bottles stood on shelves. The village official looked about thirty-five and made a tremendous effort to rise to the occasion, lurching forward and propping himself in the door frame, straining to compose his features. I wanted to explain that my visit was a return to a place I had once viewed as idyllic, to tell about the women with the brilliant lifeless birds in their hair—perhaps his mother was among them? But conversation was useless.

At the schoolroom, however, the teacher invited me inside, to the nearly uncontainable delight of seven students in the midst of a spelling lesson. *"Traste, trozo, trigo, triste."* Plate, broken piece, wheat, sad.

The kids, all with long, flowing hair, had become too excited at the appearance of a stranger to continue classes. The teacher decided we would all walk toward the lake. Boys lifted their small white tunics to run sure-footed on the damp trail. One jumped into a pile of leaves and emerged with an iguana, its tail flapping wildly; he held it aloft like a boy back home might show off a gecko.

Many villagers were drunk today, the teacher explained, because the Lacandón had just received an eleven-hundred-peso payment from the government, a twice-yearly cash "seed" subsidy that also binds those who receive it to the ruling party. (The Institutional Revolutionary Party, known by its Spanish initials PRI, ruled without a break for seventy-one years until April 2000.)

A strong breeze blew through trees, grazing huge leaves and small, creating a music that made one forget human frailties. Electric-blue morpho butterflies quivered in the air. At the sight of the lake, nothing else mattered. Gray herons waded peacefully, close to shore. Two girls sat on a rock to skip stones, while the boys threw off their tunics and used a banked dugout as a diving platform, splashing into the lake, scattering the birds. The herons recovered their dignity, regrouped, and flew in formation across the glassy surface. The teacher became oblivious to my presence, settling onto some boulders as if they were a chaise lounge, looking absorbed in thought.

There was no reason to stay. I waved to the kids, a finger at my lips to signal they should not wake the teacher, who seemed to have fallen asleep. I left to search out the driver, walking slowly. With the pictures of Bonampak so recent, I began to realize what the long hair might have meant to the ancient Maya. On the painted walls, victors had held captives by their straight black locks, a sign they were truly defeated. Surely ancient warriors deliberately wore their hair long, daring the world to conquer them, declaring fearlessness, a living statement that they would not be overcome. I wondered how Lacandón at Naha would be wearing their hair—long, like Kin Bor, or short, like young Pepe.

———

From the red pickup, the landscape between Metzabok and Naha looked like a negative film of that long-ago trek I had made on foot with the Etcher and the young Lacandón named Bor. Where I recalled dark canopy, now there was light, open sky. In place of the sweetly suffocating closeness of growing vegetation, Traven's "confused, intertwined matted mass," ran a wide, dun sash of road.

Even in 1973, believing I was experiencing a world both primeval and everlasting, events were unfolding in Mexico City that would turn much of the matted green mass into a thing of the past. Luis Echeverria, president of Mexico from 1970 to 1976, was the most visible mover.

Like most Mexican presidents, Echeverria thought of himself as an imperial figure. He played upon Mexicans' historic political antipathy to the United States, the big brother to the north. Once he demanded that Coca-Cola, sometimes called the sugar-water of imperialism, hand over its secret formula to his government, threatening reprisals if the company failed to comply. Echeverria wore ersatz Aztec robes to some events, while the First Lady could don native costume to greet dignitaries, mortifying fashionable Mexican women, leaving indigenous women wryly shaking their heads.

Before becoming president, Echeverria presided over the slaughter of young men and women peacefully protesting government corruption at the Tlatelolco Plaza in Mexico City on the eve of the 1968 Olympic Games. The number cited by trustworthy sources varies, from forty-four dead (in a study made forty-two years after the fact) to more than three hundred (in contemporary accounts). Hosting the Olympics was supposed to be Mexico's moment to appear an important player on the world stage. President Gustavo Diaz Ordaz regarded the protest, part of the growing demand for democracy that students represented, as intolerable. With

Minister of Government Echeverria in command of the government's response, helicopters opened fire as the army's Olimpia battalion shot at the crowd of thousands from positions in surrounding buildings. Echeverria's performance so pleased the president that Diaz chose him as the *tapado*, the anointed presidential candidate of the official party.

After inauguration, Echeverria began negotiating with the Lacandón to make about 7 percent of the state of Chiapas into a "protected area," carrying their name. It sounded good. Trudy Blom allied herself with the president. She too had an imperious streak, vulnerable to the flattery of government honors (the yellowing certificates grace NaBolom's entrance).

When the Mexican legislature created the protected area, Echeverria and other notables, including the governor of Chiapas, became partners in the Lacandón Forestry Company on behalf of the government, which eventually cut and sold the Lacandónes' trees. (Trudy Blom, it is said, had not truly understood Echeverria's plan and felt betrayed both personally and on behalf of the Indians.) With considerable fanfare, the government designated the area the "Lacandón Zone," a 1.5-million-acre rainforest territory also populated by thousands of Chol and Tzeltal Indians. Echeverria, however, gave collective title to just sixty-six Lacandón families because "it has been perfectly established that the Lacandón tribe has possessed this zone since time immemorial." They received some cash, too. The trade-off: they signed away the right to fell mahogany and cedar at far below its market value. As if it were theirs to give.

Echeverria's team exploited rivalries that existed even among the small number of Lacandón families, recognizing one man, then another as their leader, until finding one who would sign on the dotted line. There were lies, cunning, and empty promises on the part of Mexico City, the usual, wrenchingly sad story. And probably some thoughtful Lacandónes hoped that official demarcation might help them defend against Tzeltal and Chol settlers, to them invaders of a forest that, in recent memory, had been only theirs.

And there was money. The Lacandón are forest dwellers who thrived on a simple existence, but they were also just poor people. They lived without the goods and medical care they knew others could get. Chan

K'in might have called money "shit of the sun," but neither he nor others disparaged cash. If there were some who did not want to sell (Chan K'in is said to have been reticent), they did not have the power to convince others.

Six years after my first trip to the Lacandón, my late friend, the Guatemala-born writer Victor Perera, visited Naha with anthropologist Robert Bruce. Perera recorded Chan K'in, who told him, "What the men of the city do not know is that the roots of all living things are tied together. When a mighty tree falls in the forest, a star drops from the sky. That is why, before you cut down a mahogany, you must ask permission of the keeper of the forest, and you must ask permission of the keeper of the stars."

———

Pulling into Naha, I saw a television satellite reception dish and a truck filled with army troops in camouflage. With their Tzeltal and Chol neighbors supporting the Zapatistas, the Lacandón had invited the government army to build a garrison. The driver dropped me, turned tail, and sped away, leaving a cloud of fine dust.

Where to go first? Chan K'in, of the ever-present cigar, three wives, and deep knowledge of Lacandón cosmology, was recently dead. At NaBalom, one of the aficionados who had studied and befriended the Lacandón had said a certain one of Chan K'in's sons would likely give me a place to sleep. The house was an open gallery with a couple of rooms on either side, enclosed by a dirt yard, quiet except for the presence of two long-haired boys in tunics, aged about ten and fourteen.

"*Balché*—sacred drink—long ceremony all night," said the older child, explaining why his father was still asleep in the late afternoon.

"Is your mother here?" I asked.

I wanted to leave my pack and wander about the village before dark. The older child hesitated, then shrugged, and led me to a detached kitchen. The cooking fire had burned down to a few smoldering sticks.

"Mother," announced the boy.

A woman lay curled on the dirt floor, reeking of alcohol, sacred or not I could not say. A toddler awkwardly bent at the waist, attempting to suckle from one of the woman's breasts, which was hanging outside her unbuttoned dress. Embarrassed, aware nobody had truly invited me into this house, I backed away.

"My father—he's awake!"

The younger boy came running from the opposite side of the gallery, his face flush with small victory. "Stay!" he said.

Behind him, a man emerged barefoot from a dark room. He looked groggy, as if navigating entrance into the real world. He bore that flagrant head of long black hair that marked him as one still undefeated. I believe I had never met this man in my life and know I had sent no message ahead to say I was coming. Nevertheless, he regarded me with a look of familiarity.

"So, you've arrived," he said, with finality, as if he had been expecting me.

Either this son of Chan K'in really had been drinking ceremonial *balché* all night and saw me coming in a dream or this was his way of greeting any visitor. I would never know the truth. In the next instant he tumbled backward into the hammock, apparently unconscious. His groin lay exposed. The youngest boy hurried over to pull down his father's tunic.

I said good-bye to the boys and walked away. The elder caught up to me and asked for a present. "Trudy Blom always gave us presents," he said.

I had nothing to give him, I said (although I would have given something to his father). I told him I was sorry about the death of his grandfather, Chan K'in.

"Yes, he is buried over there," he said, with a broad gesture toward the jungle.

"Will you take me to his grave?" I asked.

"It's about fifty miles away," he said, which would put the grave in the middle of the Usumacinta River, or inside Guatemala. I took my leave.

Looking for information about the bus, I stopped at a house-front shop. I met two young Israeli men who were camping nearby, on vacation before they returned to do military service. A costume designer from Hollywood and her boyfriend, both dressed in white Lacandón tunics, were in the midst of an inebriated disagreement with a Lacandón guide over the price of a canoe ride they had taken. Another Lacandón came to the window. I recognized José Bor, a big, gentle man whom I had met briefly at NaBalom, who still wore his hair long, and the white tunic. He offered me a place to hang my hammock.

That night, my host insisted I listen to his two children read, a boy and a girl about seven and eight. José Bor was a doting single father whose wife—not a Lacandón—had left him and the children, moving to Ocosingo. Both youngsters read from a single primary school book, rhymes and non-Indian fables. They proceeded haltingly, but José Bor, who was illiterate, looked up at nearly every phrase to make sure I admired their ability. Once in a while, he took the volume into his own hands to look at a page, shaking his head in defeat and amazement.

When the children went to bed, José Bor strung up his own hammock in front of the TV set. We finished the evening together watching the news from Mexico City and a rerun of Princess Diana's funeral.

I slept late, exhausted from the nearly sleepless night before. Before I left the village, I wanted to look up Chan K'in's widows. I needed to do it.

I found two of the wives in a smoky cookhouse. The wife senior to them, the mother of Kin Bor's wife, Nuk, had died. Now the older of the remaining Kohs received me, still slapping tortillas onto a hot *comal*, her eyes gray and watery from preparing meals over fire and smoke for more than sixty years. She called across the cookhouse to the younger Koh, who came to us, gazing at me as the other spoke.

The younger wife was still beautiful, as I had remembered, with softness in her features that age had only made more tranquil-looking. "I remember you, your visit," she said.

Both wives spoke Spanish now, and they seemed to understand much more than they had on my first visit. At first, I took what the young wife said as a kind gesture. On second thought, I wondered if the appearance of a young woman from the outside, not much older than herself, unmarried and apparently aimless, could have made a lasting impression.

Washing my hands, I stepped up to help the Kohs make tortillas. I was no better now than I had been twenty-five years before when they had tried to teach me. It was an art, to take just the right amount from a mound of corn dough, place it in the hollow of one hand, and slap it between both without dropping the *masa*, creating a perfect circle, perfectly thin, equal in size to dozens of others in the batch, an art I would never master. Laughing agreeably, the Kohs changed my task. I held their infant grandchildren, one after another.

A teenager appeared and hung over the younger Koh's shoulder. He was quiet but attentive to our faces in a way unusual for a youngster, an albino, like several youngsters in Naha. Koh said the boy was the last son of Chan K'in, who sired more than thirty.

The boy had never left his father's side, she said. "He learned much." Maybe this pale adolescent would some day take over Chan K'in's role, I thought, and become the spiritual guardian of the Lacandón.

When they finished with the corn dough, I asked the women to come outside so we could take a picture together before the sun set. Following their steps toward the door, I noticed their confident, big bare feet, and heard the sharp-voiced call of a bird flying over the roof. I already knew some of what I had loved about that first visit continued to exist. Now I thought the spirit of the rainforest might live most in women like these, and in the young Koh's pale son, a sense of connection with life that goes back generations, merging with the life of the forest, where one felt best.

The two surviving Kohs walked out before me into the roseate light, and I noticed: they wore dead birds in their hair, where it was gathered at the nape of the necks. The younger wore gray *codornices* dappled with pure white, quiet and elegant. The older had jeweled her hair with a kind of parrot, whose feathers shimmered mostly yellow but also scarlet and iridescent blue.

I handed the camera to the boy. The photo he took of the three of us in the fading afternoon sits on my desk. In the picture I stand between the two women in white togas. I look absurdly tall. They smile. The dead birds are not visible, but I know they are there.

7

Welcome Aboard

IN THE DARK HOURS OF NEW YEAR'S DAY MORNING, 1994, hundreds of masked Indians, carrying rifles across their chests, marched onto the cobblestone streets of San Cristóbal de las Casas. Tourists and *coletos*, still merrymaking, some dazed by drink, stood aside and watched, as if the event were an unexpected parade. Other witnesses rubbed their eyes fiercely, like sleepers trying to clear their minds of an unnerving dream. Turning points in history, at their first moments, are experienced in various ways.

The armed Indians advanced silently, deliberately, into the heart of the capital of the vice-regency, the jewel of Mexico's southernmost state. Their eyes burned intently above kerchiefs tied to disguise their faces. Weapons and uniforms were mismatched, but the Indians maintained distance from one another military-style, two files per street, past banks and jewelry store displays of amber and jade. They did not even turn their heads to look when passing the charming central plaza, built over years by their grandfathers, whom authorities then forbade to set foot inside. The Indians entered the colonial municipal building and trashed it, beginning an occupation that would last all day. Reports reached San Cristóbal that armed indigenous were entering other Chiapas towns.

When it became light, a Tzeltal Maya, colored ribbons floating down from the brim of his straw hat, stepped outside to a second-floor terrace of the municipal building. A crowd had gathered in the plaza. The Tzeltal announced eleven demands, along the lines of health, education, and democracy.

Demands? Indians did not make demands in Chiapas.

Landowners, and their allies in the military and PRI government, still ruled in the country's poorest state. Virtual slavery on ranches and timber camps lived in recent Maya memory. In the 1970s and 1980s, *chiapanecos* answered questions about living conditions with a bitter comment: *La revolución no ha llegada todavía.* "The revolution hasn't got here yet." The revolution they referred to was that of Pancho Villa and Emiliano Zapata, which produced the Mexican constitution in 1917. The armed Indians called themselves Zapatistas after their hero, whose cry was "Land and Liberty!"

Going public on January 1, 1994, had been no accident. NAFTA, the North American Free Trade Agreement, went into effect that day. The treaty, pushed by Washington, benefited private business by mandating a free flow of goods (not people) among the United States, Canada, and Mexico. Mexico City would look to the world like an equal partner with Washington and Ottawa. The cost: president Carlos Salinas agreed to privatize state enterprises, abandoning the country's mix of capitalism and soft socialism for a strict neoliberal economic model. For small farmers, NAFTA would reduce credit for seed and fertilizer, limiting price guarantees for corn, destroying the livelihoods of two million *campesinos*. With scarce funds, the Mexican cultivators could not compete in a single market with US farmers, whose agricultural product input and technology produced four times the corn on the same amount of land.

The president's most draconian measure was repealing the land reform in place since the Mexican Revolution. *Ejidos*, communal lands that could not be sold, ensured Indian peasants' survival from one generation to the next. Opening them up for private development had been the last straw. Zapatista Subcomandante Marcos, a non-Indian spokesman for the movement, called NAFTA "a death sentence for the indigenous."

Six months after the New Year's Day uprising, the Zapatistas called for a "National Democratic Convention," where civil society would join the rebels' demands for nationwide democracy. They invited teachers, labor activists, peasant union leaders, students, the country's famous authors and artists, and even masked wrestlers, icons of the common man's just fight.

The spectacle was set for the month of August 1994. It aimed to symbolize national support for the rebels, which would help protect them. Most important, the gathering would emphasize what Zapatistas had wanted from the beginning: that all Mexicans demand clean elections and an end to corruption. After seventy years of unbroken rule by the PRI, the Institutional Revolutionary Party, the Maya called for an end to the hegemony of a single, tight political class.

From my house in Antigua, Guatemala, I followed the Zapatista insurrection in the newspapers. When I heard about the Zapatista National Democratic Convention, I decided this was the time to see it up close and made the ten-hour trip to Chiapas. In San Cristóbal, where I had friends, it was not difficult to find out how to begin. Zapatista civilians—and there were plenty of them outside Indian villages—were discreet about participating in the movement but did not live clandestinely. Association alone was not officially against the law. I went to the Zapatista offices in "San Kris."

"I don't have an invitation or a Mexican press identification card," I told one of the Convention's organizers. "But I would like to go." I launched into a recitation of my Central American reporting experience, interest in Maya lands, anything I thought might help.

"Don't worry, we know who you are," said the Zapatista, filling out a Convention pass. I tried not to look surprised. San Cristóbal was not a big place, but rebel intelligence was excellent, too. The organizer marked a thin piece of paper with a bus number and seat assignment.

A few days later, I rose in the middle of the night in a small San Cristóbal hotel room, picked up my pack, and walked to the edge of town. There, buses rented by the Zapatistas had turned the streets into a massive parking lot. I wandered among thousands of other conferees to find my assigned place. By early morning our line of vehicles was on its way, probably the longest caravan Central America has ever seen. The buses were draped with red, green, and white Mexican flags and painted banners carrying Zapatista sayings such as NEVER AGAIN A MEXICO WITHOUT US. Farmers on country roads waved and cheered. In towns, entire families stood on the curbs, adults holding signs of encouragement and solidarity, children waving paper flags or pictures of Marcos. Students in school uniforms lined the sidewalks, as if their teachers placed the caravan to the Zapatista redoubt in a framework of current events or history.

As we descended the mountains toward the Lacandón jungle, there were no more onlookers. The hours became harrowing, crawling along the edge of steep cliffs. Parts of the narrow, twisting roads lay strewn with loose rocks. Drivers repeatedly tried their brakes. Some buses broke down. It was such a relief to reach the lowlands that I heard no complaints about the warm, clammy air.

After twenty-seven hours of travel, we looked upon a surreal scene. Against the rainforest backdrop, rebels had constructed a stage, with banks of boxy black speakers ready for action, albeit blocking the sight lines for the first rows of chairs. They had carved banks of seats into a hill for an amphitheater that resembled the prow of a ship. A mammoth white roof tarp had been rigged overhead. It lifted and fell with the breeze like a sail.

"Welcome aboard," said Subcomandante Marcos from the stage.

Over the next two days I chatted informally with fellow mud-spattered attendees, including a world-class historian, a pair of Basque nationalists, an elderly veteran of Zapata's original fighters, and grand Mexican literary figures like Elena Poniatowska and Carlos Monsiváis. The most memorable orchestrated moments of the Zapatista National Democratic Convention to me, however, were wordless.

Hundreds of civilians, introduced by Marcos as "the companions of the jungle," marched by in silent parade between the stage and rows where we, the visitors, sat. The Indians wore masks, carrying sticks across their bodies like rifles. They struggled to keep orderly lines, men and women from adolescents to elderly, individual Maya ethnicities revealed by the weave of a shirt or color of a skirt—Tzotzil, Tzeltal, Chol, Tojolabal. The rainforest residents had hidden Marcos and a few others from the outside for a decade, nurturing two thousand Maya guerrillas as they trained to become the EZLN, the Zapatista National Liberation Army. Marcos looked over the heads of the marching Indians at us, the audience. A black ski mask disguised his features, but everyone knew Marcos gazed with clear, green eyes.

The EZLN answers to Zapatista civilians. The Indians passing were masters of the combatants, as civilians command the military in a democracy, deciding when it should join battle, when to treat. It didn't start out that way, but that's how it had become. The Indian peasants needed an armed force to eject drug runners and timber thieves from the jungle, to defend their land. When NAFTA loomed, the Chiapas Maya said they must push back, make a public stand, backed by weapons. Marcos and others demurred, saying forces were not ready to take on the Mexican army, which would surely respond. But the peasants said, "We cannot wait any longer."

The long minutes watching the indigenous marchers felt eerie, revelatory, as if the passing lines were endless, the Indians supernumerary, telegraphing a message of resistance to subjugation with every step. The only sound came from their feet hitting the soft jungle floor, feet bare, feet in sandals, feet in rubber boots.

Later, EZLN combatants paraded. They had tied strips of white cloth to the business end of their rifles, carried upright, aiming at the sky as they marched. It was a sign, the world was meant to understand, that they did not want to use arms again. Instead, the EZLN wanted the episodic peace negotiations to satisfy the need for land and services, demands that had not changed since New Year's Day. By now everyone knew *zapatismo* was not about taking power. Face-to-face fighting with the army had stopped January 12, 1994.

The night before we left the Zapatista redoubt, a tempest arose. I fled for the sleeping pavilion but did not sleep. Noises of straining, cracking, thunder broke on all sides. The wind roared.

"The sail is gone!" someone yelled.

I moved to the periphery of the massive tent, where hundreds attempted to rest, or at least stay warm, in blankets, sleeping bags, hammocks. Looking outside, I could see the white tarp roof blowing in shreds, its metal poles bent and disjointed by the force of the gale.

Wind was taking the shelter's side flaps, too, tossing them into the air, carrying rain and chill inside. I dreaded the upcoming return trip, when I would be tired and probably still wet, another uncomfortable twenty-seven hours. Had the Zapatistas planned to offer a taste of what they regularly experienced, they could not have done better than opening the sky to the raging storm.

————

From the time of the Zapatista uprising in 1994 to 2010, I made eight more journeys to Chiapas, some as a journalist, some to ancient Maya sites, once to revisit the Lacandón village, Naha. Each time, I stepped into a mirror of the wars I had thought were over, those in Central America more than a decade before. Revolution in Mesoamerica was a wheel, not unlike the Maya concept of the cycles of time, renewable. In each place, suffering led to rebellion, which brought on counterinsurgency, including civilian massacres, and dislocation of communities whose roots went back a thousand years. The US role in each conflict—El Salvador, Guatemala, Nicaragua—aimed to repress genuine change, to maintain an antebellum status quo. When Chiapas erupted, Washington increased aid to the Mexican army.

What was different in Chiapas from rebellions farther south was that Zapatistas did not want to take over the government. Instead, their purpose was to draw attention to the death in life of Maya, existing in worse conditions in the twentieth century than the sixteenth. Mexico City, and Washington, treated the insurrection as the revolution the Zapatista movement wanted to bring, even though a democratic revolution had been envisioned.

In 1995, the year after the uprising, I returned to Chiapas, intending to visit the Maya city of Palenque. On the Mexican side of the Usumacinta River, I passed through immigration. Luckily, there I met two women coming upriver from Yaxchilan, an American and a Guatemalan, who had arranged a lift with a government worker. I piggybacked, four of us in a double-seat pickup.

In the year since the National Democratic Convention, Chiapas had turned into a militarized state. More than a third of the Mexican army—thirty thousand soldiers—were hunkering behind sandbags, plowing into villages with tanks, controlling every main road and junction. (Later, the number of Mexican soldiers stationed in Chiapas would reach seventy thousand.) Meanwhile, a Mexican general who had received training in psychological warfare at Fort Bragg, North Carolina, began a system of paramilitary units made up largely of armed ruling party members to harass pro-Zapatista neighbors.

We three women and the driver rode contentedly toward the ancient ruins for more than an hour, feeling none of this, until we hit a spot where other cars had stopped, engines off.

Bare-chested men in green shorts occupied the road in several lines of half a dozen each. They hopped, touched their left feet with right hands, then right with left, windmill style. Tall, with narrow noses and lips, they did not look Maya. Perhaps they came from the north, an elite, the best the Mexican army had. They jogged in place. Their drilling blocked the road, so there was nothing to do but to watch. Perfect biceps, perfect chests, handsome, perspiring, shining. In a quarter of an hour, they stopped and stood with arms at their sides, action figures at rest, skin like bright plastic, expressionless.

A fully uniformed soldier led the men from the road. Another motioned for the cars to proceed. In less than a mile, a third flagged us down. He ordered us out of the car, toward a set of tables under a banner announcing KIOSK OF ECOLOGICAL INSPECTION AND VIGILANCE. The soldiers and officers wore camouflage. Sandbags filled with clay protected the "kiosk." An officer reviewed our passports while lumber trucks passed without stopping. Why couldn't the government just admit it was at war?

When the officer returned the driver's documents and my passport, I remarked, "There are many of you."

"*Hecho y derecho para batalla,*" he replied, the environmental vigilance banner flapping above his head. "Right and ready for battle."

When we crossed the Chankala River, close to Palenque, the driver used a car phone to call his office, but there was no answer. I tried to tune in the local radio station, but only static spat from the dial.

"This road usually has more cars," the driver said.

He dropped us at the edge of Palenque town, where I said good-bye to my fellow passengers. It was too early for siesta but the shops were closed, CERRADO signs in windows or rolling metal doors pulled down to the sidewalk. I smelled the odor of burning. As I walked toward the town center, the smell became sharper. In the central *parque*, a pile of glowing ashes held the remains of sandals, tortillas, a one-legged doll. Shoeshine boys and newspaper vendors stood together in knots.

They said Indian farmer families had been camped in the park, a protest of some kind. Armed men had arrived in jeeps, tore down the sheets of plastic the families had raised to protect themselves at night, kicked belongings into piles, and set it all afire. They pushed the campers, men, women, and children, into the back of a cattle truck. No police or soldiers were in sight, although a police station stood nearby.

At the hotel, a small place surrounded by palms and flowering jacaranda, the receptionist told me the ruins at Palenque had been closed, at least for the day. "They think the Zapatistas are going to invade the temples," she said.

This sounded ridiculous, but if trouble from any quarter spread two miles down the road, it would be hard to protect stelae and fifteen-hundred-year-old structures. Whatever had happened in the park was like other violent events taking place across Chiapas. This was the closest I had come to one of them. Counterinsurgency, like the roadblock en route, unfolds below the radar of news organizations. So do local confrontations between landowners and indigenous. Yet both fed the atmosphere of war like spitting twigs feed a fire.

There is absolutely nothing to do in the town of Palenque except eat and sleep after a day at the ruins. When explorers John Stephens and Frederick Catherwood came in 1840, dengue fever had recently passed through, leaving many dead. Stephens set forth to know the quiet place and found stones from the ancient city incorporated into the church and a house face. He met the town's outstanding personages. I put on a hat against the sun and stepped into the street.

The peasants taken away by force in the truck belonged to Xinich, the Ants, a shoeshine boy had told me. I had heard Xinich described as one of the strongest farmers' organizations in Chiapas. I looked for their office, which turned out to be an ordinary-looking house in a residential neighborhood. It was doubtful the incident in the park would become a full-fledged newspaper story, but perhaps Xinich represented groups—besides Zapatistas—rebelling against the status quo in their own way. I wanted to know more, what journalists sometimes call "saving string." Even presenting myself as a reporter, I had to pass an interview on an outside porch to enter Xinich headquarters.

Inside, a 1992 photo blown up to a large size hung on one wall. It showed Xinich members arriving in Mexico City, at the end of a six-week trek on foot from Palenque, to draw attention to the need for land titles. On another wall hung a poster of Rigoberta Menchú, the indigenous woman who received the Nobel Peace Prize in 1992. Menchu was not Mexican; she was Guatemalan. But she was Maya.

Men who appeared to be rural farmers sat in chairs lined against the walls, hats in hand. Two others worked at desks. One introduced himself as Efrain Gutierrez Gomez, *un campesino*, a peasant, Chol Maya; the other was a Mexican priest. The priest shook hands and went back to receiving the farmers at his desk. Some looked shaken. The "peasant" official wore sandals. Had he been bent over carrying a sack of corn, he would have looked no different from the Chol Indians I once saw shuffling in and out of the warehouse on the Usumacinta River. Instead Gutierrez stood erect, offering a chair.

He was waiting to hear from members out looking for the missing peasants, he said. Police were hesitant to become involved. Meanwhile, Gutierrez said, the Xinich farmers I saw in the office had arrived after risky trips on back trails. They reported that soldiers at roadblocks had lists of suspect persons, including members of cooperatives and peasant organizations. Quietly he indicated a pale man with gnarled hands. He had been detained, Gutierrez said, until officers realized his last name was spelled differently from one on the list. He did not want to leave the office, afraid of being stopped again.

"We are in a state without law," Gutierrez said. "There is no end to the agrarian problem—the demand doesn't stop. But we have been telling the *compañeros* to maintain calm. We tell them civilian organizations like ours are working on it."

It seemed the job of keeping Xinich members from picking up guns was as difficult as defending land. Their founding rules, in 1986, said the Ants would be nonviolent.

"We named it Xinich because ants work together," said Gutierrez.

The peasants taken from the park belonged to a group of 250 families living on a stretch of rural land since 1945. The ranchers who took them had also appeared recently on the land, telling residents to leave, swearing to give the *tiro de gracia*, a shot to the head, if they did not. The local ranchers and cattlemen had surrounded the settlement for a couple of days, refusing to let anyone leave by road, even a young couple with a feverish infant. The parents walked a mountainous route at night, Gutierrez said, but the baby died before they reached the hospital.

The Indians' protest in the park placed them in a five-hundred-year cycle of historical fights over land, taken brutally or by the stroke of a pen or by chicanery. Indigenous rebellions began almost as soon as the Conquest was complete. The Zapatista insurrection was a point in the cycle, too, but its reach seemed greater than its predecessors, affecting or inspiring indigenous statewide, even in other heavily Indian states. By calling upon countrymen to demand democracy, *zapatismo* approached solidarity with nonindigenous groups, another aspect distinguishing it from most other uprisings.

Government and landowners together quashed previous rebellions with torture and gore to teach the lesson. But President Salinas could not oversee a sweeping massacre of Zapatistas, or any other Indians, because NAFTA partners Ottawa and Washington would have found it intolerable. (Soldiers might easily have erased rebel combatants, which they outnumbered eighteen to one.) Instead, the Mexican government launched the counterinsurgency, the hidden war.

I had walked into the Xinich office at crisis time, and the strain was palpable. The army was using the Zapatista uprising as an excuse to go after any Indian peasants who raised their heads in the name of a more decent life. Among members of Xinich, the temptation to respond violently, out of self-defense, simmered just below the surface.

The priest working in the office said to me in Spanish: "They are profoundly indignant right now, but at this point they are still thinking with their heads."

He put his fingers to his temples as if calling up the effort to stay rational, calm. Gutierrez heard and saw. He would not leave the non-Indian priest with the last word.

"We give them no provocation, but they have beat us and shot at us anyway," he said. "How long can this be withstood?"

I stopped in again the next day. Gutierrez wasn't there, but the priest who had been taking reports from farmers worked on them at his desk. The families taken from the park had been dumped twenty miles away, the *padre* said, huddling until dawn, when they walked to places they could hide, at least for a few days. In the baroque parlance of armed conflict this is called low-intensity warfare. Multiply by hundreds the atomization of this single community, the displacement of a thousand persons, the infant's death, the trauma of being kidnapped. For those on the receiving end, this is low-intensity warfare.

———

For the first hours of the trip from Palenque to San Cristóbal, the bus traveled along nauseating curves. Passengers watched a Mexican Western on TV monitors dangling from the ceiling. We passed scruffy dirt yards where barefoot Indian women wore only skirts. A line of shacks advertising amber for sale perched along a precipice above a river. Children walked bent forward along the road, tumplines around small foreheads, wood on their backs, carrying their own sources of warmth.

The bus slowed. The movie images froze and then broke apart on the screen. We stopped at a lonely spot, no sign of a town. The driver cursed.

About eighty men, bandannas tied around their faces, were blocking the highway. Their large number, and the disguises that revealed only the eyes, inspired fear. They carried sticks with nails stuck into them, like weapons wielded by rebellious serfs in medieval Europe. Half a dozen men broke away from the rest and approached the bus.

Their leader possessed the body and gait of a young peasant farmer. He motioned with a twist of the hand for the driver to open the door. He did not carry one of the homemade weapons; the compact gesture suggested he was used to being obeyed. A few men from the group followed him aboard.

"We are Zapatistas," he said. "Civilians. Remain calm, quiet."

I was sure the bus driver carried a gun under the dashboard or in his boot. Maybe some of the Zapatistas did, too, concealed. The situation was sickeningly out of one's control. My stomach hurt. I was less concerned about the masked men than that someone on board would balk, show anger, make a stand.

"The government must negotiate . . . " the lead fellow was saying. Raw nerves prevented me from following the pep talk.

Slow, simple Spanish signaled that the leader's first language was a Maya tongue. One of his *compañeros* walked down the aisle passing a basket, as if collecting donations from pews at church. No one refused to contribute.

During the shakedown, the driver fumed so obviously I thought he would draw notice from the intruders. They left backing down the stairs, and the gauntlet of men outside split down the middle, opening the road. The driver shut the door with a string of expletives, gunning the engine angrily as we sped away. One of the passengers asked him to restart the Western.

———

When I returned to Palenque, the ancient city was open, its excavated ruins surrounded by forested hills where hundreds more temples and buildings lay sleeping. Coming upon the great plaza can overwhelm a visitor, not just with its beauty—temples massive and delicate at once, framed so softly by the calling jungle—but also for the sense of human history that passed there. When Stephens and Catherwood arrived in the middle of the nineteenth century, the city was mightily overgrown, yet even then Stephens could register Palenque's strong sense of place. "What we had before our eyes was grand, curious, and remarkable enough," he wrote. "Here were the remains of a cultivated, polished, and peculiar people, who had passed through all the stages incident to the rise and fall of nations; reached their golden age, and perished."

I wandered without a plan, walking slowly through the plaza. On my right rose the Palace of the Inscriptions, where the ruler Pacal lay buried deep inside in a finely carved sarcophagus showing him tumbling backward into the underworld. Across stood the Temple of the Sun, in ancient time painted red, much of its roof comb still extant. At the top of its steps, a sculpture commemorated a royal ascension. Not only is the new king pictured but his dead father, too, as if the scene would be incomplete without including the forbearer. The tablet brought to mind Kin Bor's first personal question to me. Not, as we might ask, "What do you do?" or "Are you married?" but "Who is your father?"

It was as if, in Maya thinking, the presence of the father lived on in a real way, was part of who a person was. In the second half of my life, I had begun to feel how this works in a way I could not in my youth. I had realized it—why must it happen like this?—as my father, who really was a rocket scientist, sat wrapped in a blanket, beginning to die. "We have the same sense of humor!" I thought then.

Instead of eating, the last time I visited he wanted to tell me again about early meetings of the Rocket Club, where engineers drank cocktails and spun dreams out loud, such as how a man might go to the moon. "Lot of crazies then," he said. "Volunteering to go. Before we had a way to bring them back." He laughed wryly, I uproariously, scandalizing others in the next room who had been trying to speak in whispers. A couple of days later I felt something of myself disappearing with my father as, before me, he died. *To die, OCH-bi-j(i), to enter the road.* Every day I see more that something of him is left behind, in me.

Kin Bor's question about my mother had been different. "Is she alive?" he asked, as if to him that real everyday presence, not the blood the father gave, were the more significant fact to know about a woman.

Near the Temple of the Sun stands the Temple of the Foliated Cross, named for its huge tablet showing a cross-like Tree of Life, whose outstretched limbs are not branches but ears of maize draped with leaves and flowing corn silk. The image holds symbols for ceremonial bloodletting that helps the corn grow, and gruesome masks, topped by a sharp-beaked mythological bird. In the end, the picture consoles. At their outer tips the corncobs become human heads, faces turned up to the sky.

From atop the Temple of the Cross, looking out at the forest, the world felt right, the connection between us and growing things graven exquisitely in stone, the growing things alive. The doleful massive pockmarks where the forest had disappeared could not be seen from the vantage. Instead, the earth to its curvature was an endless green and growing mass, as if the trees grew forever and there was nothing about which to worry.

The city-state of Palenque endured six hundred years; probably its residents thought it too was endless, maybe even until near its very end. To look at the tablets and friezes was to wish we could read glyphs, as if some secret might be contained there to answer questions we still have about how long our own world might last. Or how far we might watch rainforests evaporate into lamp stands and chopsticks and expect it not to matter. The myriad cubes and curls of Maya writing mesmerized. "The impression made upon our minds by these speaking but unintelligible tablets I shall not attempt to describe," wrote Stephens, who was never otherwise at a loss to describe an object, personality, or landscape in all his Mesoamerican travels.

For the Maya, writing about the events of the world kept it in order. In the *Popol Vuh*, the attempt to create men out of wood failed because the creatures couldn't remember to praise and thank the gods but also because they didn't acknowledge their origins, didn't know their own history. That was why they were not worthy of being human, and turned into monkeys.

We shared this impulse with the ancient Maya, writing to impose order on the world around us. For them such writing was a sacred duty; now it feels presumptuous to think any order can be made at all. I climbed around the temple under a hot sun to sit upon cool stones before the smoker god. I pulled a Kretek from a vest pocket. I carried around the small, hand-rolled Indonesian cigarettes, smelling of cloves, to light up on special occasions, true to the original idea of smoking as a way of communing with others or with the gods.

The plaza at the temple's feet spread bright under the sun, almost vibrating, perhaps holding the energy of so many that had used it. All the sculptures and inscribed slabs I had spent the day touching and observing melted in my mind into the one theme they seemed aimed at showing: the power of connection with family, the significance of having come from somewhere, having roots. That was why the Maya of Chiapas fought so hard for their land, which meant connection, memory, survival.

In the public art of Palenque, "family" meant the royal family, genealogy slabs erected to shore up its claim to power. But even Maya who came later referred to their leaders as "those who have mothers and fathers." Not only was it informative to possess a written or graven account of who your progenitors were, where they were from, and what they did, but it was something that gifted you with a set place in a chaotic world.

I considered how much I was writing about this journey for myself and how much, more deeply, for my daughter. I wanted her to know the beauty of being in places close to the creation. She has to realize that everything possible must be done to stop war before it starts, that once begun it has a mind of its own, uncontrollable, creating a million unique, heart-corroding stories. That it takes life, which is never restored. The line of smoke from the brown cigarette rose sinewy and sensuous into the air, carrying away thought.

8

They Never Came, and They Never Left

ON DECEMBER 21, 1997, PARAMILITARY GUNMEN KILLED EIGHT unarmed men, twenty-one women, fourteen children, and an infant in a Chiapas village called Acteal. I heard the news at my house in Antigua, Guatemala, on the shortwave radio, the regular 8:00 P.M. BBC broadcast. Shortly after, I received a call from a clergyman in California, a good friend with Mexican and Central American parishioners. He asked me to meet him in Chiapas, where he wanted to find out the facts about the killings. Two weeks after the massacre, I took a bus to San Cristóbal, met my friend, and rented a car.

When I have a chance to travel with Father Bill O'Donnell, I take it, partly because his Irish sense of humor is like my father's was, raising laughs even at rough moments. Once a California farmboy, now in his sixties, with clear blue eyes in a face still handsome, Bill has a physically large presence like a former football player might have. He believes in Gandhi-like, nonviolent protest "when my government misbehaves." That is why he has been jailed with César Chávez, keeps vigil outside San Quentin on nights when prisoners await execution, has lain upon tracks to stop trains with weapons for Central America, walks picket lines with workers, once or twice on the wrong end of billy clubs. Father Bill has been arrested 240 times for nonviolent resistance. When we first met I asked how he came to be a priest.

"I was thirteen, running a plow in the hot sun," he said. "I prayed, 'Please God, show me an easier life.'"

Father Bill had been in Chiapas once before, visiting a hospital that received support from a nonprofit foundation he helped to establish. This time, barely arrived, he had already managed to meet three Tzotzil Maya Indians with an urgent need to go to a village called X'oyep, where Acteal massacre survivors gathered. The Tzotzil needed to know whether relatives from Acteal were dead or alive. Bill said they told him they belonged to the same Christian pacifist group as those who had been attacked, Las Abejas, the Bees. Like Xinich, the peasant organization based in Palenque, the Bees supported the Zapatistas while advocating nonviolence.

"They are afraid of the soldiers and paramilitaries," said Bill of his new friends. "They're afraid of being pulled off a bus."

"Sure," I said, "Let's go."

From San Cristóbal, the route entered a cloud forest. Only bright white lilies burned through the grayness, marking the edge of the road. The diaphanous mist made mountainside huts look imaginary, as if they might disappear if you came too close. Crosses with distinctive rounded arms, the way Maya here carved them, were planted on hills in threes. Through the humid curtain they looked like druidical outposts, not symbols of an established religion. We passed a store where fellows sat smoking on the porch, rifles across their laps. Paramilitaries. In the rearview mirror, I saw my Indian passengers turn their heads away.

About fifty miles into the clouds, we stopped at a trail too narrow for a car. The Tzotzil men piled out first. Bill followed, wearing not clerical garb but a black T-shirt, jeans, and his favorite black leather motorcycle jacket. He carried a priest's white collar, should it be needed, in his pocket. I had just locked the door and stepped away from the car when we heard the sound of tumbling stones. Dark-clad government troops spilled down the trail, holding rifles. We all froze. The soldiers, however, huffing and glassy-eyed under their packs, merely jogged a few yards on flat ground and ascended another trail to the west.

The Tzotzil took to the path like thirsty men who smell a lake, anxious for the sight of the mothers and siblings they hoped to find in X'oyep. Father Bill followed them closely despite the fact he was twice their age. There was no way I could keep up, thanks to my damned lungs.

"Just keep to this path and you can't get lost," one of the men called back. I hate hearing that because it is almost never true.

For the next hour and a half I climbed slowly but without problems. The route they had taken was steep but easy to follow at a reduced pace. The mist lifted. I could see mountains running to the south, riddled with streams and thin waterfalls, scenes of such tranquility they belied a land at war with itself.

Across the mountains somewhere Zapatista guerrillas melted into the Lacandón jungle, camouflaged among civilians. Peasants there had lived as Zapatistas in the forest for years, many related to EZLN combatants. The cause was so much part of their lives that even a massacre among them like the one at Acteal would be unlikely to shake their open commitment. A counterinsurgency tactic such as naked violence would not frighten that population into conformity. Elsewhere, however, it could intimidate Zapatista sympathizers.

Under my feet the path changed, becoming less rocky and easier to walk upon. Around a bend I saw four soldiers wearing the yellow armbands of the army's Social Work unit laboring with picks and shovels, smoothing the trail. They moved aside courteously to let me pass. I smelled the rich aroma of cooking meat.

"*Tiene hambre?*" "Hungry?" asked a man in full white apron. He minded a bubbling cauldron set atop a fire.

I had come upon a Mexican army civic action station in full view of the path. Men and women in the uniform of army medics sat at tables covered with medicine boxes and bottles. To their right, the chef dipped into the stew with his ladle, lifting it so its contents fell back into the pot, broadcasting the alluring smell. Overhead, a white plastic tarp protected the tables from sun and rain. A tableau meant to capture hearts and minds.

Out of curiosity, I walked up to an officer with a stethoscope hanging around his neck. "How long have you been here?" I asked.

"This is the third day," he replied.

"Any customers?"

"No one wants the medicine or even food," he said. "It makes no sense."

The trail served several hamlets where the officer imagined conditions were "difficult." Yet so far he had treated only one patient, a member of his own Social Work unit who had slipped in the mud and fractured a wrist.

"I don't understand," he said.

He sounded annoyed, as if it were he and his troops who were being wronged. "We are doing this in good faith," he said.

Less than half an hour later, I reached X'oyep, a town of only a few dozen families, filled now with tents and other temporary shelters. A village of two hundred souls had recently grown to two thousand with frightened newcomers who were fleeing their own villages lest they meet the fate of Acteal. I found the Tzotzil men from the car reunited with relatives. Father Bill was inside a roofed shelter with dozens of cots. He was conversing animatedly with Indians, although he spoke little Spanish and not a word of Tzotzil.

Wherever I went in X'oyep, the sound of coughing was more ubiquitous than birdsong. At a makeshift clinic, an Indian teenager who had become an instant medic in the crisis distributed available treatment, a mixture of bougainvillea, eucalyptus, camphor, red onion, garlic, and pine bark shavings. I thought of the packaged medicines stacked on the tables along the trail, suspecting it would not be long before some desperate father with an ailing child would break ranks and approach the Social Work soldiers for help. That is the way counterinsurgency works. You make goods and services available, often for the first time, to a poor and rebellious people and then sit back and watch how long they can resist the seduction.

"They just want to offer some services so we'll be happy and not feel our problems anymore, not feel anything, just be quiet," a young man told us in Spanish when I rejoined Father Bill. "But that is not the way. We want a solution to the problems, the fulfillment of the accord of San Andres."

The San Andres pact, which called for indigenous rights and local autonomy, was signed in 1996 after months of negotiations between representatives of the Zapatistas and the Mexican government. In far-away Mexico City, Congress vetoed it.

"If we accept those crumbs of help," the young man said, "it does not mean a problem is resolved."

———

Mornings, San Cristóbal de las Casas may be one of the loveliest cities in the Americas. Its mountain elevation means the sun does not so much rise over softly colored houses but rather lightens the cloud into which residents wake.

I went to an office near the yellow cathedral because I wanted to talk to bishop Samuel Ruiz. I wanted his wisdom on the cycles of war in Central America, on where a line of nonviolence legitimately might be crossed.

The best I could do was to catch him on the fly in the cold foyer, where he wore a pullover sweater and his distinctive beret. There was time for one question. Why didn't he encourage Indians to accept aid from the army, at least for the sake of the children?

"How can they," he asked, "when they see the army as accomplices of the paramilitaries?"

Chiapas Maya call bishop Samuel Ruiz *Tatic*, an endearment for "father," meaning the blood relation, not the religious title. Ruiz shares the spirit of his long-ago predecessor, a Dominican friar named Bartolomé de las Casas, San Cristóbal's first bishop. A humanist and man of fairness, de las Casas's letters convinced the Spanish king that New World Indians ought to be considered beings with souls. It meant they were subjects for conversion to be sure, but also—and this was the revolutionary part of his thinking—they must not be subject to slavery or inhumane treatment.

Samuel Ruiz came to the city in 1960 at age thirty-five with a mission to evangelize the Maya, considered hardly more Christian than they had been at the time of the Conquest. A conservative cleric, Ruiz called in those with more local experience, Marist brothers who had long worked in the outlands. They told the young bishop stories about feudal-style exploitation, places where debt peonage continued.

Ruiz was a hands-on administrator. To do the job, he learned Indian languages and spent rough time in the countryside, eating only beans and tortillas and sleeping in the houses of those he was supposed to be confirming in the flock. He witnessed firsthand the conditions in which the Indians lived, the daily round.

It has been said of Ruiz that by going out like a missionary to fully convert the Maya, he himself experienced a conversion; that is, he was so impressed with how they bore up under meager compensation for work, in the face of hunger and landlessness, that his point of view was transformed. He came to believe that the Indians possessed the answers to their own problems, if only they might be given a chance to solve them.

These new understandings did not mean Ruiz became unorthodox. Among the ways Chiapas politicians attempted to stem his influence in the early 1990s was to frame a law permitting abortion, which is anathema to Church doctrine. Ruiz put up a dogfight. The law never took effect.

Having lived in Guatemala, I knew Ruiz was beloved there by Indians for taking in one hundred thousand Maya who fled on foot through jungles and over rivers to Chiapas for safety during the Guatemalan war. He was the first public figure to call the Guatemalan army campaign against civilians, mostly Indians, genocide.

"Thank you for sending us your best," I once heard him say in Guatemala City to a group of nuns and catechists from Indian communities. "It fertilized, and made more conscious, our Indians."

Decades before, Ruiz had been sent to confirm indigenous in their faith. Now he seemed to believe that the natives' vision of the world, of balance in life and nature, might be a positive force for the rest of Latin America.

"The indigenous must evangelize the continent," he said to the religious workers, many of them indigenous Maya. "You are the emergent subjects of development and integration, and an emerging people has a renovating effect: to bring about not just peace but a system that is just."

In Chiapas, the elite, old guard residents of San Cristóbal accused the bishop of being a revolutionary, especially when he began mediating the peace talks between the government and Zapatistas. The talks took place in the yellow cathedral, the only place the Zapatistas felt safe. Death threats arrived for the bishop. *Coletos* openly carried a coffin through city streets, branded with Ruiz's name, and set it afire. Once, when the bishop attempted to visit displaced Indians in the countryside, the paramilitary group called Peace and Justice tried to kill him as he rode in a car. Ruiz and his auxiliary bishop survived; their driver was killed. Even the papal nuncio in Mexico City tried to convince Rome to remove Ruiz from office. It didn't work.

When Father Bill returned to San Cristóbal after a couple of days visiting the hospital in the countryside, I accompanied him to the cathedral, where Bishop Ruiz was saying Mass. The pews were already full with *coletos* and indigenous in various local dress, and we stood for a while until worshippers in a back pew squeezed together and invited us in. "Heaven begins here," Ruiz said in the homily. "It is not a promised land for later. It is the weave of human actions performed for the service of the Lord that gets us into heaven." After the service, as we stepped outside, Father Bill asked whether I wanted to accompany him to a meeting with the bishop.

"You have a meeting with Ruiz?" I said.

"Come along," Bill said. "I always like the questions you ask."

It had not occurred to me that Ruiz and Bill O'Donnell were in contact, might be friends. But it made sense. Both were unassuming yet unbowed before authority. Each spoke for those with little voice, Bishop Ruiz for the indigenous, Father Bill for immigrants, the jailed, and "the lads," alcoholics and drug abusers trying to go straight.

Inside the nearby chancery, Bishop Ruiz's sister guided us down a short hall. She seemed to walk well, after having opened the door some months earlier to an attacker gunning for her brother. The would-be assassin shot her in the leg and ran.

The bishop rose to receive us in a quiet reception room, wearing a simple white soutane and a plain cross of Chiapas amber on a chain around his neck. Bill had donned his clerical white collar for the occasion but otherwise looked less like a priest than a Hell's Angel. The men warmly embraced. I wished I had a camera just for the aesthetic of the scene, one man all in white, the other all black.

When Bill introduced me to the bishop, Ruiz disarmingly spoke some English in greeting. His parents, he said, once had been farm workers in the United States.

We sat in straight-backed chairs while Father Bill and the bishop discussed the situation of the hospital he and his colleagues had just visited, located at a gateway to the Lacandón jungle. Their nonprofit had helped support the place for years. Nuns told him of sick forest dwellers who did not come to the hospital because paramilitary vigilantes roamed the town. The bishop seemed troubled, and he spoke of other places where divisions tore at the social fabric.

"I told the nuns I would walk medical supplies into the jungle," Father Bill said. I nearly fell off my chair. I knew he had a life-threatening heart condition that he sometimes ignored. "But the good sisters said they would search for some other way to do it."

The bishop nodded gravely, and I noticed the satiny white skullcap on his balding head. "Mary Jo has some questions," Bill said. "She always has good questions." He gave a quick rundown of my work.

"Of course," said the bishop.

Almost immediately, my tape recorder jammed. I became flustered. Ruiz reached for the wretched thing.

"No, no, *Monseñor*. It's broken, the worst possible time, it's broken."

"Even so, perhaps something can be done," he said, adjusting large, black-rimmed glasses. He fiddled with buttons and a lever. He handed the machine back, working. "I believe you're ready now?"

I asked whether Chiapas was on its way to duplicating Guatemala's "development poles," a tactic based on the US strategic hamlet policy during the well-known Phoenix counterinsurgency program in Vietnam. Suspect civilian populations are separated from guerrillas, "draining the sea" in which rebels swim, as Mao would have it. Military or paramilitary forces then isolate the civilian hamlets by occupying or surrounding them. Those living outside become outlaws by definition, targets for government forces.

Ruiz warned against parallels with other rebellions. There should be no political outlaws, he said, thanks to a key piece of legislation, the Law of Concord and Pacification, passed in 1995. As long as it was honored, the law protected Zapatistas from being arrested merely on grounds they were Zapatistas, as long as the peace process continued. Instead, he said, the thick military presence in Chiapas was the problem, destroying the "climate of trust" necessary for dialogue.

"They sure scare me," said Bill, raising his arms as if ordered to "get 'em up." He feigned fright by shaking from head to torso in the straight-backed chair.

"Oh, oh, excuse me," he said as we laughed. "I didn't mean to interrupt."

The bishop said peasants forced from their homes who returned found them pillaged of what few goods families had managed to accumulate in a lifetime. I realized how deeply Ruiz had come to understand the Indians' lives when he dwelt at length upon the seeds lost in burned villages or looted from storage sheds. It seemed at the same time he was lamenting the attack upon his own labor, diocesan teams who had worked closely with indigenous communities over thirty years.

"Those seeds aren't the kind you can buy," he said. "They are seeds acclimatized after years of work, special seeds kept from year to year, those which have become most fruitful, adapted to the particular niche of each farmer's soil."

When Father Bill and I left the chancery, my friend seemed wrapped in thought as we walked toward the hotel. I mused silently, too. Samuel Ruiz, now in his seventies, reminded me of the Maya Time Bearer, who carries the responsibility of time on his back. A glyph shows him bent under the bundle, carrying its weight with a tumpline around his forehead.

I said good night when we reached the hotel, telling Bill I would walk around the central square, lit at this hour like a fairyland. It seemed his mind remained in the church where we had heard Mass and in the bishop's chancery room, because he only nodded in confirmation that he heard me, saying as he turned into the lobby, "A good man."

The little city still bustled at 9:00 P.M. In the park a marimba band played on the second floor of the gazebo as middle-aged couples danced and drank beer. Youngsters chatted on benches, some in indigenous *traje*, others in jeans and sweaters. Tourists showed each other Zapatista dolls they bought from Chamula women on the street, of Comandante Ramona on her horse, Subcomandante Marcos, Comandante Tacho wearing a straw hat with miniature ribbons hanging from its brim.

San Cristóbal was no longer the same place to which its leading citizens, *autenticos coletos*, had welcomed young Samuel Ruiz in 1960. Too much history—not just years—had passed. Indians had organized themselves into peasant unions beginning in the 1970s. By 1992, the five-hundredth anniversary of Columbus in the New World, thousands from villages across Chiapas peacefully marched for indigenous rights, removing the statue of the conquerer Diego de Mazariegos, tradition-ally called the city's founder. By the end of the twentieth century, resi-dents could no longer consider Indian protesters or radical peasant unions phenomena to crush or ignore. Zapatista or not, popular organi-zations might be backed by an army.

For centuries, *coletos* had kept indigenous Maya from settling within town limits, but now Indians walked the streets—even sidewalks—like anyone else. Some residents still paid little or no salaries to Indian girls working as maids, claiming they did the *muchacha* a favor by putting a roof over her head. But now, behind every Indian face, there might be a Zapatista.

Heading back to my hotel, I passed another where I had stayed in 1994, catching sight of the owner. I recalled that he would not allow me to reregister at the time when I returned from the Zapatista National Democratic Convention, even though he had vacant rooms. In the first months of 1994 *coletos* did not speak of the uprising and occupation of San Cristóbal; even now they belittle key events such as the Peace Accords. Yet they must serve those who bring in dollars: Zapatista proj-ect volunteers, human rights observers, journalists, and "Zapatourists," travelers who thrill to drink coffee on the same streets once taken by the charismatic Marcos and revolutionary Maya. The regal old city wavered between denial and the reality of its new identification as a Zapatista town.

"They never came," *coletos* say of the Zapatistas. "And they never left."

With Chiapas militarized like occupied territory, Zapatistas and their sympathizers felt shut in, like the Bats in the underworld. "And then they descended the road to Xibalba," says the *Popol Vuh*. "Then they came to water again, to blood: Blood River. . . . Bat House is the name of the fourth test. . . . The Bats are shut inside; they can't get out." The United States had sent Mexico helicopters and other weapons for the "drug war." The Mexican army used them against Zapatista combatants and civilians. Zapatistas possessed no advanced weapons, no air power.

Under president George H. W. Bush, Washington shipped $212 million in military supplies to Mexico. Under president Bill Clinton, the first of seventy-three promised Huey helicopters arrived. The list of additional US material supplies for transfer to Mexico included four C-26 reconnaissance planes, five hundred bulletproof armored personnel transports, $10 million in night vision and communications equipment, global positioning satellite equipment, radar, machine guns, semiautomatic rifles, grenades, ammunition, flame throwers, gas masks, nightsticks, uniforms, and rations.

After another ceasefire went into effect in 1996, the Mexican government stationed tens of thousands of soldiers in Chiapas on bases, along roads, in villages, backed up by armored personnel carriers, Humvees mounted with sixty-caliber machine guns, and air reconnaissance.

Government loyalists began carrying better guns, including automatic weapons too expensive for ordinary farmers. In many places half a village aligned with the PRI might be pitted against supporters of the opposition PRD (Party of the Democratic Revolution) or outright Zapatista sympathizers.

Despite the firepower lined up on the ruling party's side, pro-Zapatista Maya villages began declaring themselves "autonomous," out of bounds to the government and the PRI. You did not have to be Zapatista to live in one of them or to be part of its governing council, but you had to accept the authority of the council, elected by consensus. The San Andres accords recognized the right of indigenous communities to elect authorities "according to their uses and customs." By 1998, the Zapatistas said, a thousand towns had set up their own systems of governing.

Indigenous people in Panama, Brazil, Nicaragua, and other countries governed with some form of local autonomy. Mexico, however, said its history had forged a "cosmic race," a mixed population capable of rising above categories of race and class. Thus distinctions such as "indigenous" were irrelevant, "autonomy" out of the question.

Besides, Chiapas supplied over half of Mexico's hydroelectric power, 70 percent of its timber, and shared a geological shelf with its oil-rich neighbor, Tabasco. If indigenous autonomy were recognized, what would happen to resources? And what example would autonomous Maya communities set for the other ten million Indians in Mexico? Since the uprising, groups in the Huasteca, Guerrero, and Mixe areas had begun to speak of *autonomia*. Zapatista autonomous communities accepted no police, judges, or other authorities from outside, and no government assistance projects, either.

One day when Father Bill could not come with me, I visited one of the autonomous towns, an ancient Tzotzil place called Polhó (pre-Columbian name: *Poyol ob*, Tree on the River). It stood an easy drive from San Cristóbal, in view of lush peaks reaching into moving clouds, its hills rich with coffee groves. Since the massacre at Acteal, Polhó's population had swollen from one thousand to seven thousand. The refugees lived in bizarre shelters made from donated canvas that had been used for billboard advertisements.

Thus a shivering woman bent to enter her tent through a slit in a painted canvas eye, its lashes thick with mascara. Next door, a teenage girl sat in the dirt trying to weave, thread looped around the big toe of her outstretched leg for want of a loom. She looked dwarfed by a light-skinned couple on the canvas wall of her shelter, bright teeth big enough to eat you with, brand-name cigarettes in manicured fingers.

I walked the alleys among the tents, watching near-naked children steer rocks with sticks, apparently their only toys. When a kind-looking fellow emerged from one of the shelters and bid me good day, I stopped to talk.

"All the chairs are left back in the village," he said. "We had to leave quickly." Armed townspeople chased out neutrals or those who sided with the opposition to the government. With formality, the man offered a rough-hewn block of wood as a seat, pulling up another for himself.

His name was Antonio Vasquez, he said. His hair was the flat black of the Maya. Like many other indigenous men in Chiapas, he wore no distinctive *traje*, but cotton pants and a faded shirt. His coffee trees had begun to produce in recent years, he said, but middlemen connected to the official party took such a cut that "I saw for all the work, I had no future." Vasquez said he was "one hundred percent Zapatista."

"All we want is to find a way to give food to our children, to have a little something more." Like almost everyone I talked to in three days at Polhó, Vasquez painstakingly listed what he had left behind fleeing his home village: shoes, a radio, a pulping machine, good rope.

"Yesterday afternoon we buried my son, up on this hill behind us," he said, startling me. The boy had been three months old.

Sometimes Vasquez could only say what he meant in Tzotzil. I wished I understood. Behind the words, I sensed sadness and frustration. He suspected that medics who were not indigenous cared little for Indians' lives. On the canvas wall of Vasquez's painted tent, three fine-featured women threw back heads of freshly shampooed hair, delirious with joy. From inside came the sound of weeping.

Vasquez bent to speak close to my ear. "My wife," he said. He put his fingertips to his breast and whispered. "She still has milk."

———

With the army occupying Chiapas, roadblocks were frequent. "Are you carrying weapons? Why are you on this road?" soldiers asked.

When I tried to reach Acteal, where the massacre had occurred, soldiers on a public highway stopped me, confiscated my passport, and sent me back to San Cristóbal. I was not allowed to leave the limits of the city until they decided what to do, even though I had broken no rules, a virtual town arrest. I spent hours in a drab office struggling to make sense of the situation with a dull bureaucrat. Another journalist, the author

Sebastian Junger, was there, too, in similar circumstances, and even gift-
ing the bureaucrat with a bright copy of his international bestseller, *A
Perfect Storm*, made little impression. When my passport was returned,
it carried a notice to leave the country within forty-eight hours.

I left the country and returned shortly thereafter, during a window
when military units had disappeared from the road. The respite fell into
the counterinsurgency category of psychological operations. A landscape without soldiers tricked the mind into thinking the world was
once more a safe and quiet place. The illusion of peace might lure the
wanted out of hiding, to see whether houses still stood or to grab coffee beans from their trees. Within a few days the window would close
again, but in the meantime the road to Acteal was free. This time I
travelled with Father Bill.

Residents showed us bullet holes in houses and shops. Police had stood
on the highway and shot weapons into the air, they said, but did not
descend to the western part of town, where paramilitaries were invading.

They showed us a path that led to a white-haired Indian, perhaps in
his sixties, repairing a corrugated roof. He climbed down and bent low
in salutation. Had he been more nimble, his head would have brushed
the ground. He was a throwback, one who had spent his young years
in debt peonage, virtual slavery. His partner at the roofing work volunteered to accompany me to the chapel where the shooting had begun.

I want to say a wave of comprehension swept over me at Acteal. That
feeling its dirt under my boots, hearing the wind in its trees, brought
some understanding about evil and innocence and endless war, an illumination I had hoped for in coming. But that was not the case.

"See, they had no chance," said Agustin, our guide.

The simple chapel's wooden boards were splintered where the shots
entered. Without warning, gunmen had stood outside and fired blindly
into the praying congregation.

Agustin led us to a shallow ravine where he said he had found bodies
of some who ran, trying to hide in caves or reach the river. He described
too much, the conditions in which he found this one, that one. The
paramilitaries had used machetes, too. Powdered lime was still visible
where it had been dusted onto puddled blood.

I wanted to thank him, tell him we had the picture, had to go. But he wouldn't stop.

"I saw all the poor people, then I heard something," Agustin said. "'Llevame. Take me with you.' It was a small boy. His mother was dead. 'All right,' I said. I picked him up and carried him out.

"The rest, I couldn't do anything for them," Agustin said. "They were *puros hermanos*," real brothers and sisters. "*Fue mucho, fue mucho.*" It has been too much.

Bill didn't wait for a translation but put his hands on the man's shoulders. Agustin began to weep. "Ask him if he wants to pray," said Bill, but before I could open my mouth, he took his hands from Agustin's shoulders and asked him with hand signals, palms together, then lifted to the sky.

"*Si, si,*" said Agustin, bending his head to receive a blessing. Then the two prayed at the same time, Agustin in his native Maya language, Bill directly addressing God for a little help for the suffering poor of this place.

I didn't join. I believe in prayer, but this all seemed, as Agustin had said, too much. Bill was famous for his righteous anger on a labor picket line or for standing on railroad tracks with a fist in the air as a train carrying war weapons screeched to a stop. Yet here he was praying. I don't believe his outrage was less than mine. Clearly his faith was more.

The wind rose, making whistling sounds. It tumbled several vigil candles someone had placed to honor the dead. Flames hissed in the running wax, turning to wisps of black smoke. From the caves came a great disordered flapping. Bats flew from the ravine. The last birds of the day hurried to the darkening trees.

In 2002, Father Bill was arrested at the US Army base at Fort Benning, Georgia, during a protest against the School of the Americas, where many of the worst human rights offenders in Latin America received military training. The judge appeared disposed to leniency if he apologized, but instead Bill gave a statement to the courtroom about the obligation to protest in the face of evil, which ended with him addressing the judge.

"And you, sir," he said, "are a pimp for the Pentagon."

They gave him six months in federal prison. The warden assigned him toilet cleaning duty and a top bunk despite his age and heart condition. They forbade him to say Mass. He refused an offer to finish the sentence under a kind of home arrest. Prison was hard on Bill. Six months after his release, he was dead of a heart attack.

———

Since 2000, paramilitary units like the one that murdered at Acteal, supported by the army, have become embedded in the network of Chiapas villages. They are following a plan to crush the EZLN, the Zapatistas, pushed by a regional Mexican general who attended the School of the Americas. "The strategic operational objective is to destroy the will to fight of the EZLN," the plan reads, "isolating it from the civilian population, and achieving their support." The plan says the army will "secretly organize" civilians such as ranchers, small property owners, and others "characterized by a high sense of patriotism, who will be used under orders in support of our operations. . . . Where self defense forces do not exist, it is necessary to create them . . . "

Now forces are woven through the Chiapas fabric like woof on warp. They discourage the kind of unified action among neighbors that might lead to forming groups like the pacifist Christians who died at Acteal or other pro-Zapatistas. No longer is it necessary to drain the sea; instead, throw in the biggest, baddest fish and the situation comes under control.

"That way," the Chiapas chronicler Andrés Aubry wrote in 2007, "revolution which becomes a social movement is fractioned, and anger becomes rooted inside the community."

———

In 2010, the last time I went to San Cristóbal, a shaman told me that real change indeed has come to Chiapas for the Maya in the last thirty years, but it is incomplete. He also said, "Things will never go backward, and the Zapatistas have a lot to do with it."

Javier, the shaman, receives visitors in a large colonial house that has been in his extended family for generations. He regularly wears a green jade jaguar medallion around his neck, sometimes drawing it up on its chain and fingering the carved stone softly, as if the texture gave him comfort or information. Javier said "profound" change is at hand, not only in Chiapas but the world beyond. More than the word "change," *cambio*, he used the words *acomodarse*, to accommodate one's self to something, and *corregir*, to correct, adjust, realign.

"Beaches will flood, and there will be eruption of volcanoes, earthquakes," he said.

With a gift, a *don*, for healing with stones, Javier, who is seventy-five, apprenticed with a Maya spiritual guide who died at age 106. Javier led me along a corridor to a back room of the house, the chamber where he works. In its center is a narrow, high white platform on which the seeker lies while Javier places pieces of white jade, green, multicolored, on the body. Jaguar figures, large and small, rest upon an altar, on tables and shelves. They are carved from jade and precious woods or made of ceramic.

I walked slowly around the room until stopping before a rendering of the sacred cat in dark blond wood. "Go on," Javier said. Tall and unbent, he smiled from under the wide-brimmed straw hat he wears even indoors. I picked up the figure, heavier than I imagined, letting it rest in my palm. With the other hand, I stroked it, warm and smooth.

Javier says before his master died, the elderly man told him, "My soul is in the jaguar." He would remain present in a certain mask, he said, the animal's face in wood, its mouth open and tongue extended, real whiskers, eyes of amber so rich they look real. The mask hangs on the wall.

Javier says the coming change may be "brutal." Nevertheless, he believes we have the opportunity to "prepare," as a student prepares for an examination. The more who are aware of the moment, of our connection to the cosmos, the more likely we will accommodate ourselves, act more at one with the earth.

"My teacher told me this time does not give him concern. It is a period of correction on earth, but for other planets, too, an adjustment such as tectonic plates make when they move." The sun, most prominent of the celestial bodies to us, is especially affected, he said. The change will be slow, however, "so there will be no mass killing by the sun, no tragedy."

Scientists say solar activity is more intense now than it has been in ten thousand years, that it will peak in the year 2012. On its winter solstice, December 21, the sun, earth, and Milky Way align in a way that happens only once in twenty-six thousand years. By the Maya long count calendar, the date of that solstice, 13.0.0.0.0, is the final day of the *baktun*, or time period, ending the fourth era of man, the age in which we live.

For Javier, and some other guides, the period of change and volatility does not begin and end at that moment. Instead, it has already begun, and it will continue for ten or twenty years.

"My master said it would be a spiritual change, that we can become less animal, more human, in Maya, *hach winik*, true man," Javier said. "A truer balance of body, mind, and spirit than what we are now."

We left the room, returning along the corridor. A light rain began to fall. We sheltered at a wrought iron table, under a roof that circled the open courtyard. We watched the drizzle on flowers.

"What does it mean to be a true person?" I asked.

"To be able to counsel another man, another woman," he said. "Without *envidia*, envy, covetousness, fear, hate."

Like many rainfalls in the tropics, this one was short-lived. I shook hands softly with Javier, really just a touching of palms.

"I shall have a ceremony the night of the full moon," he said, as I left. "Come. The night of the twenty-seventh."

Acting at one with the earth, keeping the balance in nature that is part of the Maya cosmology, is the way we will keep from destroying ourselves, Javier had said. I walked the streets of San Cristóbal for a while, observing that peculiar way even old pastel walls can shine in the light that comes after rain. Soon I hit one of the smart new pedestrian walkways near the central plaza, which used to carry cars and once echoed with the footfalls of armed Indians marching into town. Reaching the central *parque*, I looked up at the municipal building taken over by the Zapatistas in the uprising of January 1, 1994. It looked the same except repainted, from blue to white. When the Zapatistas called attention that day to the miserable lives and deaths of tens of millions of Mexicans, defense of Mother Earth was absent from their list of demands.

For Zapatistas, the rainforest is a place to farm. Many who pioneered the movement originally migrated to the jungle in the 1960s and 1970s, encouraged by the government. Mexico City sent the landless there under legislation like our nineteenth-century Homestead Act. Maya grow food, try to keep a hold on their land, and, at the outside, find a way to school children. The fact that they must honor *Madre Tierra*, that their culture demands awareness of the interrelationship of all living things, can only bring pain when it is necessary to act otherwise.

Once I asked Nobel Prize laureate Rigoberta Menchú how the growing Maya identity movement in Guatemala might arrest rainforest destruction in Petén. She became testy.

"Why do others always think it is Maya who have responsibility for the environment?" she said. Other issues, she implied, are more urgent.

At the headquarters of the Morelia municipality, one of five autonomous Zapatista municipal districts operating in Chiapas in 2010, I asked the governing council member in charge what he believed the Zapatistas' achievement had been over sixteen years. *Educacion, salud,* he said. Education, health.

I had seen it right away, when two husky security officials interviewed me to permit access to the municipality headquarters compound. Sitting side by side at a long table, they wrote my answers to their questions with pen on paper—the municipality operates without computers. It was slow going, and I ached to see how painstakingly they formed the words, sometimes checking with each other on spelling. They were former combatants in the EZLN, in their late thirties. As Zapatistas, they said, they learned to read and write.

"We can do the writing," joked one. "It's the Spanish that trips us up."

"If we would have been taught in school, things would have been different," said the governing council member. Notoriously, many government teachers attempted little with Indian children, showing up at schools only to take attendance and then leaving for two weeks, or dismissing indigenous youngsters' abilities.

"We were always told we couldn't learn, but yes, we can. We can do all this," the council member said, gesturing to include piles of handwritten municipal proceedings and the wider compound outside. "We have learned to read."

Zapatismo and new official government attention have not changed the fact that most Chiapas Indians—71 percent—suffer from malnutrition. Seven out of ten live in one- or two-room houses with dirt floors. Sewage systems and potable water remain dreams.

Generally, Indian children born in Zapatista communities since 1994 read and write. There is a secondary school in Morelia. Likewise, every Zapatista has access to free medical care. Outsiders can use the clinics, too, for a modest fee. This is progress, every drop of it squeezed into existence by the peasants themselves.

When the gates of the Morelia Autonomous Municipality compound closed behind me, I drove slowly, partly because the road was rocky and full of holes, partly for the pleasure of looking at the mountainous landscape that separated the cattle ranching region from the Lacandón jungle. I contemplated what Arthur Demarest once said, that he believed ecological awareness is growing to the point where it can act as a force against war and human destruction. But what if we continue to destroy the earth at the same pace we are doing now? Will awareness catch up in time? In life, we know there are moments to grasp or they never return. This moment may be saying to us, either we turn it around now or no more chances.

In two hours on the road, I saw signs indicating the presence of other autonomous communities, with messages such as: YOU ARE IN ZAPATISTA TERRITORY, WHERE THE PEOPLE COMMAND, AND THE GOVERNMENT OBEYS. Or: AUTONOMOUS MUNICIPALITY IN REBELLION. Notices forbade drugs or alcohol, for Zapatista communities are dry. Zapatista markers appeared on the highway, at least a few near Mexican army bases, vying with billboards announcing official government projects like replacing dirt floors with concrete. The effect of crossing dueling territories is discombobulating, like driving across squares on a giant checkerboard, half an hour in black, half an hour in red.

I was heading toward the ancient Maya city of Toniná, a bellicose kingdom that once warred with Palenque. I wanted to see a particular twelve-hundred-year-old mural, discovered by archaeologists only in 1992, called the Frieze of the Dream Lords. Perhaps, it was said, the figures on the frieze illustrate the four eras of man, three prior to our own, and the fourth in which we live, which is about to end.

The entry to Toniná runs along a broad pedestrian avenue, shaded by trees. In the classic Maya rainforest world, from Mexico to Honduras, this city-state may have held off the Great Collapse longer than any other. A slim, sandstone-look stela, with a single extant row of five glyphs, bears the long count date 10.4.0.0.0, corresponding to our year AD 909, the latest Maya date ever found. A visitors' sign says Toniná means "House of Stone" in Tzeltal. "Metaphorically, the name refers to the home of celestial lights and deities of time: Toniná was a site of calendars and rituals," it says. The frieze. The Dream Lords.

The first sight of the great temple from the pedestrian road is a shock, it seems so mammoth. The Maya of Toniná had used a natural hill to create their sacred mountain, a seven-terrace temple built into the rise like a stepped pyramid. When Stephens and Catherwood arrived on horseback in 1840, they rode breaches on the temple face where the stucco had fallen, among wild lemon trees growing from the stones, as high as the third terrace.

I crossed a small stream and stood at the bottom of the pyramid. To see the frieze today means climbing uncountable steps. I ascended snake-style, as I once saw two elderly *ajq'ijab'* climb steep Temple II at Tikal, weaving diagonally in one direction, softly turning along several steps, weaving in the other direction. That way, the old priests said, you never confront the deity on top straight on, which would be irreverent.

Climbing like a snake gave a feeling of better balance than climbing straight up, less sensation that gravity was pulling at my back. But it was still hard on the lungs. On the flat first terrace, I rested. In the distance rolled miles of gentle cattle pasture, soft green grass, beautiful in its way. What would have been lovelier would have been trees.

In time, I reached the fifth terrace. The remains of the Dream Lords mural rose twelve feet high and almost fifty feet wide. A giant bench throne—it looked big enough for three regents—had been built in a later age, only a few feet in front of the wall carving; a roof put up by archaeologists to protect the mural cut out even more light. The figures on the wall live in eternal dusk, like the twilight just under the watery barrier that separates the underworld from the living.

The hero twins who slog their way through Xibalba in the *Popol Vuh* appear in the mural across from each other, Hunapu at the feet of a magnificent mythical bird with its mouth wide open, Xbalanque near a snappy rodent standing on hind legs. Decapitated heads with individuated features hang from the feathery frame, perhaps prisoners sacrificed, representing the newly dead. Broken and incomplete, the wall draws in the viewer anyway. With effort, I found the snake, following its twisting body up and around other creatures from the realm of darkness, linking them like a scaly thread.

The scaffolding in which the Dream Lords live is made of feathers, as if springing from timbers crossing each other in a giant X. The feeling of movement forbids calling the scene a tableau. Its dissonance disturbs. Giant twin suns with human faces do not rise but are falling through space, eyes closed, upside down. That is how the sun expires as an era ends.

Death is a skinless dancer with lively bones, face macabre with joy. He is the one I most remember when I think of the wall. I feel torn between delight at the music to which I know he dances and horror at the darkness he represents, at the sight of the remains of the murdered, which the specter wears like bangles.

This is how I have come to feel about Chiapas, with beauty and spirit as stunning as the temple growing from the hill, but inside, underneath, a darkness ready to rise up. On another terrace of the great palace a labyrinth of passageways imitates the roads in the underworld. I climbed down, avoiding its entrance, descending instead to the wide, grassy plaza in the open air.

9

The River, the Stars

THE TEMPLE OF THE GREAT JAGUAR RISES STONY AND HIGH
from the main plaza at Tikal. Just outside the plaza the jungle begins.
It is not unheard of for travelers to become lost only a couple of hundred feet from the trail, so thick and tricky is the forest. It grows above,
around, and behind the ancient structures, towering trees making a
dense green backdrop to every building of stone.

At the base of the Jaguar Temple's grand stairway, Ramona swept
with a palm branch, cleansing the space that would become sacred.
Elderly twin *ajq'ijab'*, heads wrapped in red cloths, knelt and prayed.

"There could be energy here of others, bad or good," Ramona said,
sweeping as if the grass were the floor of a house. "You never know."

Ramona and I have been friends for more than twenty years. She
was already consecrated as a Maya *ajq'ij*, a kind of priest, when we met
and from the beginning has kindly explained what is happening when
I attend a Maya New Year (on the 260-day calendar, the Short Count) or
a ceremony of petition. When she asked me to meet her and other spiritual guides in Flores on a certain day in 1994, I said OK.

I guessed they were going to pray in a place, or a way, that might draw sensitive official attention. At such times, it was always good to have a foreigner around. Such an invitation from Maya had come more than once as the war died down and the indigenous became less secretive about traditional religious observance. For years, discretion had been their watchword. When the army suspected all natives of being rebel supporters, a low profile was best. Never did I think that Ramona would attempt a full-on religious display at Tikal, the gem in the crown of Guatemala's sites, a symbol of the country to the outside world. It would probably be the first religious ceremony among the temples of Tikal in a thousand years.

"It's for the design," Ramona said, opening a five-pound bag of white sugar.

She poured it on the grass in a thin, wide circle, connecting the perimeter to the center with radial lines. For the next hour, Ramona, the twin K'iche Maya–speaking *ajq'ijab'*, and a couple of other spiritual guides I did not know prepared the sacred fire. They placed small items inside and around the circle: stones of heady copal incense, squares of chocolate, clean-burning pine sticks called *ocote*, aromatic sap.

"Don't worry," Ramona had assured me when I discovered what we would be doing in the national park, where fires, of course, were not allowed. "I have been speaking to the *abuelos*, the grandfathers and grandmothers, for more than a year, to hear their counsel."

They consulted the calendar, she said. They prayed.

Some Maya who survived the war wanted to reclaim the religious spirit of famous archaeological sites, which were usually spiritual sites. The impulse was mixed with a so-far amorphous Maya identity movement. What was clear was that educated Maya—Ramona had two master's degrees—wanted to carve out their positions of respect in the postwar country. They would never again be *carne de cañon*, cannon fodder, for a rebellion they did not lead, one of them had told me in my house in Antigua. They wouldn't be slaughtered by the tens of thousands. Maya *abuelos* without formal education told those younger to go ahead with the ceremony on a certain day. Time and space always work together in Maya ceremonies. The place, they said, was Tikal.

Already tourists and a couple of park guards were standing close, watching. High on Temple II, mirroring the Great Jaguar Temple on the opposite side of the plaza, men in shorts and women in straw sun hats were pointing our way. The spiritual guides seemed to be in their own world, making certain the candles marked the directions proper to their colors, offering them first to the sky, then placing them on the circle: red on the east, for the rising sun; white on the north, for the air; yellow on the south, where the full sun rides; black on the west, where the sun sets at night to travel the underworld. In the center they arranged blue and green candles and those of the delicate honey color called *ceibo*. Its wax was gathered from jungle bees, like those Teresa had shown me how to place on the altar the night the skull visited, in San José Itzá.

There was no way I could refuse Ramona. I had gone to her wedding in a remote northwest highland town, prayed with her and her parents, and with the groom, when the *ajq'ij* performing the ceremony found omens against the marriage. I mourned when she lost her child, commiserated when the husband left, gave a party when she published a poetry book. Like any women friends, we drink together, talk about men, gossip. Much of it is in a mix of Spanish and the English Ramona learned in California during the war years. She had fled there to survive. Death squads in Guatemala had killed her three brothers, hanging the head of the youngest in the town square.

The spiritual guides bowed to the four directions and the center, calling on the sacred lords, praying. They lit the fire, drawing tourists away from the stelae and palaces. Ramona is two years younger than me, but she looked ageless performing the ceremony, especially among the ruins. Tall for a Maya, she wore a long blue skirt with thin white lines and a richly woven, blousy *huipil* in a deep red design that marked her roots in a Kaqchiquel Maya village. She had swept up her long, dark hair, covering it with the same kind of red bandanna scarf worn by the male *ajq'ijab'*.

The park closed at 5:00 P.M., when visitors left. We stayed. The *ajq'ijab'* repeatedly reached into their small cloth pouches, extracting pebbles of incense that they tossed into the fire. In their motions I saw the scattering glyph, *U mol*, a hand dropping small circles. They could represent maize kernels at planting or gifts to the fire or blood from his penis pierced by the king in sacrifice.

After the ceremony, we slept right there under the looming pyramid, in blankets and sleeping bags. Each person took a two-hour turn guarding the fire, making sure it did not go out. My shift came from two to four in the morning, when the sky was blackest, brightest. I watched the temple rising into the constellations, its roof comb scraping the white powder of light that is stars beyond stars. There are birds that cry at night. I stirred the fire two or three times, feeling clear and tireless. When Ramona woke to relieve me, however, I crawled into my bag and slept instantly.

Today Ramona has become mother to a ten-year-old boy who speaks only Kaqchiquel Maya, abandoned by his own mother. My friend's life is changing, so centered on the child as it must be, but she continues her work as a *guia espiritual*, a spiritual guide. We drank coffee together recently in a café that used candles for light, and spoke of that night in Tikal.

"That ceremony was to recognize part of the Maya alliance with those who came before," Ramona said. "'Here are your children,' we were saying. We could reactivate the energy of Mother Earth."

She said the days we are living now are another time of change, a time of need for reconnection with the earth. "Because of the end of the era? The end of the *baktun*, the calendar?" I asked. "The way we are lining up with the sun and the Milky Way?"

"We do not want to commit the error that some Christians made at the turn of the millennium, taking the moment for something it is not," she said. "People are so preoccupied with what will happen but not what we should do. The stories we pass on, and celestial messages, do not have all the information. The time and energy people give to spirituality will aid us in response."

She told me midwives, who deliver almost all Maya babies, tell her they have never seen infants born so happy, "children of light, of sun," they call them. Well, that's certainly unquantifiable, I thought. I said nothing, lest Ramona remind me I reflected as "an occidental."

"A transition, yes, we are going through one, but it is not only physical," she said. "Prophecies say we will suffer hunger, strong winds, thunder—it could be severe. But it does not have to be the end of the world. It depends on our response. The universe responds to the treatment it is given."

————

A month after I talked to Ramona, I sat in a bus in the Santa Elena market across from the island of Flores. Outside, a gaggle of drivers pushed the bus to get us started. From my window seat, I looked out at a blind man with gray-white eyes who cheered until the engine caught.

The trip to the river would take hours. I rolled up my rain jacket to use as a pillow and rested my head on the window. Closing my eyes, I tried to conjure up the magnetic filtered light, the matrix of the jungle. Once seen, the light is never forgotten, translucent and moist in memory.

But it wouldn't come. Instead, I thought of the hard mid-afternoon sun of the day before, falling on piles of tree trunks, some dishearteningly large, stacked in the yard of a government agency. A full third of the Petén is supposed to be off limits to commercial logging.

The offices of the agency charged with protecting the Maya Biosphere are inside a pale, cream-green building of tropical administration design, made of wood with an airy-looking cupola, the kind you see in movies about sahibs of colonial India. The advantage of the high-ceiling architecture is that rooms inside are blessedly cool without air-conditioning.

Two women in the front office looked startled when I appeared. They vied to escort me to the administrator's office, although it stood merely two doors down the hall. The administrator, in turn, welcomed me as if I were the Queen. I had a feeling the offices received few visitors.

The agency's regional chief told me six hundred thousand acres had been lost in the protected areas in the 1990s. Since 2001, he said, the rate of loss has accelerated. At that time there were eleven communities in the Laguna del Tigre National Park, three of them legal. In 2010 there are thirty-three communities inside the park, three of them legal. About twenty-five percent of the entire Biosphere is a no-go area, run by half a dozen narco-families, mostly near the Mexican border. If this

man's small office, chock-full of unfiled papers and reports, is any indi-
cation, his agency is strapped for funds.

"People are coming in from the southeast," he said. The same story,
Maya with nowhere else to go, squeezed out, burning the jungle to
farm.

Ruefully, the administrator admitted his forest guards had little
authority. They did not carry guns, and should they need to grab a law-
breaker—usually a peasant farmer cutting wood for fuel—they had to
take the police and army along.

He told me the head of one of the drug families came to the office
"and sat where you are right now." The man wanted to make a deal: the
agency stays off its back, and the drug family's goons will police depre-
dation in the area.

"I said no," said the hapless administrator.

As I was leaving, he invited me to a party being thrown for the forest
guards, an agency anniversary. I expressed my regrets.

On the bus to the river, I must have dozed off after all, because when
I opened my eyes I had a new seatmate, a child. Eventually I turned to
her to pass the time.

"How old are you?" I asked.

"Ten," she said, which was older than she looked. She wore a frayed,
but clean, blue cotton dress. On her lap rested a bunch of ugly plastic
flowers, gaudy yellow and purple tulips, of texture and size unknown
in nature.

"Are you traveling all by yourself?"

"Yes. To put these on my father's grave," she said. "Nine months ago
in Las Cruces, bad men, they killed him."

"How terrible. I'm sorry."

"*Envidia*," the child said in a matter of fact way, sighing like an old
woman who had seen much in a lifetime.

I was meant to understand this word *envidia* not in its simple dic-
tionary definition, "envy," but as an entire category of impulses that
might lead one person to harm another, to cause a spell to be cast on
another, or, in extreme cases, have him or her slain or do the deed
oneself. *Envidia* is a powerful word used to cover a range of crimes or

unexplained events born from jealousy, covetousness, or even capricious bad feelings toward someone, and even a ten-year-old understands what it means. *Envidia* is not a simple crime of *venganza* (revenge) or just *robo* (theft) but implies a murkier, more diffuse passion, a crime of the weak turned mean. For those who feel they live in a world where they have no control, who have never seen a crime investigated, with motives discovered, perpetrators punished, *envidia* is also a convenient concept to account for bad luck and random violence. It is a force from beyond, about which nothing can be done. No matter its roots, *envidia* is the expression of an evil heart. *Envidia* killed her father, the child said, and probably killed her brother, too, more recently.

"He was just two."

"What?"

"My brother. He was just two."

"Who would have *envidia* toward a two-year-old?"

The girl looked up at me with the patient expression of a child called upon to explain the world to an adult. She adjusted the awful, neon-bright tulips on her lap.

"When our father died, a neighbor said he would help my mother plant her corn and beans. So we would have something to eat. But his wife got jealous. The wife pushed my brother into a well. He drowned."

The girl said her mother had six other "small ones," whom she didn't dare leave alone anymore, so it fell to the child to take flowers to her father's grave. "My mother sells grilled meat in the market," she said, her eyes on the back of the seat in front of us. "She is mother and father to us now."

We came to a stop where passengers boarded. When we started again I felt the child turn toward me and heard her voice, now shy. "How do you like the flowers?"

"Beautiful," I said.

The bus emptied when it could go no farther, on the shores of the great river. My small seatmate had left hours before, and no other traveler seemed to be waiting for the immigration inspector to return from lunch. So I dined alone in the eatery, someone's house where three tables had been set near the kitchen. Turtle soup, I'm afraid, but there

was nothing else. By mid-afternoon, papers stamped, I was sitting on a
bench in a canopied boat, heading downstream.

————

On the Usumacinta, at a spot right about where Chan K'in's grandson
tried to convince me the old man's grave might be, the river loops to
form an omega, the final letter of the Greek alphabet, a symbol of last
things. Within the omega lie the ruins of Yaxchilan, once an important
political and religious center, to which other cities—including Bonampak—paid tributes of quetzal feathers, chocolate, jaguar hides, and
other treasures. The unusual omega formation might have convinced
the Maya to build a defensible capital here, a royal city with priests,
warriors, and working people, nearly encircled by the river, their living
moat.

These historical considerations took a backseat when I stepped from
the boat to shore. Dusk was coming on. I walked into the old city. All I
could think of were the words of poet Allen Ginsberg when he remembered this place: "Yaxchilan. . . . Resurrected in the wild . . . and all the
limbo of Xbalba still unknown . . ."

I wanted to see as much as I could in the fading light. From atop
a palace I looked across the flowing border into Guatemala's Petén,
spreading blue with haze. If the haze were gone, maybe I could see El
Mirador or the temples of Tikal, I thought, although they were probably
too far away.

El Mirador is the rage now in talk among archaeologists, a site so far
north it almost touches Mexico's Yucatán. Teams are finding extraordinarily beautiful stucco masks, the earliest-yet depictions of the hero
twins of the *Popol Vuh*, scraping away jungle to expose the Maya world's
largest pyramid temple. The center of a huge city-state, El Mirador is
connected to hundreds of smaller sites, like suburbs, by a network of
wide, white roads, the *sacbe*. The only way to reach El Mirador is by
walking three days through jungle from the nearest road. I would like
to try. There is always next year.

I climbed down from the crow's nest and walked to a grand staircase etched with glyphs, near the ceremonial ball court. Here the Maya

had re-created the cosmic struggle in the *Popol Vuh* between the hero twins and the dark lords of Xibalba. Played with a heavy rubber ball, with rules like a mix of soccer and basketball, in certain ancient versions of the game the losers, or captives, sometimes even winners promised eternal life, met ritual murder.

The sight of the staircase, even centuries after the last blood had dried, was repugnant. The victim was splayed backward over a massive stone ball, tied to it at the neck and limbs, and rolled down in sight of the multitude, blood and shredded flesh marking a course down the steps until the sphere rolled to a stop in the plaza.

While my mind was filled with gruesome imaginings, a pack of mules materialized, cantering through the plaza, mounting the stony rises. Their forbears had been left behind by some forgotten expedition, and now they jumped like thoroughbreds over the ruins. At that moment they possessed all the grace of mythological steeds. The apparition nudged everything from the mind's eye save wonder at the moves to which even nature's lowly creatures might rise. Some climbed up to the overgrown platforms, reared on hind legs for an instant, and then flew down again, sprinting across the plaza. Together the animals leaped joyously among the temple mounds in a mad, hypnotic dance.

A guard saw me watching. He was a white-haired native of Tenosique, the port to which the huge mahogany logs were once floated, sixty miles downriver as the crow flies, twice that with bends and curves. The guardian had been employed at Yaxchilan for twenty years, he said, living with his family near the old airstrip. We watched the wild animals together.

"When they run like that, they own the place," he said.

He spoke of other animals—tigrillo, ocelot, pheasant, deer, *tepesquintle*, armadillo, and as many serpents as you want—until Yaxchilan sounded like a mere island of carved rocks raised to keep the jungle at bay.

"The jaguar comes down to the beach along the river when the wind is against him, and he feels safe. He finds food there, like turtle eggs, iguana eggs, or a fish."

They swim? I hadn't considered swimming jaguars.

"Of course, swim fast and well, or else how would they cross rivers? How would they reach their mates on the other side?"

Like everyone I encountered at ruined Maya cities, from archaeology professors to indigenous workmen, the guard had a theory about the Great Collapse of the classic Maya. His was simpler, and maybe truer, than many.

"Yaxchilan did not fall to attack by an enemy city. Its humble class, all its poor, led the lives of slaves. A child began to work from the time he could carry a ten-pound block of stone. And that's the way he grew up, grew old, and died. So when they couldn't take it anymore, the people rebelled against their chiefs."

The bright young Lacandón boy I knew on my first trip into the jungle, in Naha, had told me his people made pilgrimages to Yaxchilan. Did the guard remember such a time?

In minutes we were climbing a temple on the fringe of the site. Inside a long chamber sat a stone figure, more than life-size, whose decapitated head lay nearby.

"The Lacandón, they pray here," the guard said. Their legend has it that should the head be replaced on the body, disaster will fall.

The guard said whenever the Lacandón departed, he found remnants of copal incense, stubs of burning candles. They came to Yaxchilan in small groups at long intervals, quietly, almost secretly, one or two men and a woman, and perhaps a child, carrying their incense burners. Only once had the guard actually heard them pray, he said, but it made a lasting, "very pretty" impression.

"They made the sound of the jaguar and the sound of the howler monkey and the *tecolote*, the owl."

It had been ten years "since they came that way," he said. Leaving the chamber, I noticed candle stubs melted in place on a stone block near the headless image. Surely perishable ritual objects did not remain in place for a decade?

"Lacandón have come more recently, but some only when they are contracted, paid by outsiders, who watch them pray," the old man said, no hint of judgment in his voice.

I wondered if Lacandón Maya also performed ceremonies secretly, in jungle caves or powerful places hidden from view. Or in Yaxchilan, without clients, slipping in and out without notice. Like Guatemala highland Maya did during the war.

In the evening I pitched my small tent on the unused runway. Outside, I sat on a rock, drinking coffee the guard's wife had made and poured into a metal cup for me. More stars than I had ever seen spread across the overhead dome, melting into the canopy where trees met the sky. The coffee was still warm. Its caffeine cleared my mind for a while, got me thinking.

In the years I have been coming to Petén, from the time I was a young woman to now when I will never be young again, I have watched the rainforest of Gran Petén reduced by half. I see violence erupting in cycles, as people reach the limits of indignity and cannot bear the idea their children will not lead better lives than they.

At ancient Maya sites, I no longer automatically expect to return, no longer assume the visit will be only one of a series, with more to come. This makes me observe more hungrily, try harder to take into myself the sight of graceful temples in tropical forest, signs of man's work, man's yearning to understand and leave a trace behind. Now, after an explosion of intellectual work, almost all the hieroglyphic messages can be read, the Maya code broken by eager minds driven by pure enthusiasm, each step in decipherment coming just because someone needed to know. That is the way the astronomer-priests accumulated knowledge of the night sky, watching in the dark for hundreds of generations in places like Uaxactun, thirsty to make sense of the order and pattern of the heavens.

Things have changed in Gran Petén, all right, which should be no surprise over a span of thirty years. I drank the last of the coffee, turned over the metal cup, and tapped it on a rock, scattering the dregs.

How intriguing that pictures from the past appear in my mind at the same time as scenes from today, a kind of double exposure. I am feeling like the Hero Twins in the *Popol Vuh*, who emerged from the underworld with the head of their slain father, having defeated the Lords of Death, accomplished what they had wanted to do, ready to propel themselves into the sky as the sun and the moon, to rest, knowing the journey is finished. What a grace it has been, a blessing to know one of the richest corners of creation. How peaceful to sleep in this place, one animal among many.

Around midnight, I woke to a persistent, subtle, close-by noise. Slowly, I lifted the tent's door flap for a look. The wild mules, a burro, and a horse were grazing on the grassy airstrip, chomping, smooth coats nearly silver in the moonlight. Overhead spread the Milky Way, the *sacbe*, white path, celestial road.

Comforted by the sight of the animals and familiar constellations, I dozed again. Until something, a sharper sound, perhaps a dream, pulled me upright. I looked again. The wild mules stood still, alert. Cautiously, they turned their heads, first to the river, then toward the ruins.

The animals broke into a gallop, becoming a pack, disappearing in the direction of the staircase and temples. My own human ears heard nothing. The overgrown airstrip lay empty. The moon had set, but the sky remained filled with stars. They looked far away, but they were accessible to us, I knew from my father. And they could fall as the result of the deeds of man, I knew from the words of Chan K'in.

I lay down with open eyes and listened. I heard what might have been the deep-toned tumbling sound of the river, carried on a gust of wind. When it came a second time, the sound resonated more, like a roar, but not like the lion's bellow heard at the zoo or in a movie, not a frightening, aggressive sound. Instead, it rolled on the air deep-toned, a sonorous rumbling that took into itself the sounds of all animals, all breezes and winds, all cracking branches, all creatures that crawled or climbed or flew in the dark. If the night forest itself possessed a voice, it might sound like this.

So mysterious and inclusive was the sound that the possibility it might be the voice of the jaguar, which I had never heard, did not first come to mind. Another deep roar. This time more distinctive, more clearly the call of a single, magnificent animal, kingly but plaintive too. Inside the tent, it was pitch-black. All my senses were tuned to listening. Another roar, and this time I was sure.

I felt as if I were being presented with a great prize, unexpected but gladly accepted, perhaps a prize for persistence granted to anyone who spent a requisite time in these jungles. That jaguar was somewhere down on the beach, the river running in its amber eyes, a jaguar so near, so alive, calling out. Then, the greatest gift of all. From the other side of the river, an answering roar.

Epilogue

Clearing the Breath
from the Mirror

TODAY MUCH OF THE MAYA TROPICAL JUNGLE FEELS NO MORE connected to Mexico or Guatemala than it might have a century ago. Instead, forest residents in both countries have more in common with each other than they do with compatriots in their national capitals. On both sides of the Usumacinta River, Mexican and Guatemalan inhabitants share a frontier culture marked by living close to nature, surviving by simple means and hard labor.

Peasant farmers looking for land continue to arrive in the forest while Guatemala and Mexico lay out "development" plans. Ironically, frontier farmers and government bureaucrats are alike in changing the jungle's face, so much that the rainforest I see in 2011 may be gone in the next generation. The Mexican plan for Chiapas includes strategically located instant communities, concentrating residents near new industries like palm oil and, not incidentally, drawing them away from Zapatista spheres of influence. The new housing looks monotonous, concrete boxes inappropriate for the climate, likely too hot in the dry season, mold incubators in the wet.

In Guatemala's Petén, a government tourism and development project called Cuatro Balam is anchored in the massive El Mirador archaeological project, which is supported by major businesses such as Wal-Mart Central America and the huge Progresso cement manufacturer. Introduced with fanfare in 2008, set for completion by 2023, Cuatro Balam maintains Petén should be protected for its biodiversity yet must shoulder its weight in a poor country by producing revenue. A slow train whose sound will be "imperceptible" is planned to connect jungle archaeological sites, although it is unclear to whom the train's sound will be "imperceptible." Luxury tourist destinations are on the drawing board, and strict boundaries aim to limit settlement by locals. Whether farmers and fishermen will want to work in the tourist industry is uncertain. Only the most draconian methods, without other changes, will remove hungry squatters from land some have lived on for years.

The international drug network, feeding an insatiable US market, is an immediate threat to the Maya rainforest. In Petén, ranches are being used as a screen for runways to receive drugs, especially from Colombia. Small transport planes may be damaged on landing or simply abandoned once a drop is made, leading the US Drug Enforcement Agency operations chief to characterize northern Guatemala as "an aircraft graveyard." Most cocaine destined for the United States now transits Central America, according to a 2010 US Army Strategic Studies Institute monograph. In a 2006 Congressional hearing, senator Robert Menendez asked, "What will happen to the people of Guatemala if 75 percent of the cocaine arriving in the United States continues to pass through Guatemala?" By 2008 the monograph reported the transit had jumped 47 percent. Drug traffickers own Petén.

From Guatemala most cocaine goes overland to Mexico by car, truck, horse, donkey, reportedly even inside the stomachs of cattle. Twenty-five years ago, when the Zapatistas first clandestinely occupied the Mexican Lacandón jungle, they rid it of drug runners and timber thieves. Today the masked army has made its strategic point, drawing attention to Maya demands, and has become a military reserve at the call of the *zapatismo* network. Drug routes transit Chiapas, but

Zapatistas are no longer in the policing business. Mexican authorities are corrupt or inefficient.

Trained ex-military, such as some of Guatemala's fearsome Kaibiles, once headquartered in Petén, have gone into service of the drug cartels, where pay is much higher. Gangs such as the Mara 18 and the Salvatruchas, which originated in Los Angeles among youth whose families fled Central American wars in the 1980s, are being incorporated into the drug networks to sell and transport. The Zetas, brutal enforcers for Mexican cartels, reportedly have used remote corners of Petén to train gang members brought in from elsewhere. In 2010, the Zetas went independent, becoming a cartel in competition with their former bosses.

As long as using certain drugs remains a criminal offense in the United States, by far the world's largest market, then lands such as the Maya rainforest, far from US borders, pay a price. Despite the utter failure of all attempts to control supply, and against expert counsel, Washington refuses to treat drug demand as a public health issue with resources and education, the way it treats drinking, overeating, dangerous sex, and tobacco. Meanwhile, the drug business brings $40 billion a year to Mexican cartels, now buying up the rainforest. Police, elected officials, and journalists who swim against the tide are killed.

In the *Popol Vuh*, the first men and women possessed limitless vision. "Their sight passed through trees, through rocks, through lakes, through seas, through mountains, through plains." Alarmed that the human kind might become "as great as gods," the Lords of Creation marred our sight until it became "as the face of a mirror is breathed upon." "Now it was only when they looked nearby that things were clear," says the *Popol Vuh*.

Without the long view that carries insight, we are probably condemning ourselves to lose the tropical forests that bring us the very breath of life, where life takes more forms than anywhere else on earth. Yet even now, even late, we might pull this fate from the fire. We can use the gift the Creators gave humans and did not take away.

Serpents produced only "pointless humming." Animals "haven't spoken" either, so their service is to be eaten, with respect. Creatures given words, however, became human. The Mayan term for "word," *tzi-ja*, also means truth. The first true men and women used the gift of language, given to no others, to speak first to their Creators, telling their deep gratitude. This gift, giving thanks, linked them to the Creators, and so they entered a communion with all created life, with the language of the universe. We speak. We understand. We act.

"We speak," say humans in the *Popol Vuh*. "We listen, we wonder, we move . . ."

Acknowledgments

MY SINCERE THANKS GO TO MY AGENT ANDY ROSS, WHOSE love for books and knowledge of them are pure gold, and whose loyalty and sense of humor ("I am not your psychiatrist!") have pulled me out of many difficult moments. Having Sue Brandanini Betz as my editor makes me feel among the luckiest authors of the year. Her skill and attention, as well as the work of her colleagues in that vibrant Chicago office, have been a gift to *Maya Roads*.

A special kind of gratitude goes to my dear friend, photojournalist Nancy McGirr, supportive through hell and high water, herself an inspiration. And to writers Rasa Gustaitis and Jean Molesky-Poz, with whom I meet every Friday to share our pages. Their contribution to *Maya Roads*, and to my life in these three years, has been deep and selfless. The perspicacity and encouragement of friends have made this a better book. Thank you Hilary Abrams, Dan Barrett, Mary Claire Blakeman, Rony Clements, Elaine Climpson, June Carolyn Erlick, Laura Fraser, Paul Goepfert, Jim Handy, Douglas Knapp, Ronnie Lovler, Richard Rodriguez, Tom Rosenberg, Amy Ross, Frank Viviano, and Tom Waters. And warmest thanks for his valued time and effort on the path to my colleague Peter Solomon, polymath and peerless editor.

Any writer on Chiapas and Petén stands upon the work of others. Memorable to me are books by Hermann Bellinghausen, Peter Canby,

Rosario Castellanos, Michael Coe, Jan de Vos, Jose Flores, Liza Grandia, Jim Handy, Neil Harvey, Suzanne Jonas, Stephen Kinzer and Stephen Schlesinger, Mary Ann Miller, Jean Molesky-Poz, Jim Nations, Carlos Navarette, Chiqui Ramirez, John Ross, Norman B. Schwartz, Jean-Marie Simon, Joel Simon, Luis Solano, John L. Stephens and Frederick Catherwood, George Stuart and David Stuart, Dennis Tedlock, B. Traven, and the late Linda Schele.

Over time I have shared discussions with friends and met individuals whose expertise in archaeology, anthropology, epigraphy, and other fields is far beyond the reach of my knowledge. Nevertheless, they generously shared ideas, understandings, and enthusiasms, even entertained my arguments. Only I am responsible for what I took from our conversations. But they illuminated my thinking and I thank them, from the heart: Reynaldo Acevedo, Bruce Calder, Calixta Gabriel, Nicolai Grube, Neil Harvey, Veronica Martinez-Breuil, Jorge Mario Martinez, John Ross, Jan Rus, Norman B. Schwartz, David Stoll, and (*ghoti*) Linda Schele. To Sandy Close and the late Franz Schurmann of Pacific News Service go my deep appreciation for loyalty and opportunity.

Most of the time, I travel alone. Yet there are miles on Maya roads I shared with others, who brought delight and wisdom to what we saw together: Bruce Mullins, present at the beginning (Etcher, phone home), Jake Bernstein, Daniel Chauche, Davida Coady, Cindy Karp, Will Lotter, Nancy McGirr, the unforgettable Elissa Miller and Claudia Estrada, Owen Murphy, Olga Reiche, and the late Victor Perera. I am grateful to the staffs of the San Francisco Public Library and the library at the *Centro de Investigaciones Regionales de Mesoamérica* in Antigua, both extraordinarily useful in research for this book. I owe a profound debt to dedicated research and advocacy workers in Guatemala and Mexico. I send warm *saludos* to Cristina and Carlos for *Las Puertas*, the inviting oasis they have created on the island of Flores. In particular, I thank many whose names I have promised not to use, including some who appear in this work under names I have created, lest they be exposed to danger or compromised in their work. *Gracias, hermanos.*

For the Maya, time and place intersect at destined points. I will always remember a transcendent moment leaving Monte Alban, where, for me, the road began.

Robert DeGaetano and our daughter, Maria Angelica DeGaetano, have helped not only with their own deep stores of knowledge but by being the fixed center of my life. Without them there would be no book, and without them no book would matter. I can never thank them enough.

San Francisco, November 7, 2010

9 Chik'chan, 18 Sac

12.19.17.15.5

Index

About the Author

KIM MORGAN

Journalist **Mary Jo McConahay** began covering Central America as a war correspondent in the 1980s and lived in Guatemala for eleven years. Her work has appeared in *Vogue, Rolling Stone,* the *San Francisco Chronicle,* and *Time* and is included in several anthologies. She lives in San Francisco.

JUL 1 8 2011